IMAGES
of America

AROUND THE SPANISH PEAKS

I0806139

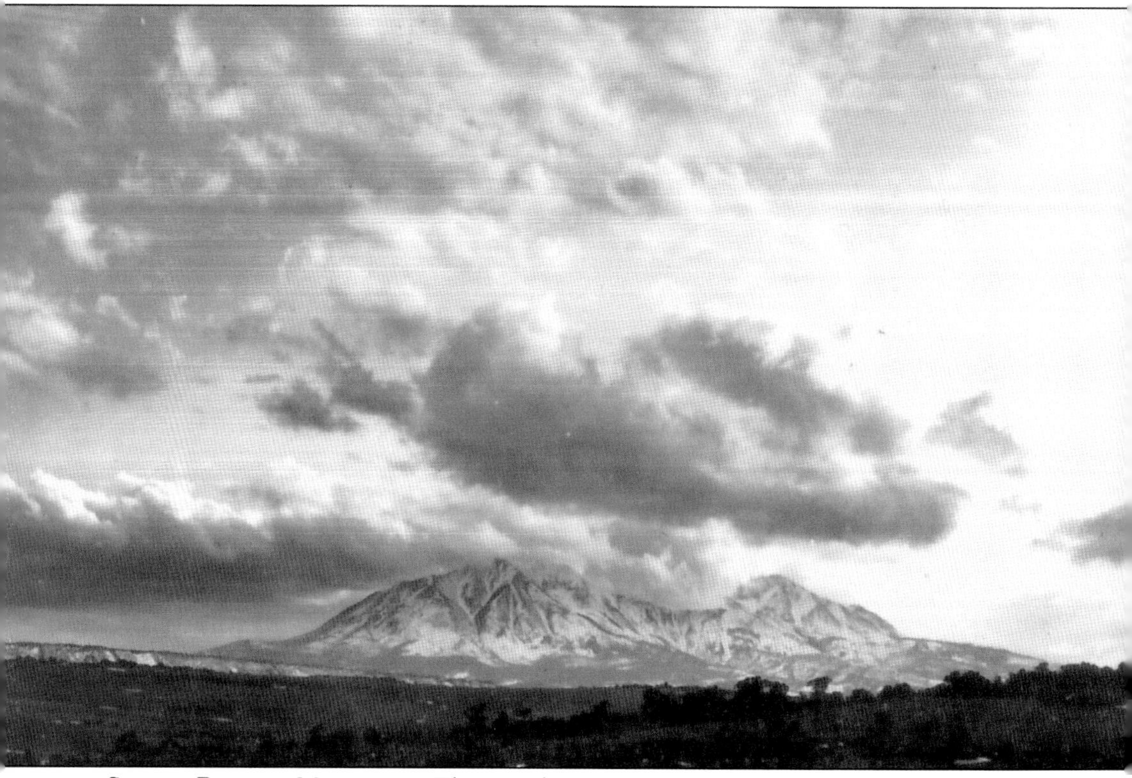

SPANISH PEAKS BY MOONLIGHT. This was the caption given by photographer Ory T. "O.T." Davis to his photograph, undoubtedly captured during a full moon in 1892. The location is north of the Spanish Peaks, looking south, with the East Spanish Peak on the left and the West Spanish Peak on the right. (Monte Vista Historical Society.)

ON THE COVER: O.T. Davis captured "Miss Ollie Hudson's picnic party at Dump Mountain, Veta Pass" on August 5, 1894. More information about this photograph can be found on page 53, and further information about O.T. Davis is on page 15. (Monte Vista Historical Society.)

IMAGES
of America

AROUND THE SPANISH PEAKS

Mike Butler

ARCADIA
PUBLISHING

Copyright © 2012 by Mike Butler
ISBN 978-0-7385-7624-4

Published by Arcadia Publishing
Charleston, South Carolina

Printed in the United States of America

Library of Congress Control Number: 2011928022

For all general information, please contact Arcadia Publishing:
Telephone 843-853-2070
Fax 843-853-0044
E-mail sales@arcadiapublishing.com
For customer service and orders:
Toll-Free 1-888-313-2665

Visit us on the Internet at www.arcadiapublishing.com

This book is dedicated to my parents, Ray and Marian Butler, who chose La Veta as their retirement home.

Contents

ACKNOWLEDGMENTS

Where does one begin to thank and acknowledge all the folks who have made this project possible? The danger is in forgetting even one person who contributed, and if that has happened I offer my sincere apologies. And while many people have helped, any errors or omissions are completely the responsibility of the author.

Katharine Emsden, of La Veta, helped me sort through photographs at Francisco Fort Museum on a cold January afternoon. Since the museum is unheated, I am truly grateful for the effort she made. Carolyn Newman, of Walsenburg, is a fountain of knowledge about Huerfano County history, and I thank her for spending an afternoon allowing me to scan photographs from the Huerfano County Historical Society collection. Eugene C. Vories, of La Veta, shared his precious family photographs with me and regaled our family with stories of the old days over dinner one evening. Mary Jean Fowler, of La Veta, has done great work with the La Veta Historic Preservation Committee, and I appreciate her prompt response in sending me its brochure. Gretchen Sporleder Orr, publisher of the *Huerfano World Journal* newspaper, shared her family photographs and gave me valuable information about the Sporleders—one of the pioneer families of Walsenburg.

The Bessemer Historical Society in Pueblo is custodian of the Colorado Fuel and Iron Company (CF&I) archives and photographs, which give an incredibly detailed look at coal-mining activities in southern Colorado. Thanks are extended to Tim Hawkins, archivist, for his assistance. Thanks also go to Kenton Forrest, of the Colorado Railroad Museum, for helping me locate rare photographs of Rio Grande Railroad operations in the La Veta Pass area. The Monte Vista (Colorado) Historical Society is the repository for a great collection of Ory T. Davis photographs, and I am grateful to Peg Schall for her assistance. Thanks go to Jennifer Halstead of Cuchara Mountain Resort for her assistance in locating Dwight Harrison, who published *The Cucharan*, and sincere thanks are given to Harrison for allowing me to reproduce photographs from the magazine.

Unless otherwise noted, the images in the book are from the author's collection. Additional images appear courtesy of Bessemer Historical Society/CF&I Archives (BHS/CFI), Colorado Railroad Museum (CRM), Denver Public Library Western History Collection (DPL), Francisco Fort Museum (FFM), History Colorado (HCO), Huerfano County Historical Society (HCHS), Library of Congress (LOC), National Archives (NAR), and the US Geological Survey (USGS). Thanks, one and all.

INTRODUCTION

The majestic Spanish Peaks, twin mountains rising more than 12,000 feet above sea level in south central Colorado, stand out high above the surrounding Great Plains and have beckoned to travelers across the centuries. The West Peak soars to 13,623 feet, while its companion East Peak rises to 12,708 feet. Walsenburg, with a population of about 4,700, is the largest town in Spanish Peaks country. Walsenburg is easily accessible today at the intersection of Interstate 25 (160 miles from Denver) and US Highway 160 (210 miles from Durango). The small town of La Veta (population about 850) is 16 miles west of Walsenburg, and the beautiful mountain village of Cuchara is 11 miles south of La Veta. The Cuchara River descends from Cuchara south through La Veta, and onward east to Walsenburg, providing sustenance to the valley.

Historically, Comanche and Ute tribes hunted and traversed Spanish Peaks country. They developed colorful legends regarding the creation of the rugged peaks and volcanic dikes, naming the two peaks Wahatoyas—breasts of the world. Great clouds formed around the peaks and brought life-giving rain to the camps below. Evidence of the Native American presence is found in the thousands of arrowheads discovered on ranches across the valley north of the peaks.

From the 1500s to the 1700s, Spaniards came to the area from Mexico looking for gold, and then looking to punish the Indians for their raids on villages in New Mexico. The Spaniards named the peaks Las Cumbres Españolas, or the Spanish Peaks. Seeking to secure the area from American settlers, the governor of New Mexico, Manuel Armijo, ceded over four million acres of land in northern New Mexico and southern Colorado to Cornelio Vigil and Ceran St. Vrain in 1843. However, the Mexicans lost their grip on the region in 1848, following their defeat by the United States in the Mexican War.

Spanish Peaks country became part of the Colorado Territory when it was formed by the federal government in 1861. Huerfano County was established in the territory that same year, and it extended north to the Arkansas River and east to the Kansas border. *Huerfano* is a Spanish word for "orphan," referring to the lone butte on the prairie a few miles north of present-day Walsenburg. The size of Huerfano County was whittled down to its present boundaries when Colorado became a state in 1876. Walsenburg had already become the county seat in 1872.

The Spanish Peaks served as guideposts for travelers on the historic Santa Fe Trail. Weary travelers, heading west by wagon train to Santa Fe and Taos, knew their endless journey across the plains would be mercifully ending when the Spanish Peaks finally appeared on the western horizon. Famous Western author Zane Grey wrote about these travelers in his novel *Raiders of the Spanish Peaks*. The federal government was also interested in this new territory and sent explorers to check it out. In 1853, John C. Fremont journeyed on a western expedition to find a pass across the Rocky Mountains that would be suitable for a railroad to cross. Fremont's party passed by Huerfano Butte, as did Ferdinand Hayden's 1869 geological survey mapping crew. Famous Western photographer William Henry Jackson accompanied Hayden's crew and recorded some of the first photographs of Spanish Peaks country.

While many travelers skirted the Spanish Peaks by turning southwest across Raton Pass, others scouted trails directly west over Abeyta Pass, which later became known as La Veta Pass. Baldy Scott opened a toll road over the pass in 1870, linking the Cuchara valley on the east with the San Luis valley on the west. The Denver & Rio Grande Western Railroad (D&RGW) followed this route when it built its narrow gauge line over the pass in 1877. The railroad was eager to continue its line west to the lucrative silver mines in Creede and Silverton. Traffic increased on the rail line to the point where the narrow gauge was no longer efficient, and the D&RGW completed a standard gauge line on a pass farther south of La Veta Pass in 1899. Today, the Rio Grande Scenic Railroad has reestablished passenger service over these same tracks between La Veta and Alamosa, bringing thousands of visitors into La Veta every summer.

The two major towns of Spanish Peaks country, La Veta and Walsenburg, have completely different histories. John Francisco, upon arriving in the beautiful Cuchara River valley on the north face of the peaks, declared: "This is paradise enough for me." He and his partners purchased land from the Vigil–St. Vrain land grant and established a ranch in the valley. He built Francisco Fort in 1862 as a defensive outpost against raiding Utes. While US Army soldiers never occupied Francisco Fort, Francisco did have to call for assistance to help fend off a Ute attack in 1863. Soldiers from nearby Fort Garland, on the west side of La Veta Pass, were unavailable because they were in New Mexico fighting a battle against Texas rebels in the Civil War, so Francisco had to call upon soldiers from Fort Lyons, 120 miles northeast on the Arkansas River. By the time the soldiers arrived, the Utes had departed. Eventually, Francisco's fort became the nucleus for the town of La Veta, which was incorporated in 1876, just after the arrival of the D&RGW railroad.

The development of Walsenburg can be traced to its status as a transportation crossroads and coal-mining center. In 1858, Hispanic settler Don Miguel Antonio Leon established La Plaza de Leones on the banks of the Cuchara River. The area also attracted Europeans, and German immigrant Fred Walsen purchased land and established a trading post in the area in 1870. Walsen became the first mayor, and the town's name was changed to Walsenburg. Coal was discovered on Walsen's land, just a mile west of town, and the Walsen Mine was established in 1876. The coal was immediately used for fuel for the steam locomotives of the D&RGW, and was also shipped north to Pueblo for use as coking coal in the steel mill there. Walsenburg grew to a population of over 12,000 people before the mines began shutting down in the 1930s.

Today, this beautiful area attracts thousands of visitors annually with year-round recreational opportunities—hunting, fishing, golfing, hiking, mountain climbing, skiing, and biking are just some of the many activities. Lathrop State Park, three miles west of Walsenburg, has over 150,000 visitors per year. Three wilderness areas are located within the county, attracting hikers and backpackers from around the country. Stretching along the western side of Huerfano County, San Isabel National Forest offers campgrounds, hiking trails, and lakes stocked for fishing. Although the scenic beauty of the county is constantly threatened by carbon-dioxide extraction, natural gas production, wind farm proposals, and gigantic high-power electric transmission towers, enough people care about the preservation of the natural and historic areas that perhaps nature may yet prevail. For all those who fought for the creation of the Spanish Peaks Wilderness Area in 2000, one can only hope so. Enjoy this journey through the geology, history, and natural beauty around the Spanish Peaks.

One

A Geologically Unique Region

The Spanish Peaks area has attracted geologists from around the world because of its high concentration of geologically unique features within a relatively small area. Many of these features are volcanic in origin, meaning that the rocks were formed from cooling magma (lava) within the earth. The magma was as hot as 2,000 degrees Fahrenheit before it started cooling. Because of all this volcanic activity, scientists first thought that the Spanish Peaks were remnants of ancient volcanoes, but later geologic study has shown them to be of sedimentary origin, chiefly sandstone.

Surrounding the Spanish Peaks and radiating out in all directions are miles of volcanic dikes. These dikes are easily visible as rock walls just south of La Veta and on Highway 12 from La Veta to Cuchara. The dikes were formed from vertical intrusions of magma into the surrounding rock and exposed when the surrounding rock eroded. It is estimated that as many as 400 dikes of various lengths radiate out from the Spanish Peaks. Hogbacks, such as the Dakota Wall (which Highway 12 passes through just north of Cuchara), are also found in the area. The Dakota Wall hogback looks like a dike, but is actually made of sandstone. The Dike Trail in Cuchara is misnamed, as it actually traverses the hogback, not a dike.

About nine miles north of Walsenburg stands the Huerfano Butte, all alone out on the prairie. *Huerfano* is the Spanish word for "orphan," and Huerfano County also takes its name from the butte. However, the butte is actually a volcanic plug—a large neck of volcanic rock much thicker than a dike. Other named buttes in Huerfano County include Goemmer's Butte, near La Veta, and Gardner Butte, near the small town of Gardner. All of these buttes are actually volcanic plugs. In contrast, an actual butte is generally a stand-alone sedimentary rock with a protective cap of harder rock. These unique geologic features have made Huerfano County an intriguing place for explorers to visit since the John C. Fremont expedition of 1853 and the Ferdinand Hayden expedition of 1869.

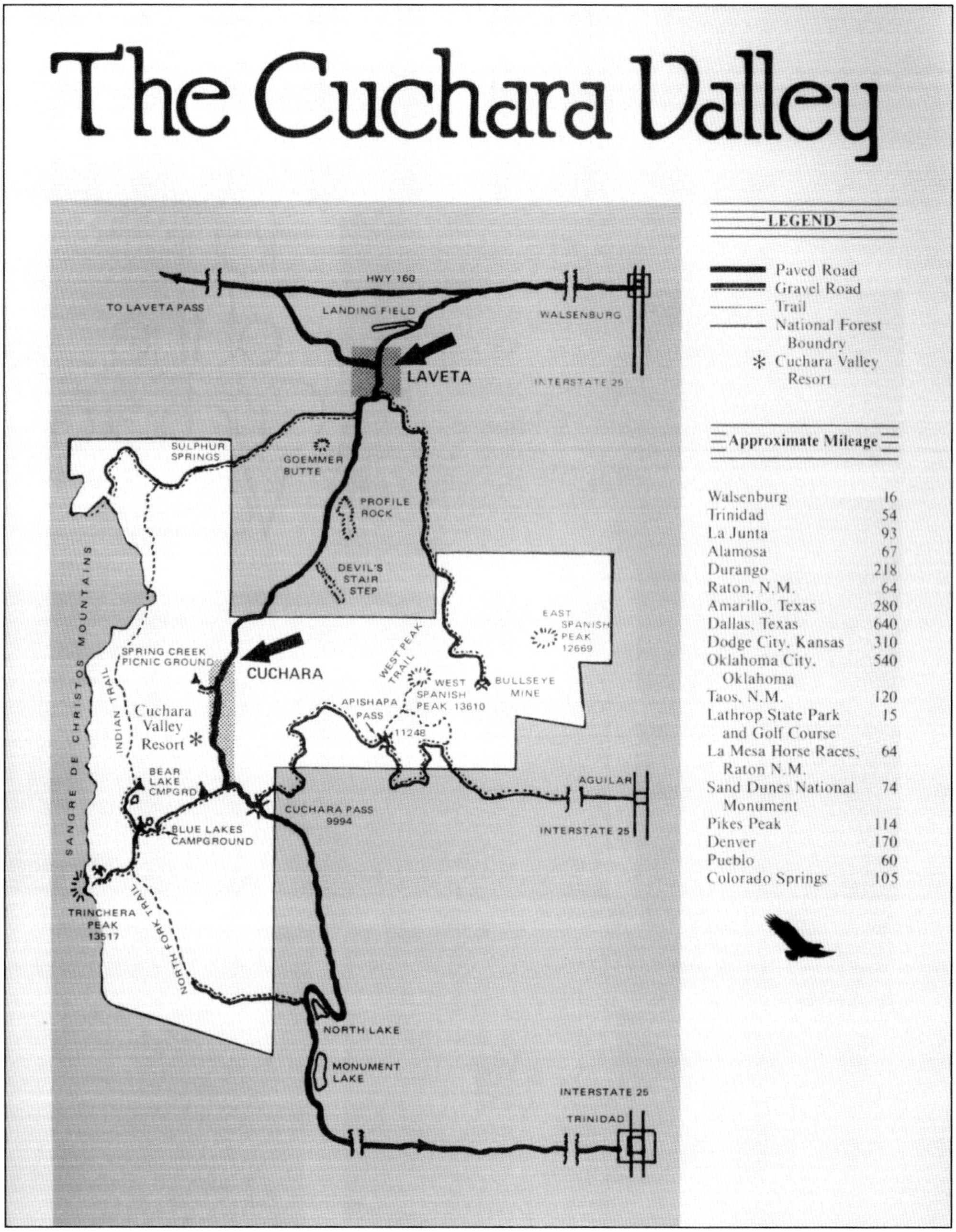

Spanish Peaks Area Map. This map offers an overview of features and locations noted throughout this book. Published by *Cucharan Magazine* in its winter 1984 issue, the map needs a little updating today: the resort is now Cuchara Mountain Resort, Apishapa Pass is now known as Cordova Pass, and the elevation of the Spanish Peaks is a bit higher according to modern surveys. (Dwight Harrison.)

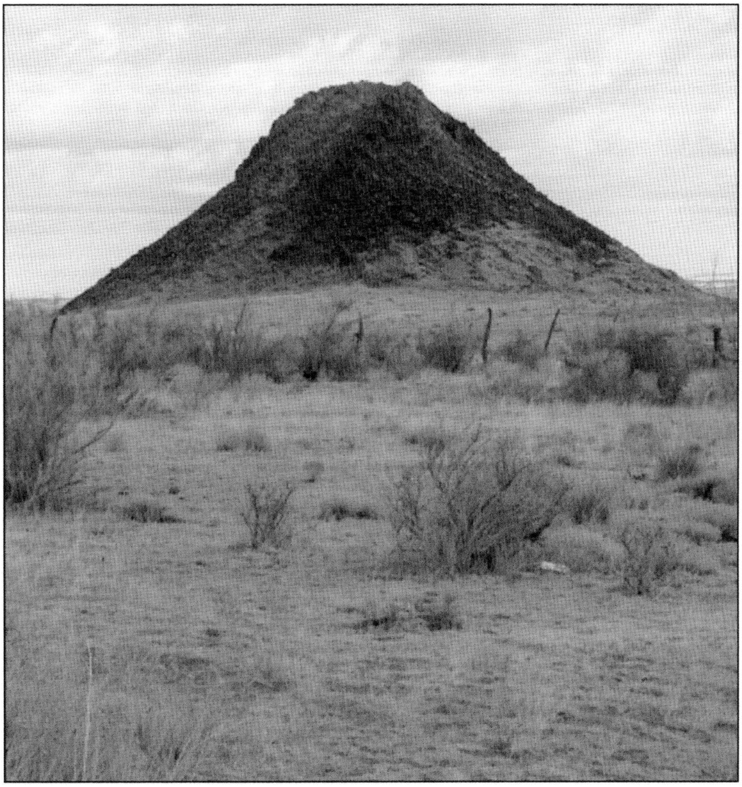

HUERFANO BUTTE. A few miles north of Walsenburg, this butte was a marker on the trapper's trail to Taos. Traders followed the Huerfano River west from the butte, to Sangre de Cristo Pass, to the San Luis Valley, and on to Taos. John C. Fremont's expedition passed Huerfano Butte in 1853 while searching for a western rail route.

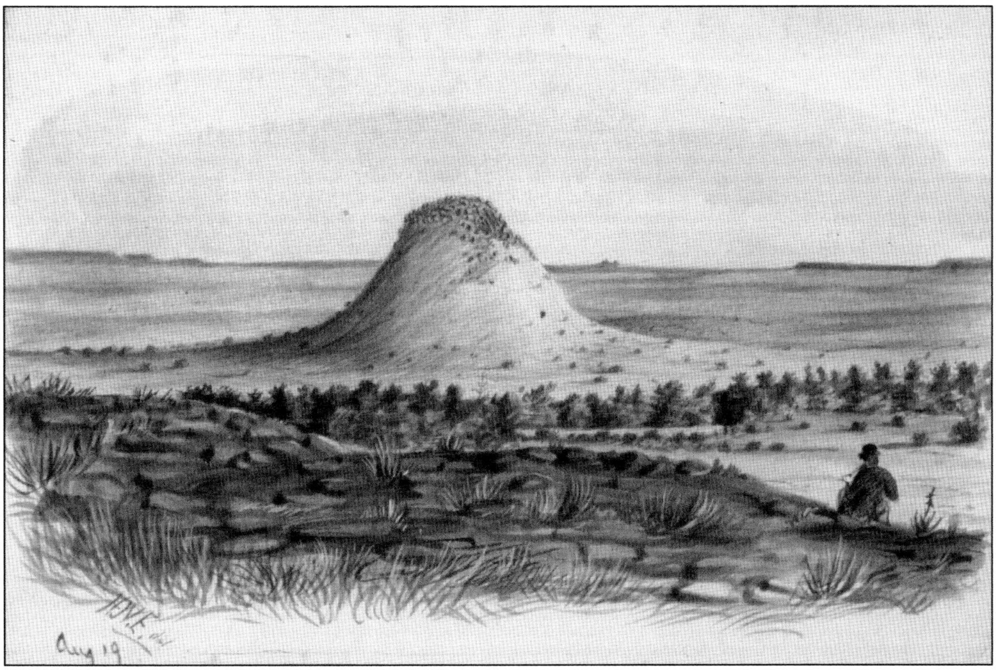

HAYDEN EXPEDITION, 1869. Ferdinand V. Hayden was a surveyor who participated in the great federal surveys of the western territories. He sketched this diagram of the Huerfano Butte on August 19, 1869. (USGS.)

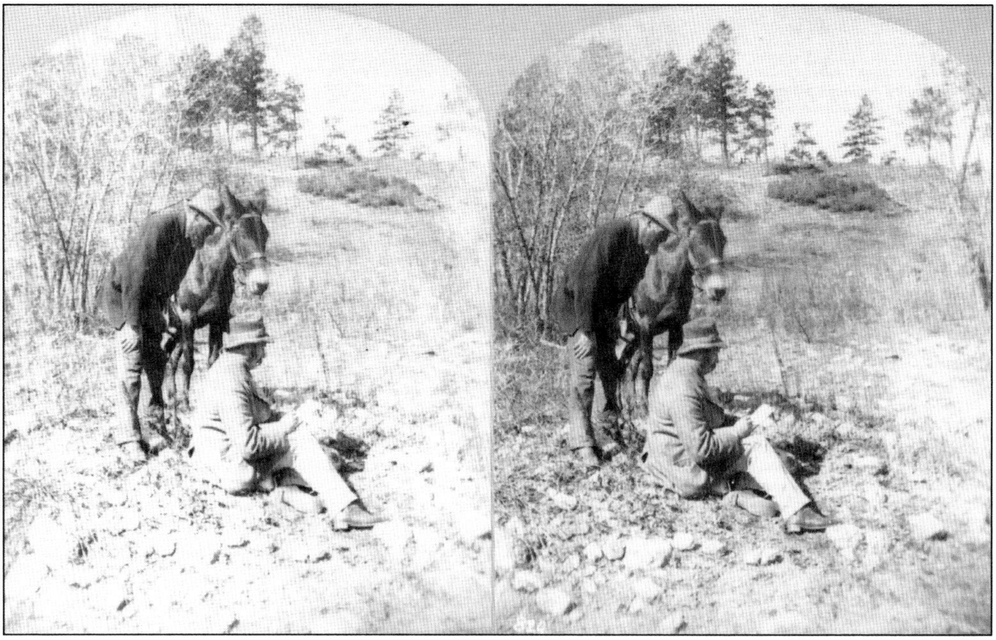

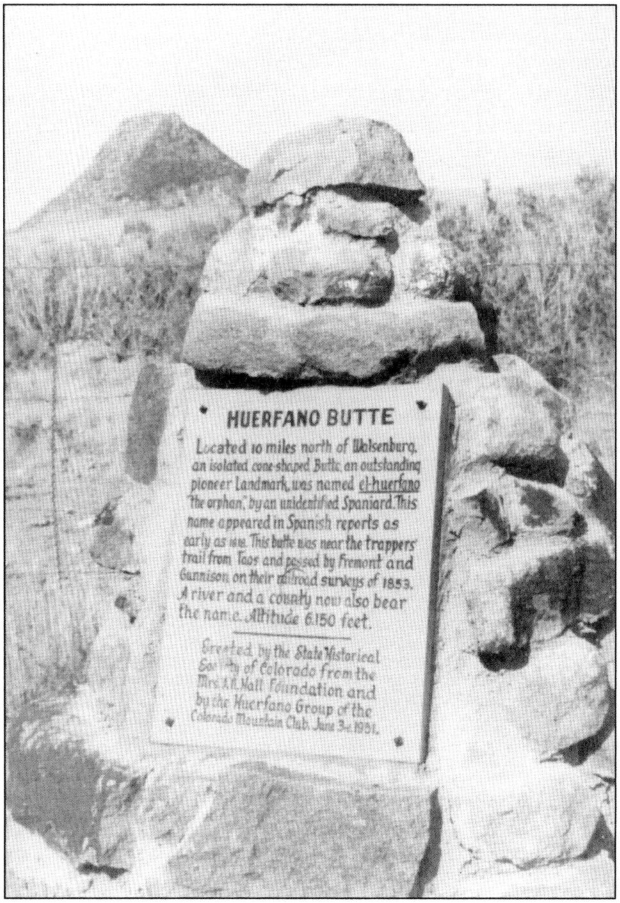

Dr. Hayden Sketching. This 1874 William Henry Jackson stereo photograph shows Ferdinand Hayden (seated) sketching western scenery for his journals. Walter Paris, another member of the US Geological Survey team, looks over Hayden's shoulder. (USGS.)

Huerfano Butte, 1951. In this close-up, the stone marker placed by the Colorado Historical Society and the Colorado Mountain Club appears to dwarf the actual butte.

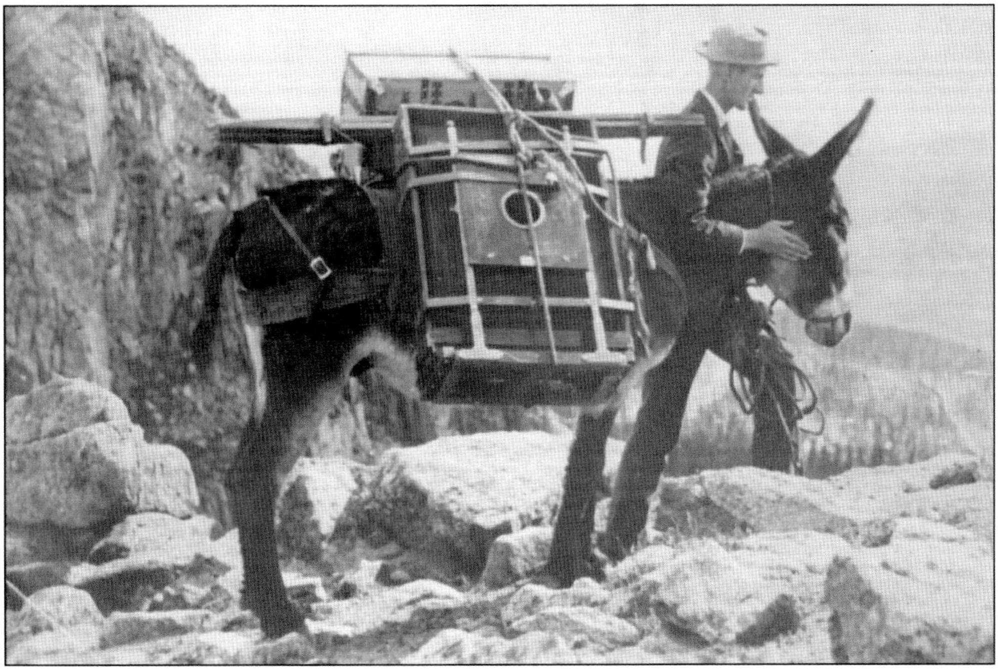

William Henry Jackson and His Pack Mule, 1873. Jackson roamed the west from the 1870s through the 1890s, taking hundreds of photographs wherever he went. His large box camera is visible strapped to the right side of the mule, with the tripod on top. The camera could take glass-plate photographs that were 20.5 inches by 16 inches in size. (LOC.)

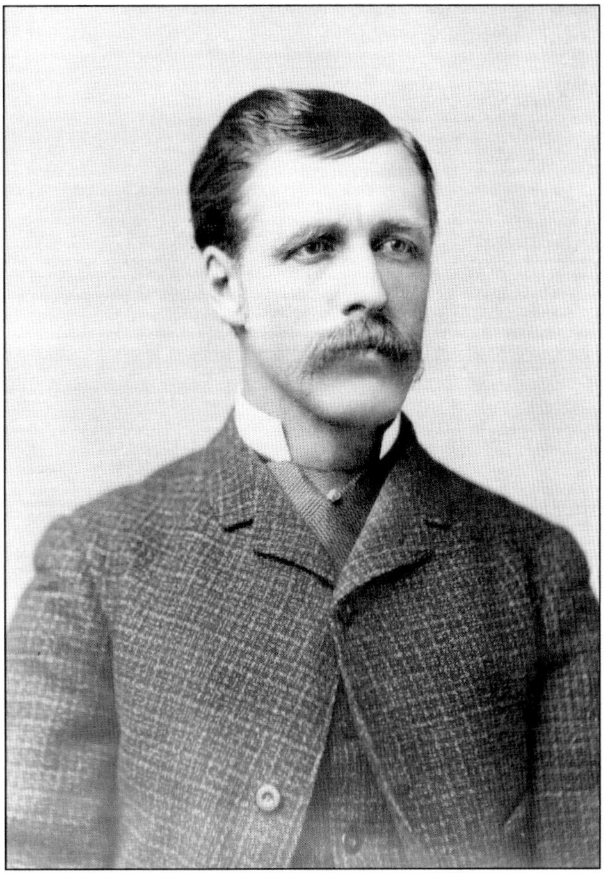

William Henry Jackson, 1880. This portrait of young Jackson was made in a studio. Jackson enjoyed venturing around the Colorado mountains with his pack mule, taking photographs of the Spanish Peaks and trains on Veta Pass. His photographs of Colorado and the west have been gathered in many modern books. (USGS.)

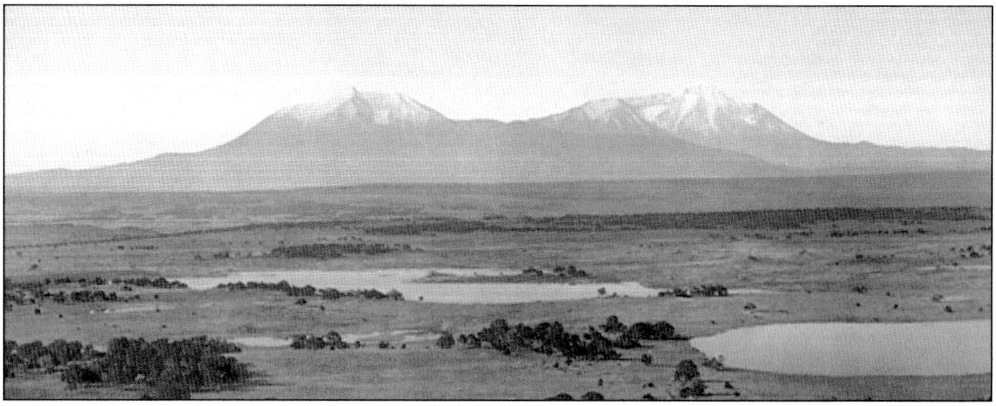

LAKES NORTH OF THE SPANISH PEAKS. The lakes in W.H. Jackson's photograph are near what is now Lathrop State Park, three miles west of Walsenburg. Note the lack of trees on the high, dry plains around 1890. The East Spanish Peak (on the left) rises to 12,708 feet, while the West Spanish Peak climbs to 13,623 feet. (LOC.)

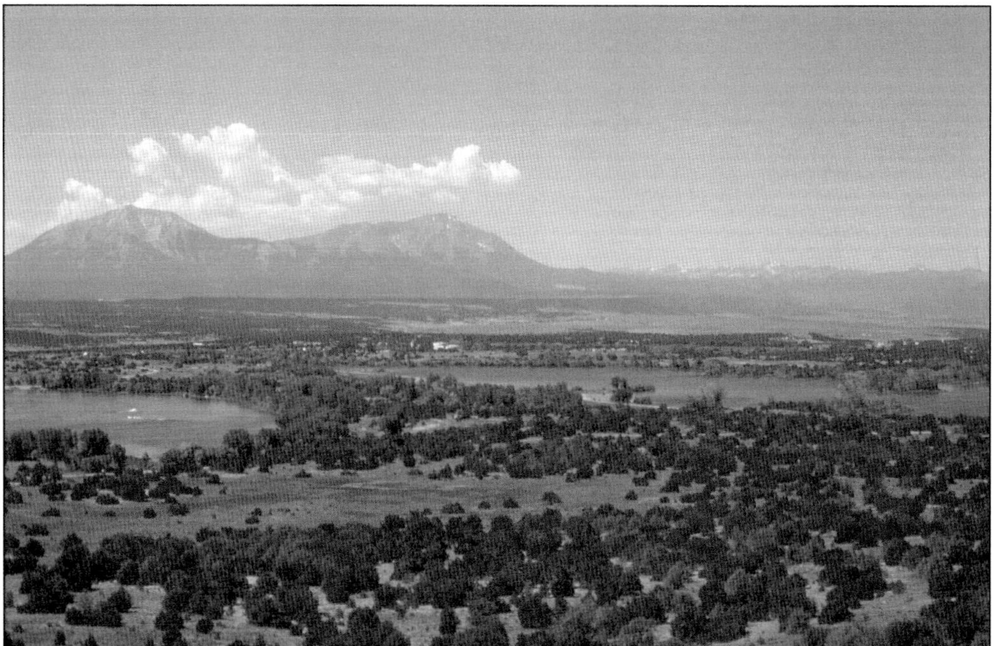

LATHROP STATE PARK LAKES. This contemporary view of the Spanish Peaks shows the predominance of piñon pine trees that have grown around the lakes since Jackson's 1890s-era photograph. The Sangre de Cristo Range stretches along to the right of the Spanish Peaks.

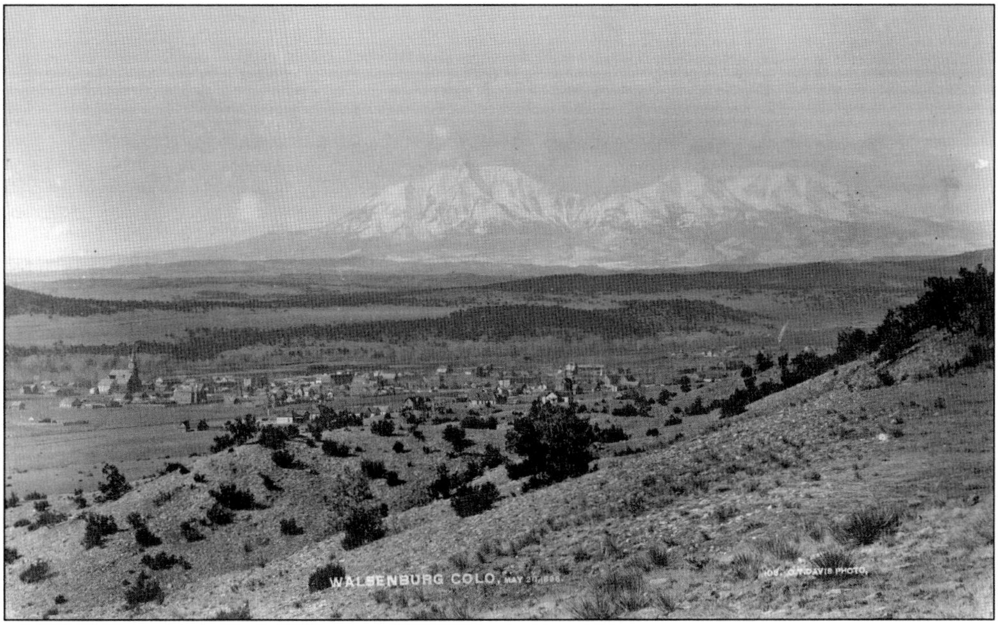

WALSENBURG AND THE SPANISH PEAKS, 1890S. Ory T. Davis took this photograph and several others that are reproduced in this book. Originally from Iowa, Davis moved to Colorado in the 1880s. He mined for copper on Pass Creek, west of La Veta Pass. When the mines played out, he became a commercial photographer in La Veta and Walsenburg, capturing the mines, railroads, and people of the area. (DPL no. X-14012.)

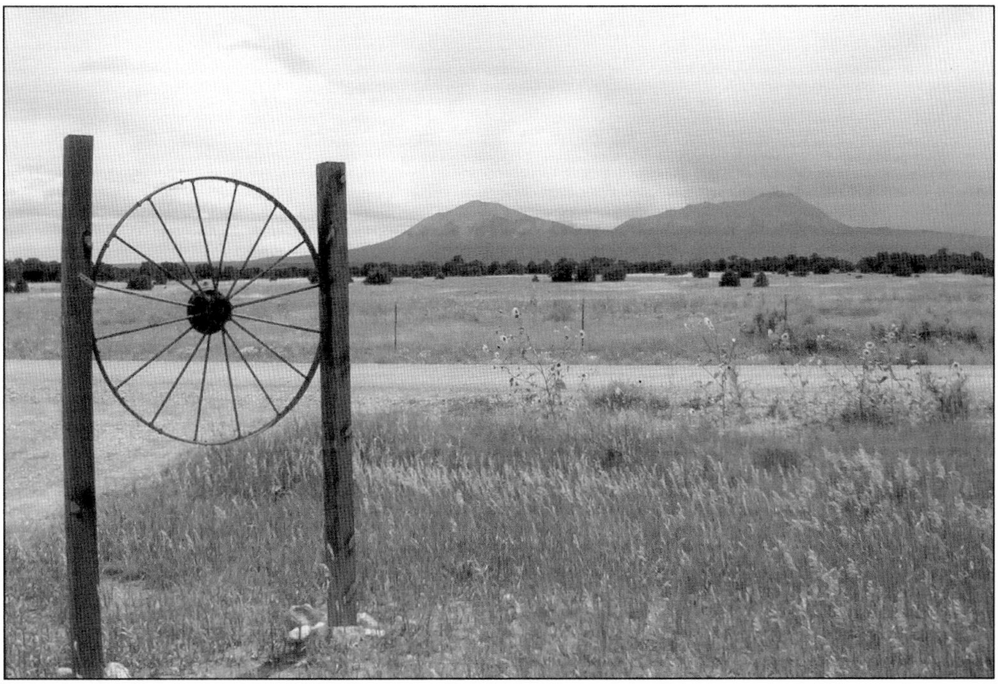

SPANISH PEAKS FROM NAVAJO RANCH. Navajo Ranch is about 10 miles west of Walsenburg and offers incredible views south toward the Spanish Peaks. The wagon wheel evokes memories of the early pioneers of the area.

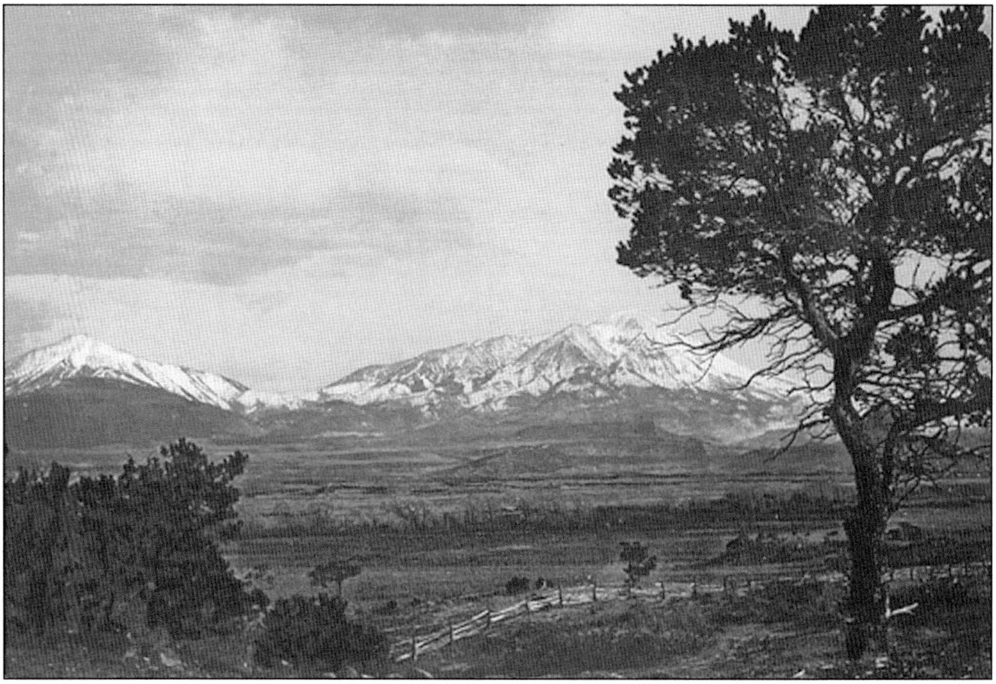

Spanish Peaks, 1880s. This William Henry Jackson photograph shows the snowcapped Spanish Peaks from a viewpoint north of La Veta. The scenic split-rail fence indicates the presence of cattle ranches, which are still predominant in the La Veta area today. (LOC.)

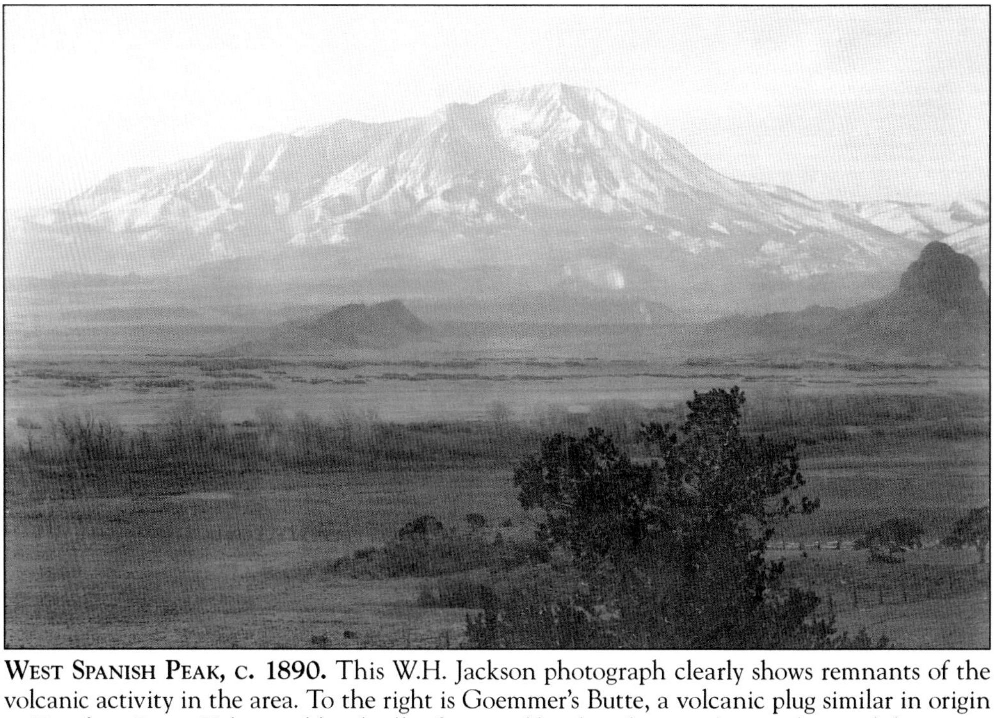

West Spanish Peak, c. 1890. This W.H. Jackson photograph clearly shows remnants of the volcanic activity in the area. To the right is Goemmer's Butte, a volcanic plug similar in origin to Huerfano Butte. Volcanic dikes (walls of exposed hardened magma) extend toward the viewer from the base of the peak. (DPL no. WHJ-1536.)

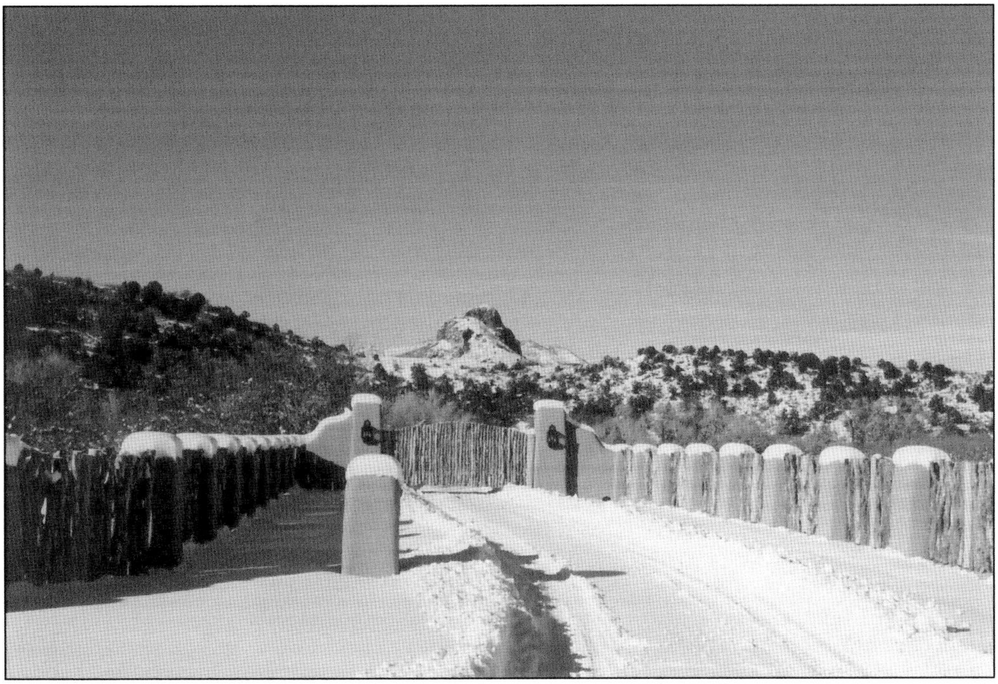

Goemmer's Butte. A winter snowfall has left about 10 inches of new snow along a ranch entrance south of Goemmer's Butte. Goemmer's Butte, a volcanic plug, is visible south of La Veta off Highway 12.

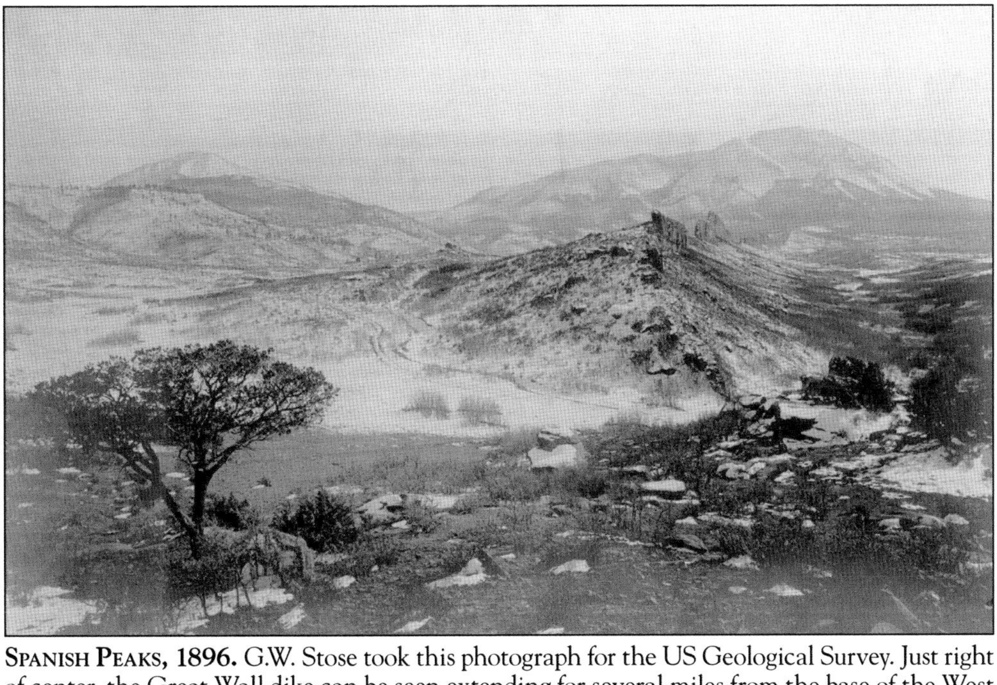

Spanish Peaks, 1896. G.W. Stose took this photograph for the US Geological Survey. Just right of center, the Great Wall dike can be seen extending for several miles from the base of the West Spanish Peak. This is the longest dike in the Spanish Peaks area. Dikes can be anywhere from a few feet to several miles in length. (USGS.)

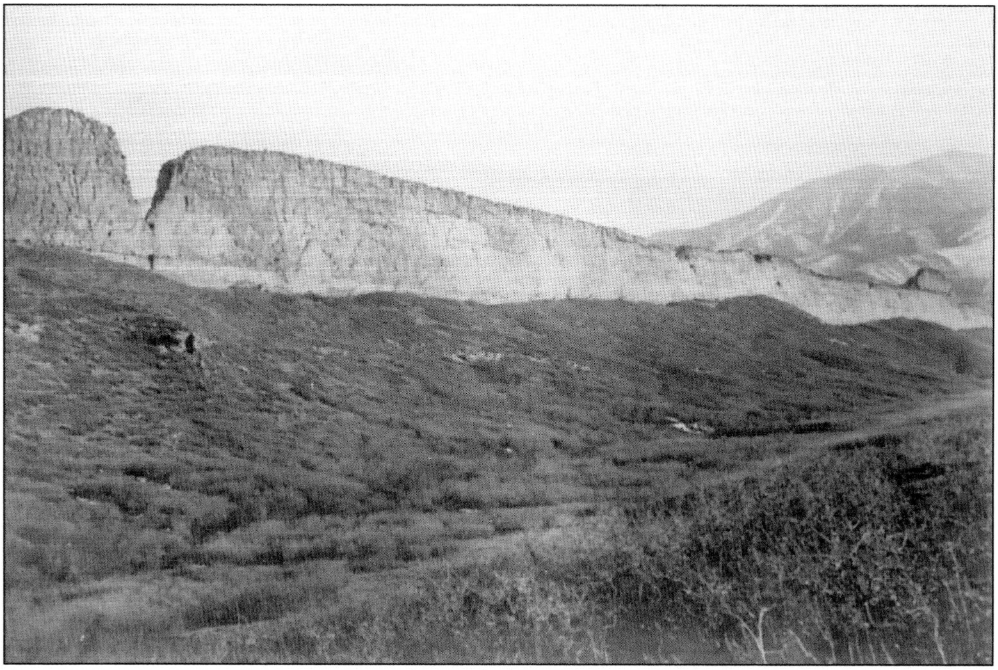

Great Wall Dike, 1896. G.W. Stose also took this spectacular photograph showing the height of the dike. This dike ranges 100 feet or more above the valley. The West Spanish Peak is visible at the right end of the dike. Smaller dikes around the Spanish Peaks may only be five to ten feet above surrounding ground. (USGS.)

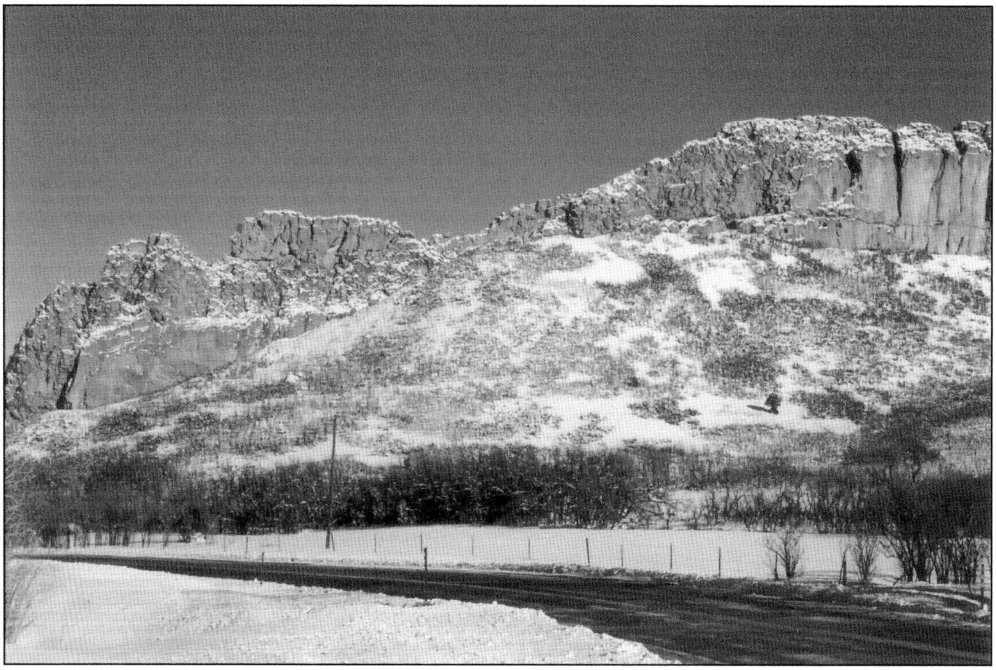

Profile Rock Dike. Snow outlines the Profile Rock dike in winter. Located just a few miles south of La Veta on Highway 12, Profile Rock takes its name from the imaginary profiles of faces seen along the ridgeline of the dike.

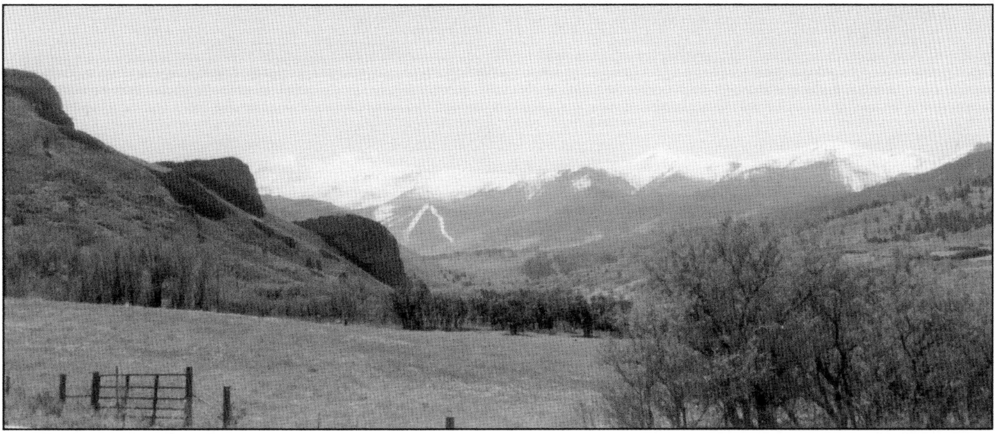

Devil's Stairsteps Dike. The dike on the left side of the photograph is known as the Devil's Stairsteps. The view is south toward the Cuchara Ski Area, with spring snow still covering the peaks and ski runs.

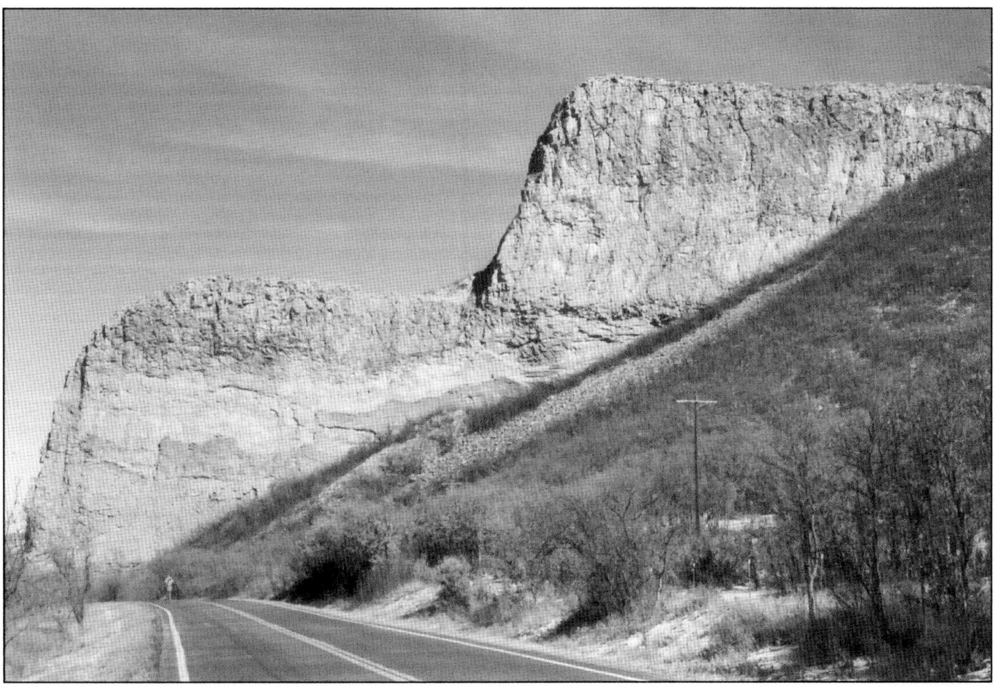

Highway 12 and the Devil's Stairsteps. In this view looking north, the dike towers hundreds of feet above the Highway of Legends. One legend has it that the devil climbed these rock stairs up to the Spanish Peaks for a better view before God banished him to the lower regions for eternity.

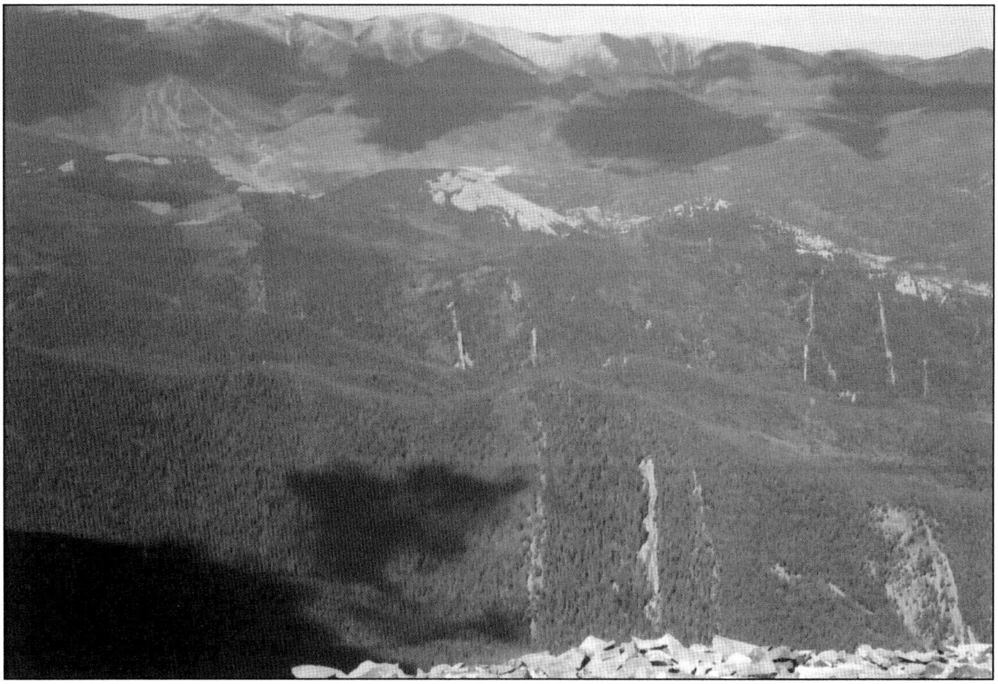

Dikes from the West Spanish Peak. The climb to the top of the West Spanish Peak rewards hikers with incredible views of dozens of dikes spreading out in all directions. The view here is west to the Cuchara Ski Area, which is visible at upper left. The dikes are visible as white lines of rock running from the bottom to halfway up the right side of the photograph.

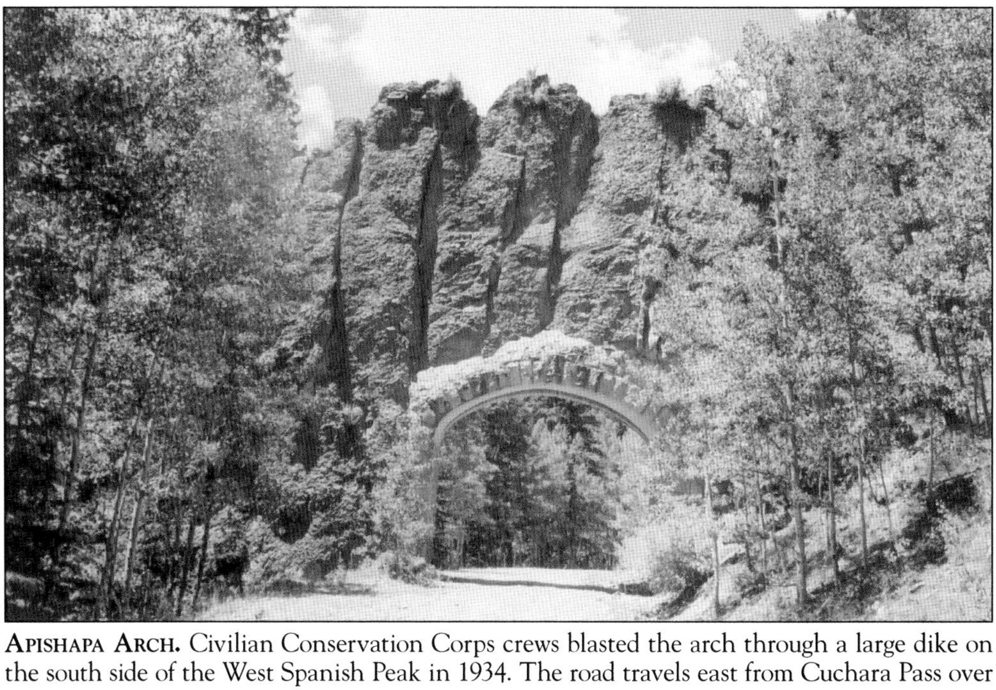

Apishapa Arch. Civilian Conservation Corps crews blasted the arch through a large dike on the south side of the West Spanish Peak in 1934. The road travels east from Cuchara Pass over Cordova Pass, then downhill through the arch and on to the town of Aguilar. The road follows Apishapa Creek—*apishapa* is an Apache word that means "stinking water."

Two

Native Americans and Francisco Fort

Comanche and Ute Indians roamed the area around the Spanish Peaks, although the harsh winters prompted a seasonal migration to warmer areas to the south. By the 1860s, the Utes were the predominant tribe in the area, and it was their presence that prompted John Francisco to build his fort in 1862. The fort was built around a plaza a few blocks east of the Cuchara River. This later became the site of the town of La Veta.

John Francisco had been a sutler (civilian supplier) at Fort Garland in the San Luis valley, west of La Veta Pass. His supply trips frequently took him east over the pass and through the lush Cuchara River valley at the north foot of the Spanish Peaks. Declaring, "this is paradise enough for me," Francisco decided to purchase land in the valley with his trading partner Henry Daigre. They raised cattle and crops there, but frequently felt threatened by marauding Utes and so began construction of an adobe fort, built in a *U* shape with a log stockade on the open east side. All doors and windows faced inward to the plaza so that there were no exposed areas on the outer adobe walls. Sharpshooters, protected by parapets built on the flat adobe roof, could fire down upon any attacking Indians.

In 1863, Francisco Fort was surrounded by Kaniache's band of Ute Indians. The Utes probably hoped to starve out Francisco and his men, but they did not know that the settlers were prepared with harvested crops (wheat, corn, beans) and a water well dug in the center of the plaza. Francisco could hold out for weeks, but nevertheless sent Hiram Vasquez out in the dark of night to ride his mule 120 miles to Fort Lyons on the Arkansas River to bring back the cavalry. By the time the soldiers arrived at Francisco Fort, Kaniache was gone, persuaded with a few sides of beef to depart. Kaniache threatened again in 1873, raiding ranches and homes, but was dispatched west to what eventually became the Ute reservation in southwestern Colorado.

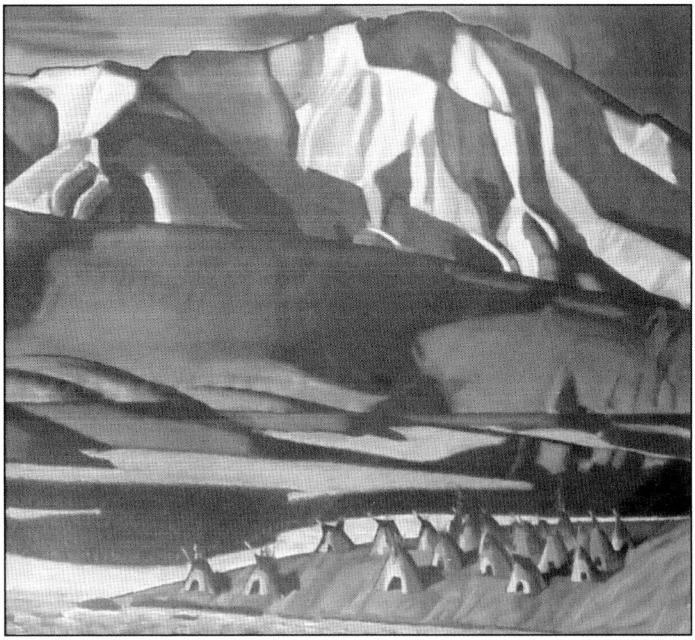

Blumenschein Mural. This close-up of a portion of Ernest Blumenschein's 1937 mural on the wall of the Walsenburg Post Office reveals Indian teepees on the plains north of the Spanish Peaks. Comanche and Ute Indians lived here, relying on the rain gods who lived atop the Wahatoyas to bring water to the valleys. (Brian Orr.)

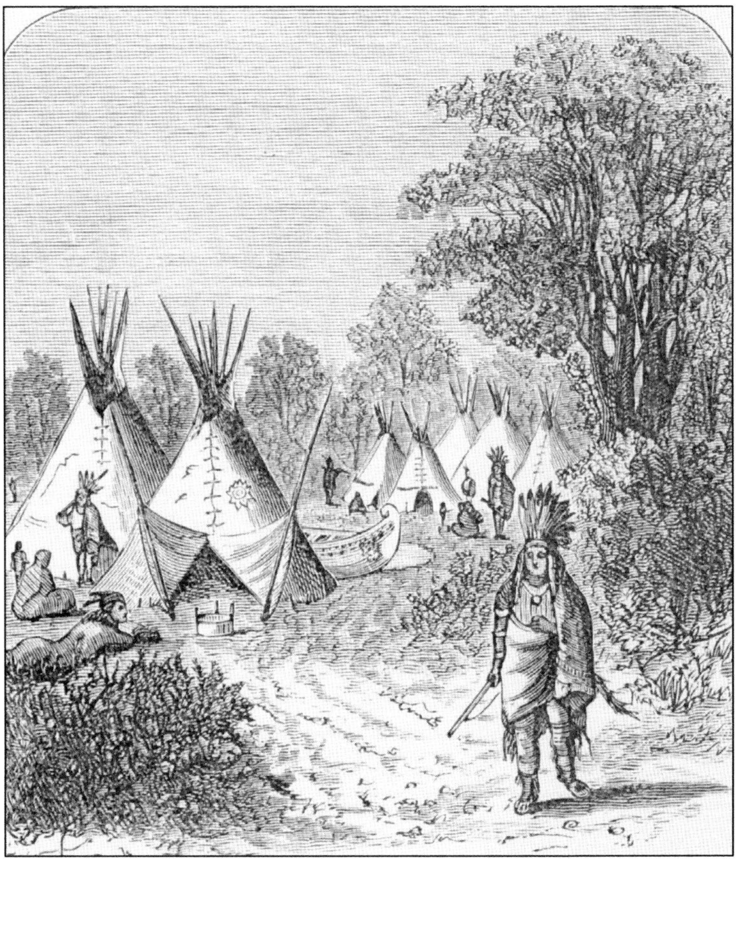

Ute Camp. This 1880s sketch illustrates a Ute camp on the White River in northwestern Colorado. Similar encampments would have existed near the Spanish Peaks along the Cuchara River.

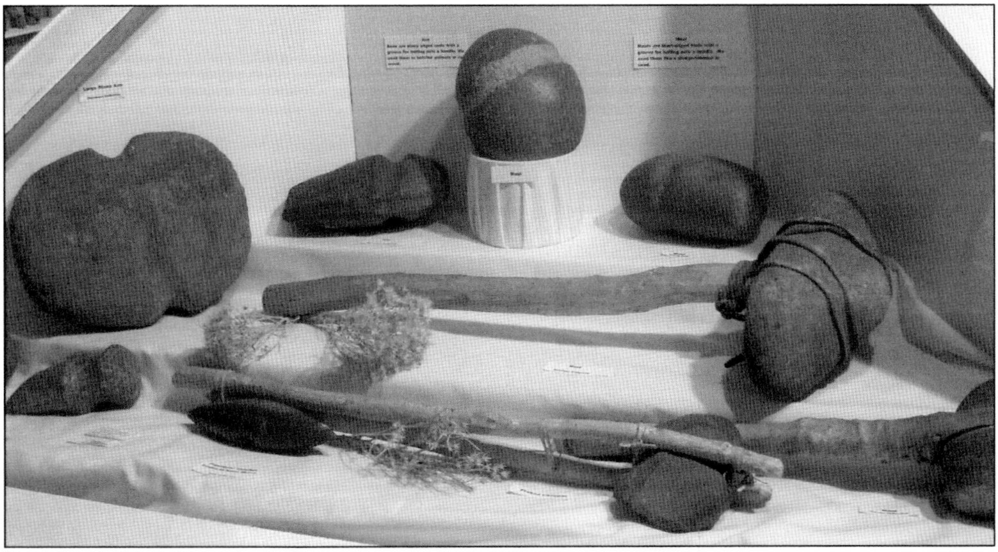

INDIAN AXES AND CLUBS. Native Americans shaped large stones into ax and club heads. These artifacts on display in Francisco Fort Museum show how the stone heads were tied to wooden handles. The stones without handles still show the grooves where they were once tied.

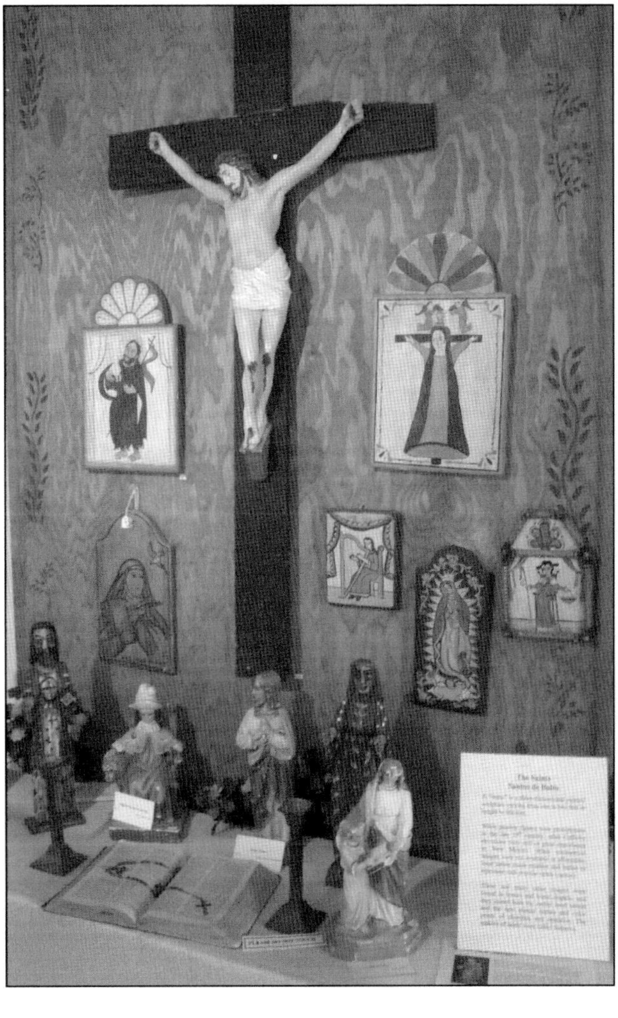

FRANCISCO FORT SANTO COLLECTION. Reminiscent of the early Hispanic settlers of the Cuchara valley, these santos (figures of saints) depict various saints revered by the devout Hispanic Catholic population. Some Hispanic men joined the Penitente brotherhood, whose members memorialized Christ's suffering by whipping themselves.

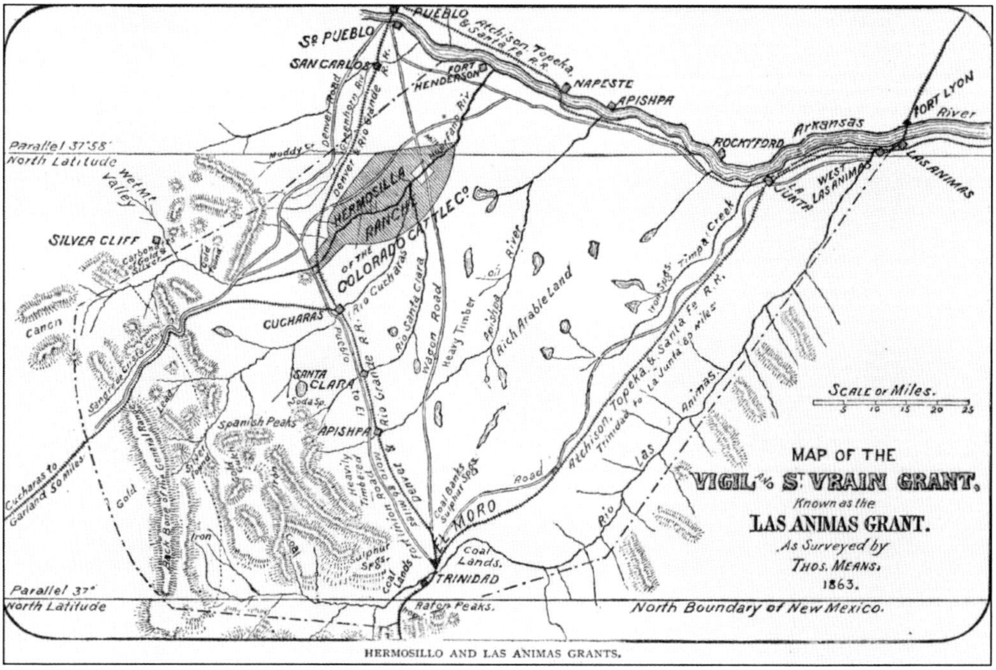

Vigil–St. Vrain Land Grant. In 1843, the governor of New Mexico ceded over four million acres of land to Cornelio Vigil and Ceran St. Vrain. This vast area ran from the northern boundary of what became New Mexico all the way north to the Arkansas River. John Francisco became partners with St. Vrain in an 1862 cattle venture and purchased land from St. Vrain in 1863 that became the location for Francisco Fort.

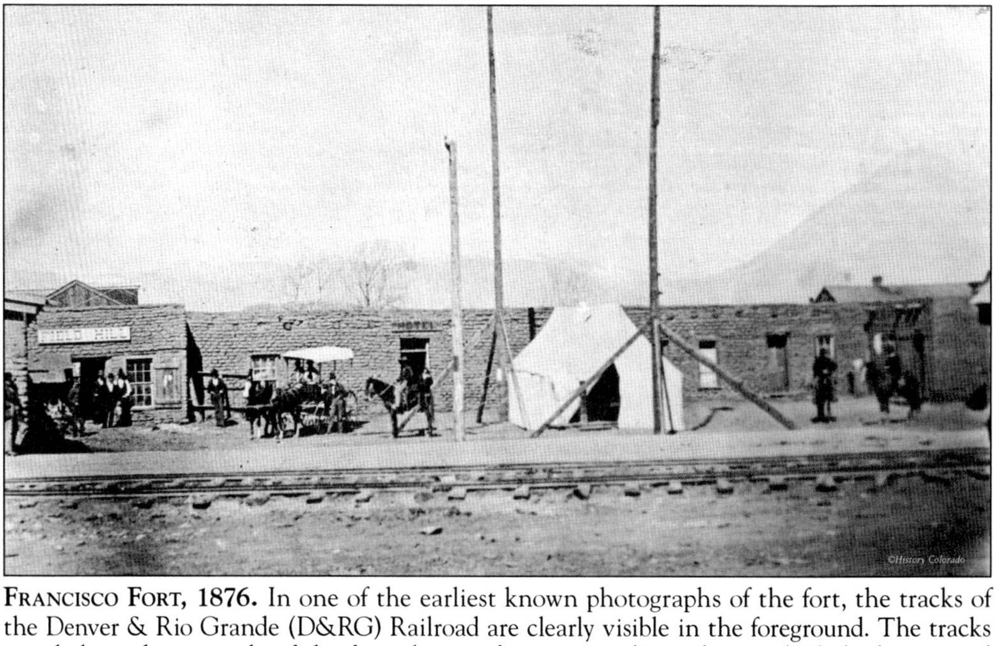

Francisco Fort, 1876. In one of the earliest known photographs of the fort, the tracks of the Denver & Rio Grande (D&RG) Railroad are clearly visible in the foreground. The tracks stand along the east side of the fort where, a few years earlier, a log stockade had protected the fort from Indian attacks. A building at the south (left) end of the fort served as a railroad depot. (HCO no. 20007638.)

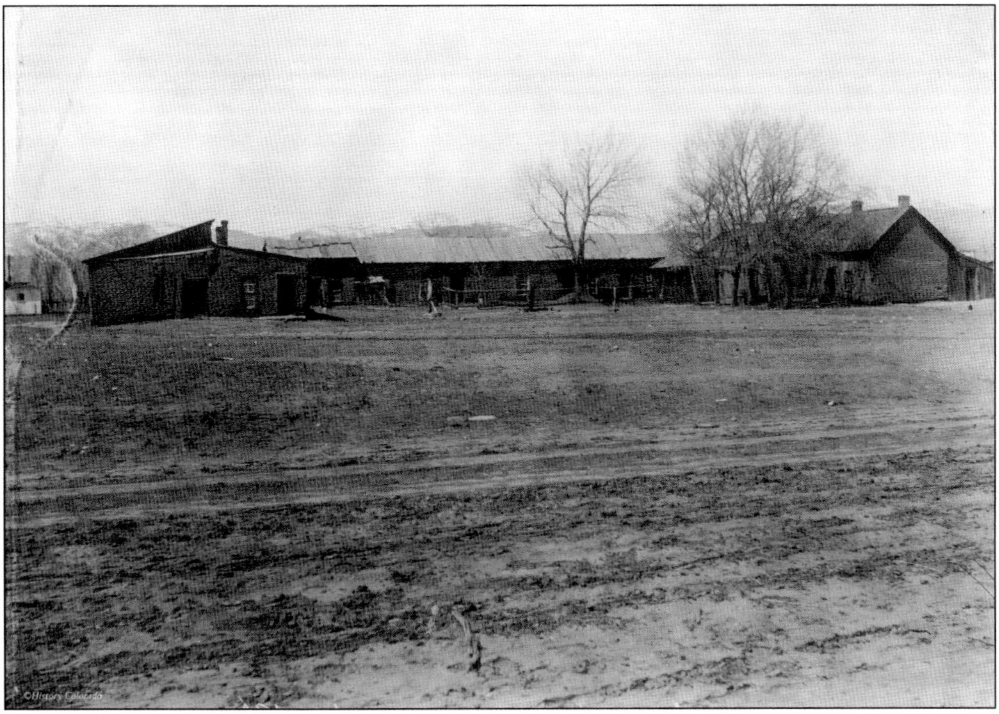

FRANCISCO PLAZA, 1890. In this O.T. Davis photograph, the U-shape of the fort is clearly visible. By 1890, the railroad tracks at the front of the "U" had been removed, with the station moved a few blocks north to D&RG Railroad property. (HCO no. 20007632.)

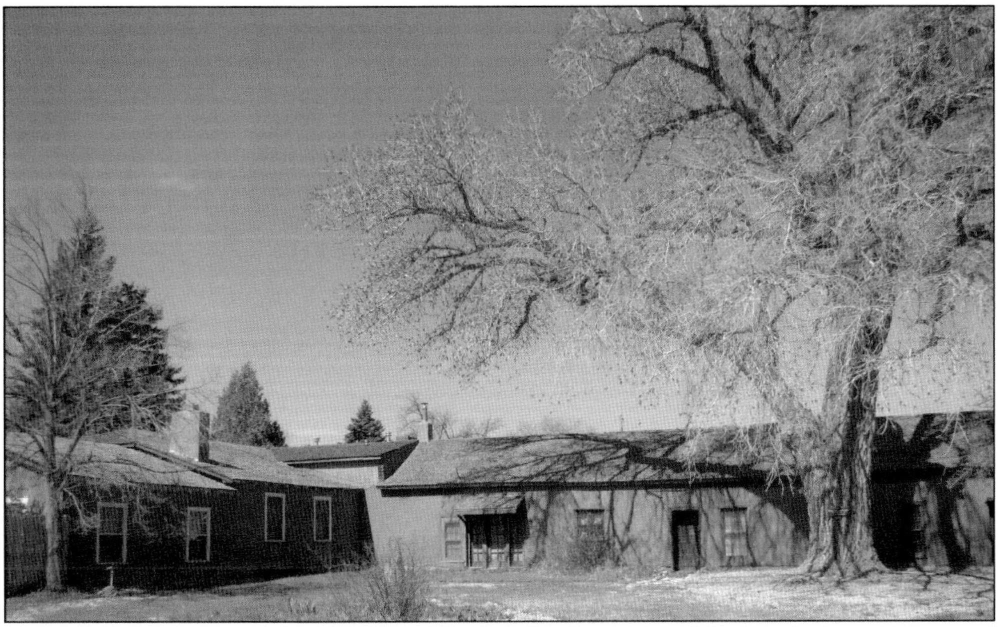

FRANCISCO FORT, SOUTHWEST CORNER. In this contemporary view of the fort, the large cottonwood tree at right is the same one visible in the 1890 O.T. Davis photograph. In 1878, John Francisco planted this tree just west of the well that supplied water to the settlers in the fort.

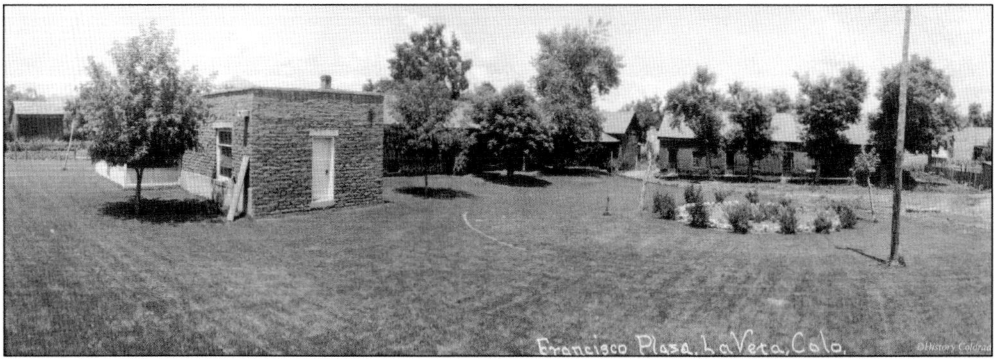

FRANCISCO PLAZA, C. 1924. This northward view shows the north and northwest wings of Francisco Fort, with a gap between the two buildings. When this served as a fort, the gap was bridged by a tall log gate that kept Indians out but allowed wagons and horses to pass through when opened. The log pole at right marks where the D&RGW Railroad tracks passed in front of the fort in 1876. (HCO no. 20007634.)

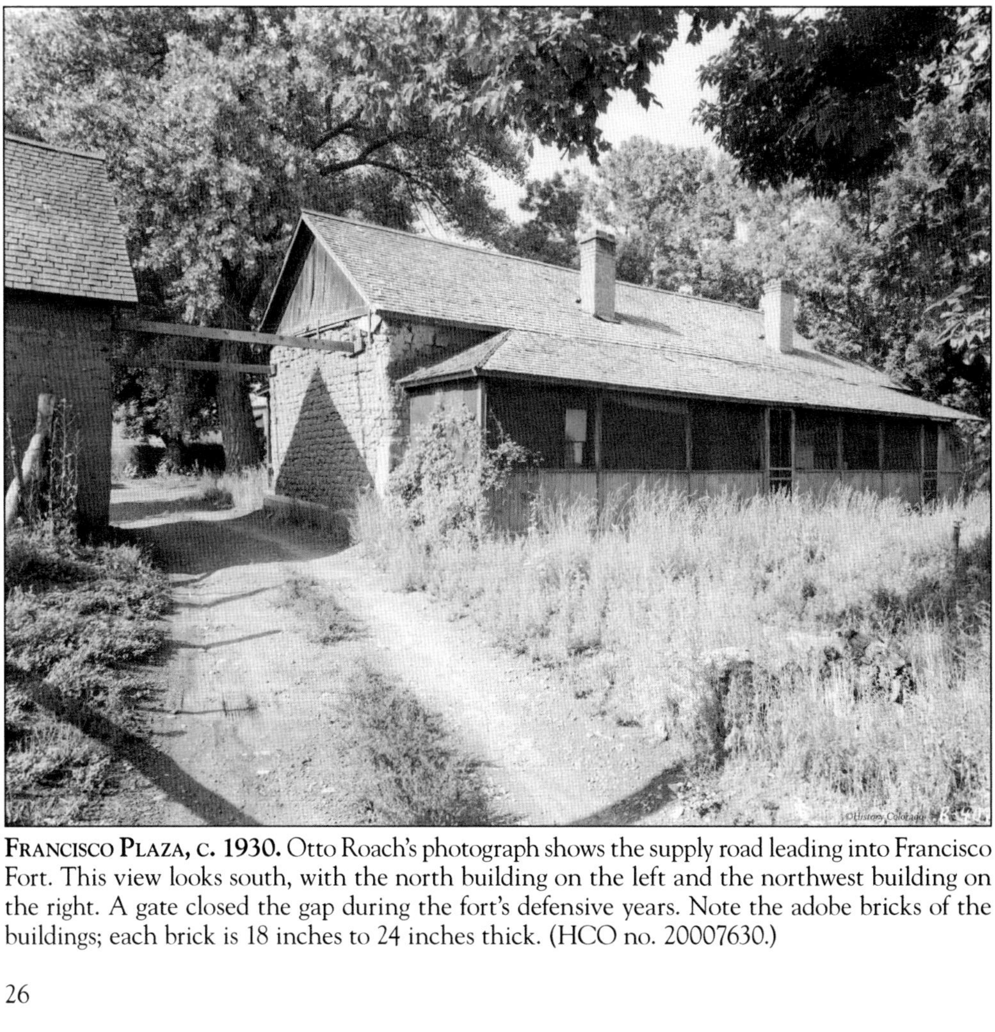

FRANCISCO PLAZA, C. 1930. Otto Roach's photograph shows the supply road leading into Francisco Fort. This view looks south, with the north building on the left and the northwest building on the right. A gate closed the gap during the fort's defensive years. Note the adobe bricks of the buildings; each brick is 18 inches to 24 inches thick. (HCO no. 20007630.)

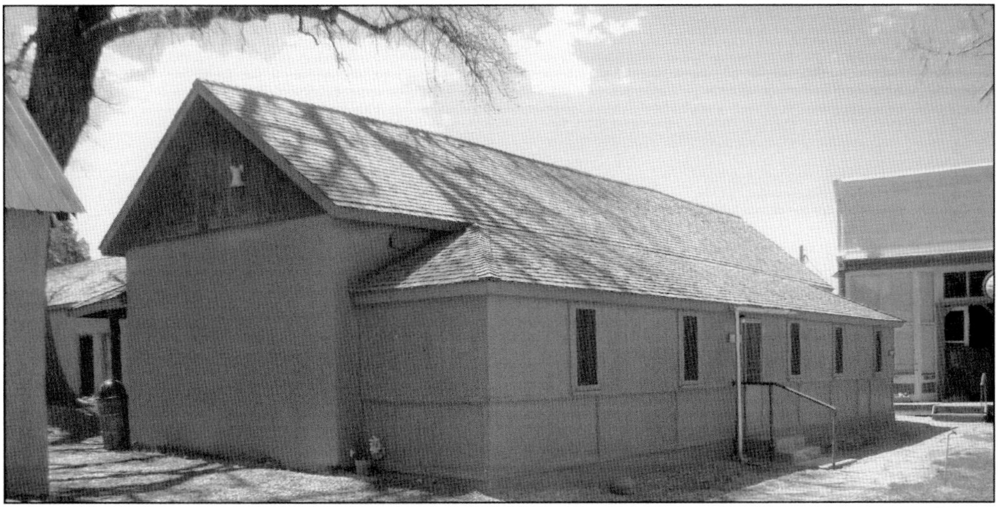

Francisco Fort, Northwest Building. This contemporary view shows the same northwest building visible in Otto Roach's 1930 photograph. Note that the adobe bricks have been plastered over, the chimneys removed, and the overhanging porch enclosed.

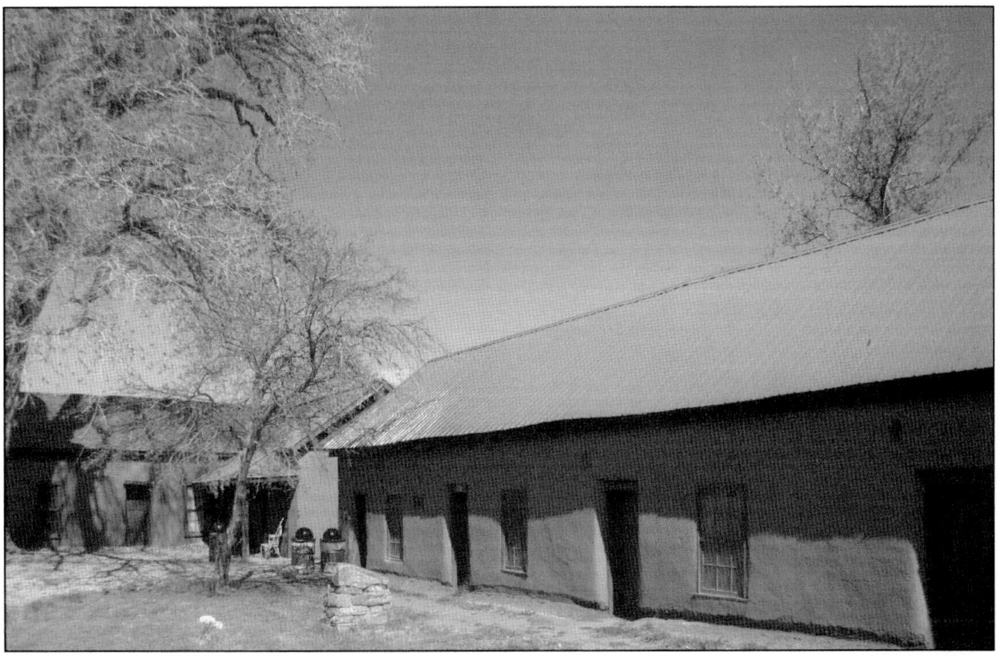

Individual Rooms in Francisco Fort. Several individual doors were set into the adobe walls. While each room currently contains separate displays within Francisco Fort Museum, originally, each room was housing for a fort occupant. Note that all doors and windows face into the plaza. The outside walls had no doors or windows, to protect against attacks.

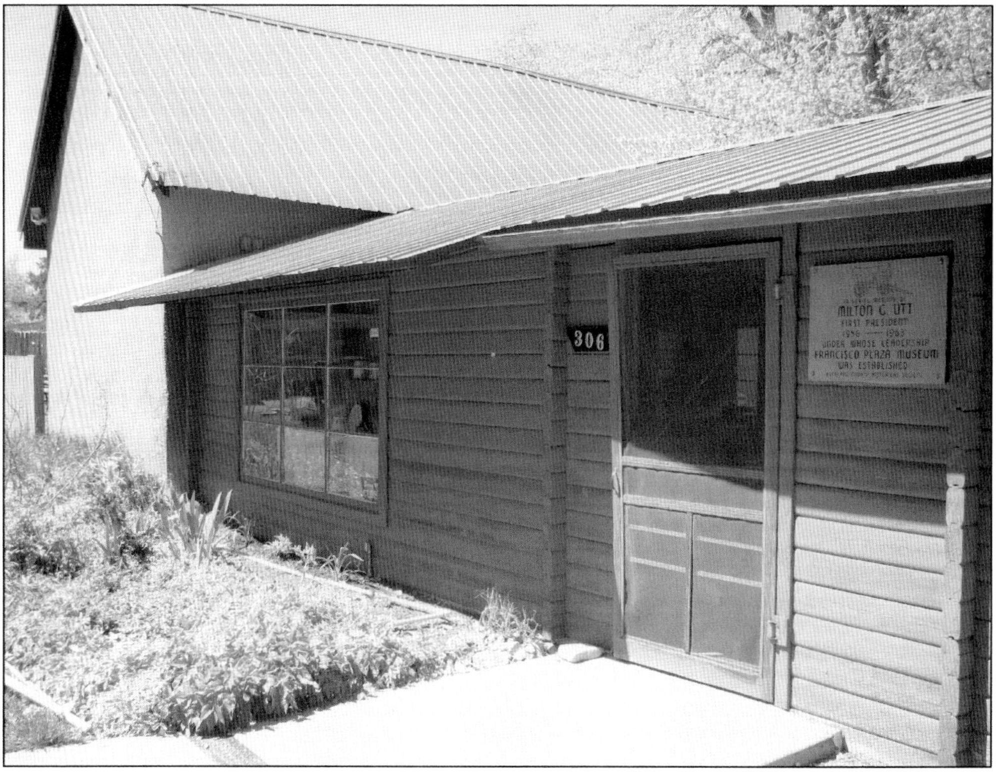

Log Cabin Entrance. This contemporary entrance to Francisco Fort Museum is a 1950s add-on to the original fort's adobe building. It serves as a visitors center, with a gift shop and office. The plaque by the door honors Milton Utt, first president of the Huerfano County Historical Society, who served from 1956 to 1963.

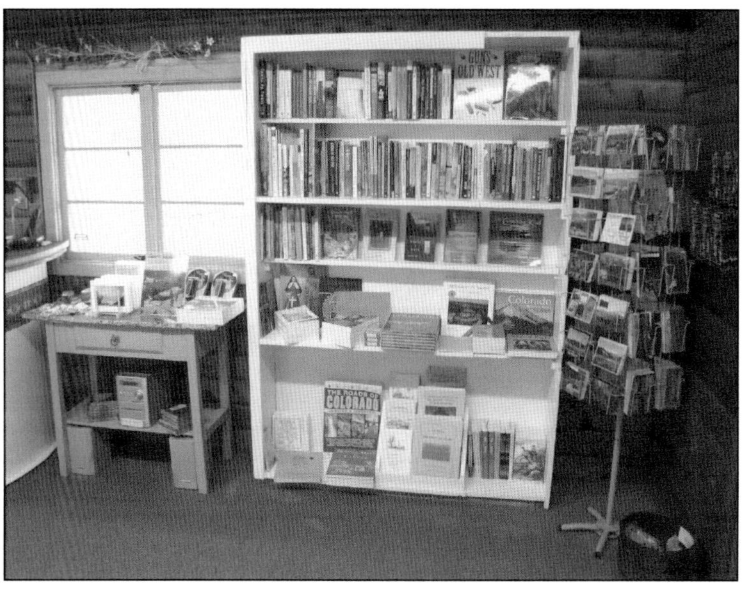

Francisco Fort Museum Gift Shop. Francisco Fort opened for public tours in 1958. In 1986, Francisco Plaza was listed in the National Register of Historic Places.

Three

La Veta and Its Stone Buildings

In 1873, after the Indian threat ended, Francisco Fort prospered. A post office named Spanish Peaks had been established in the fort in 1871. Other settlers built homes near the fort. Growth really took off, though, with the arrival of the Denver & Rio Grande Western (D&RGW) Railroad in 1876. The railroad built tracks right next to the fort, on the east side, where the old stockade had been taken down. A depot office was established in one of the southwest rooms of the fort.

As was common throughout Colorado, the railroad formed a land company to buy land around town and then built the depot on their own land. Thus, the Francisco Fort depot was abandoned, and the D&RGW built a depot two blocks further north. It was also common for the railroad to change the name of a community; Spanish Peaks became La Veta, which is Spanish for "the vein." Although the name *La Veta* was chosen by the railroad, its origin is obscure. It could refer to the dikes radiating out from the Spanish Peaks that looked like veins, or to a gold vein, or to a vein of white rock near town that was quarried, crushed, and used for whitewash on the adobe buildings.

With the construction of the D&RGW depot, development of the town shifted away from Francisco Plaza to Front Street (which fronted the depot). Merchant David Ryus arrived and built his store on the corner of Main and Front Streets. Front Street was later renamed Ryus Avenue. La Veta boomed, and 22 liquor licenses had been granted in the town by the end of 1876.

La Veta's notorious west winds played havoc with the frame buildings in town, and residents and businesses looked to nearby sandstone quarries for more substantial construction materials. The first stone building, the Masonic Hall, was erected in 1889. Many more stone structures were built through 1941. Today, more than 20 stone buildings can still be observed on a walking tour around town.

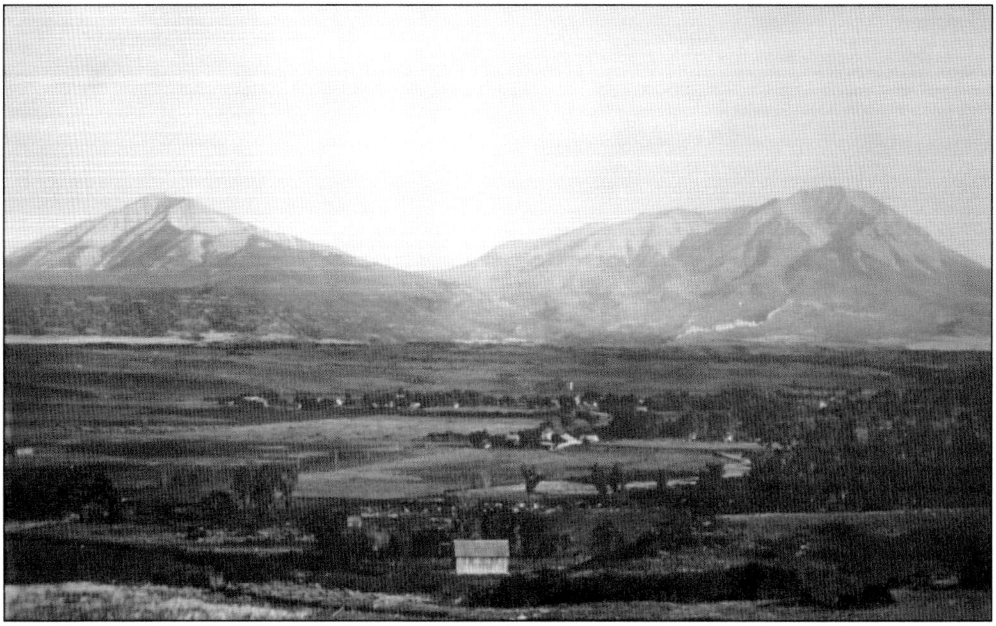

Spanish Peaks and La Veta. An unknown photographer captured this spectacular view of the Spanish Peaks and La Veta, probably in the 1880s. The Great Wall Dike is clearly visible, extending from the lower portion of the West Spanish Peak on the right. (FFM.)

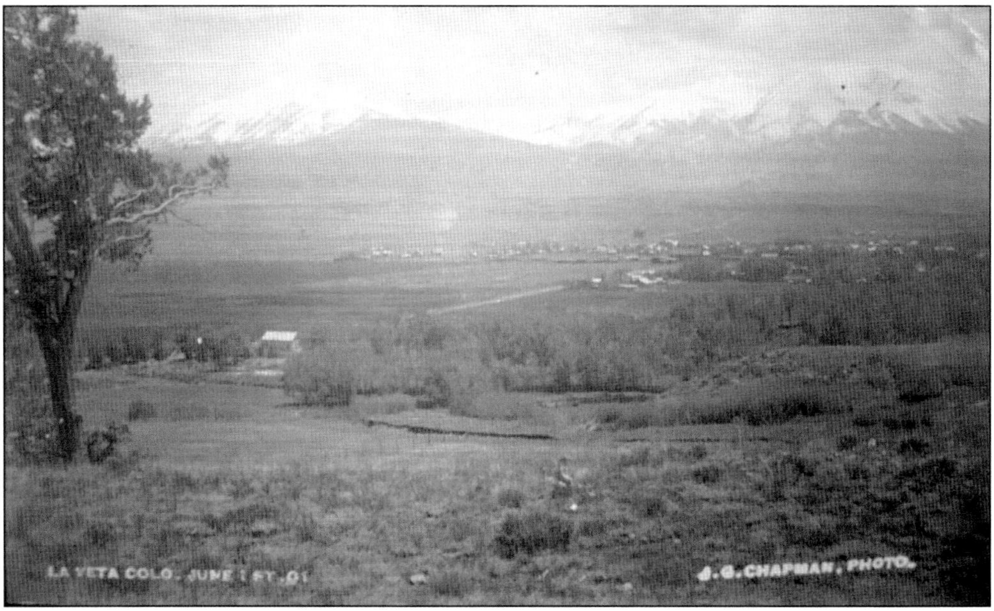

La Veta, June 1, 1901. J.G. Chapman's photograph of La Veta shows many more buildings than in the previous image. La Veta continued to grow after the narrow gauge railroad into La Veta was replaced by standard gauge in 1890. (FFM.)

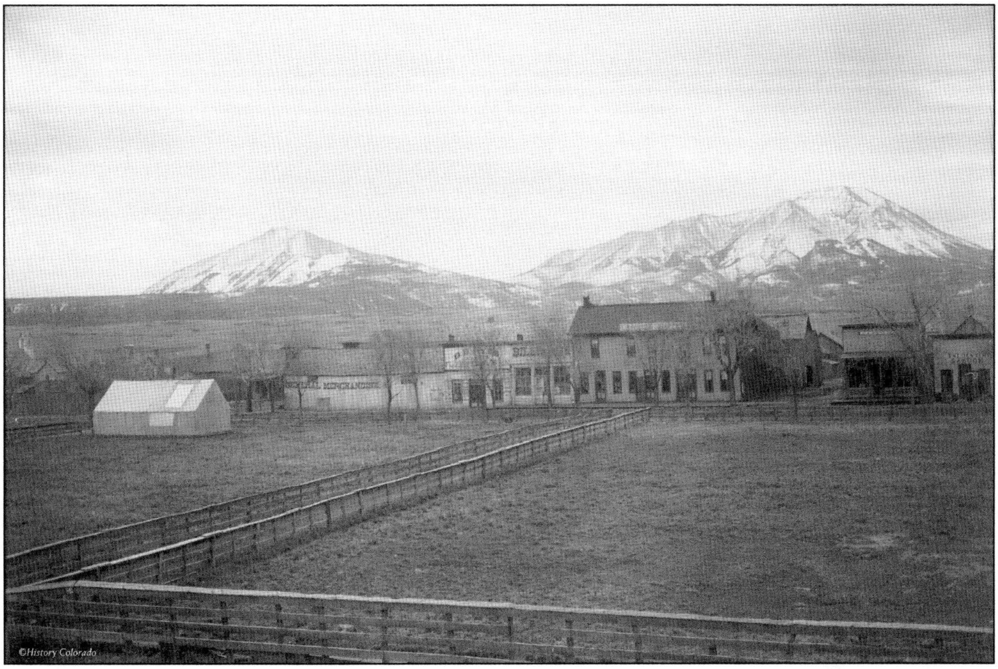

La Veta, c. 1883. The La Veta Hotel is the two-story building with two chimneys. To the left of the hotel is D.D. Ryus's general store and billiard hall. The street in front of these buildings was originally called Front Street, but the name was changed to Ryus Avenue. (HCO no. 20004940.)

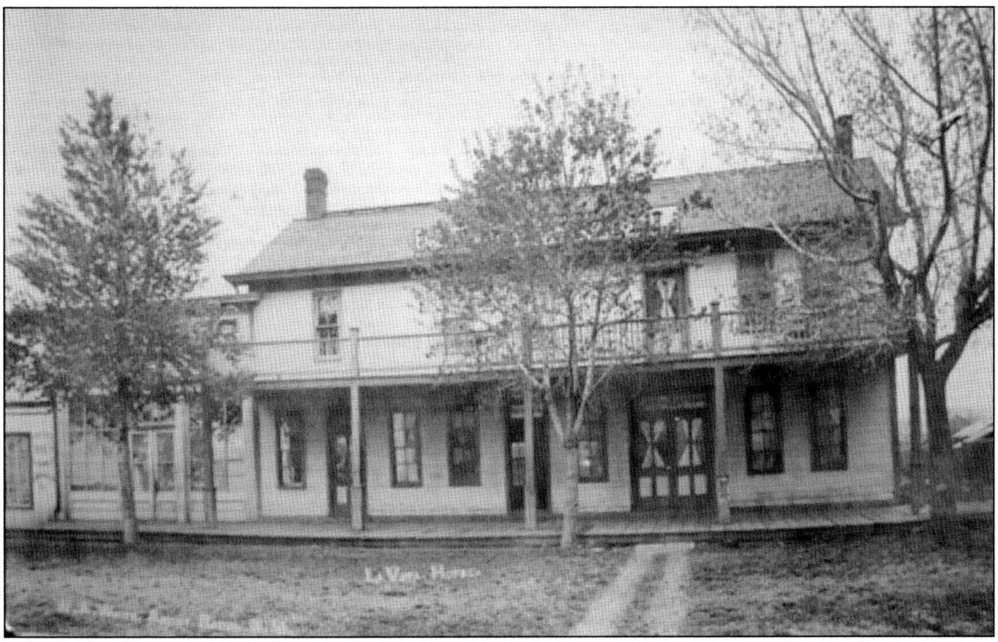

La Veta Hotel, 1897. The La Veta Hotel was completed in 1877, just a year after the D&RGW Railroad came to town. Twenty years later, as shown in this photograph, trees had grown up in front of the hotel and obscured the its sign on the roof. (FFM.)

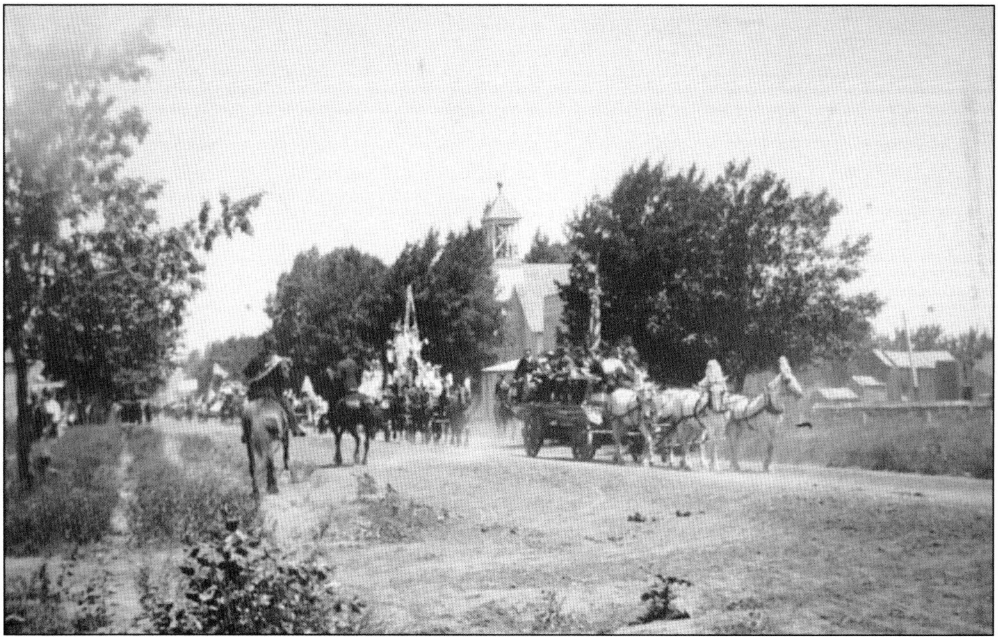

JULY 4, 1905. La Veta has always loved a parade, and the annual Fourth of July parade is a historic tradition still carried on today. The building in the center, with the steeple, is the First Baptist Church, which was constructed in 1877 and still stands today. (FFM.)

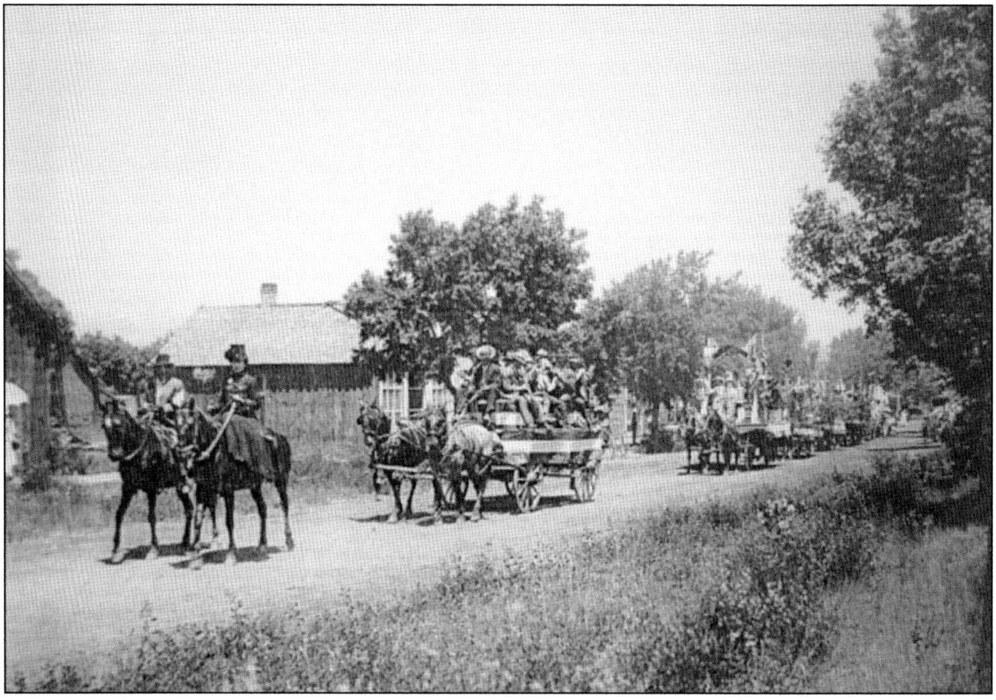

FOURTH OF JULY PARADE, 1908. Mayor Samuel J. Capps and Pearl Steele lead the parade down Main Street in La Veta. Capps had established a large cattle ranch east of the East Spanish Peak in the 1880s, but by the 1900s moved his wife and seven children to La Veta, where he served as mayor. (FFM.)

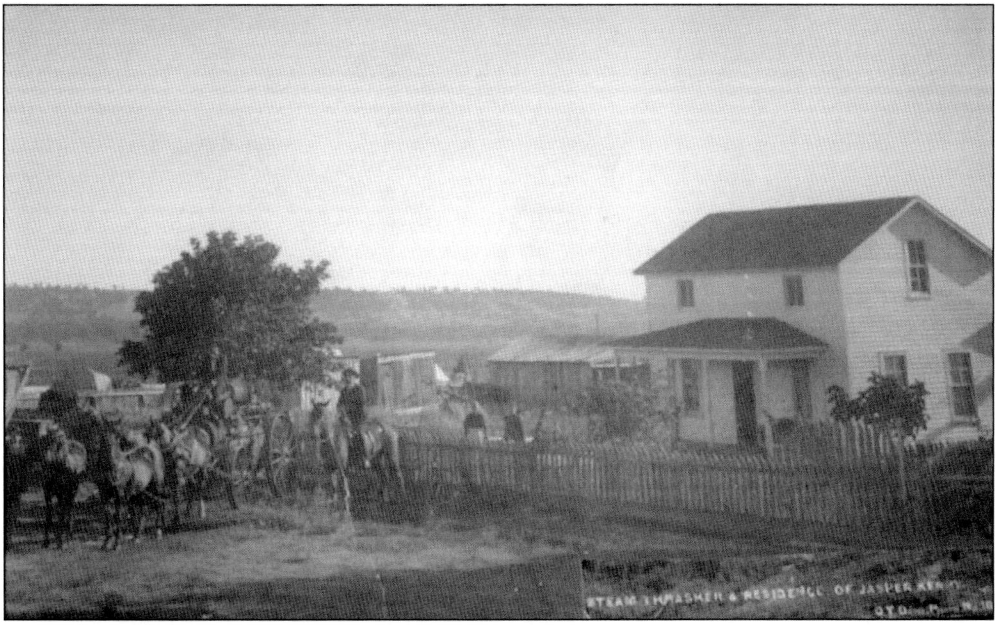

La Veta, 1899. This O.T. Davis photograph shows the residence of Jasper Kerry with a steam thrasher parked in front. The steam thrasher was mounted on wheels so a team of horses could pull it to the wheat fields to thrash the cut wheat. (FFM.)

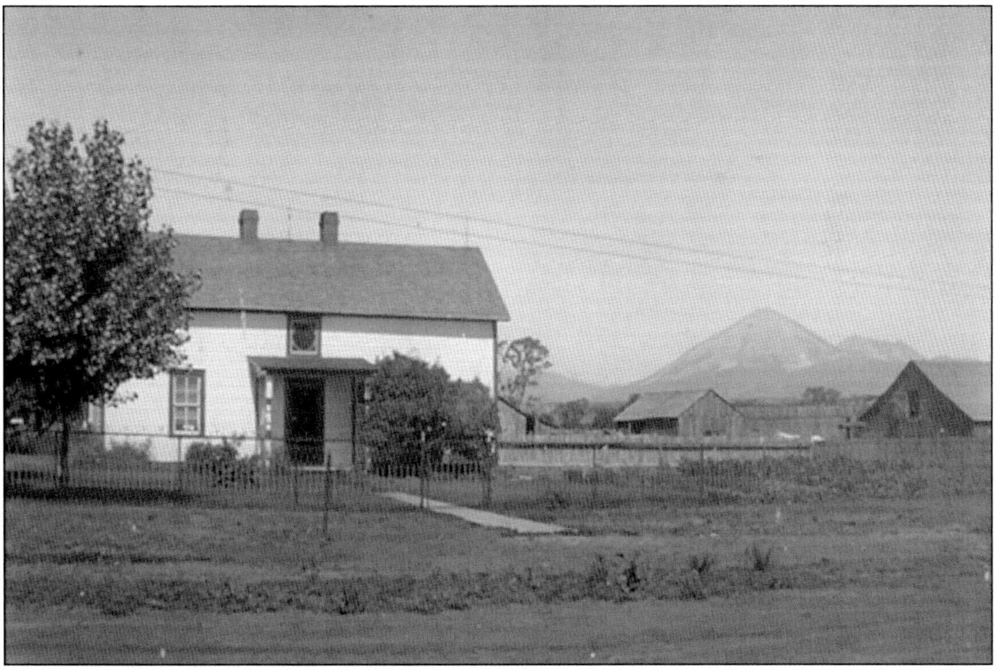

Martin Residence, La Veta. An unknown photographer captured this splendid early-1900s view of the Martin Ranch, on the west side of La Veta, with Mount Mestas rising prominently in the distance. (FFM.)

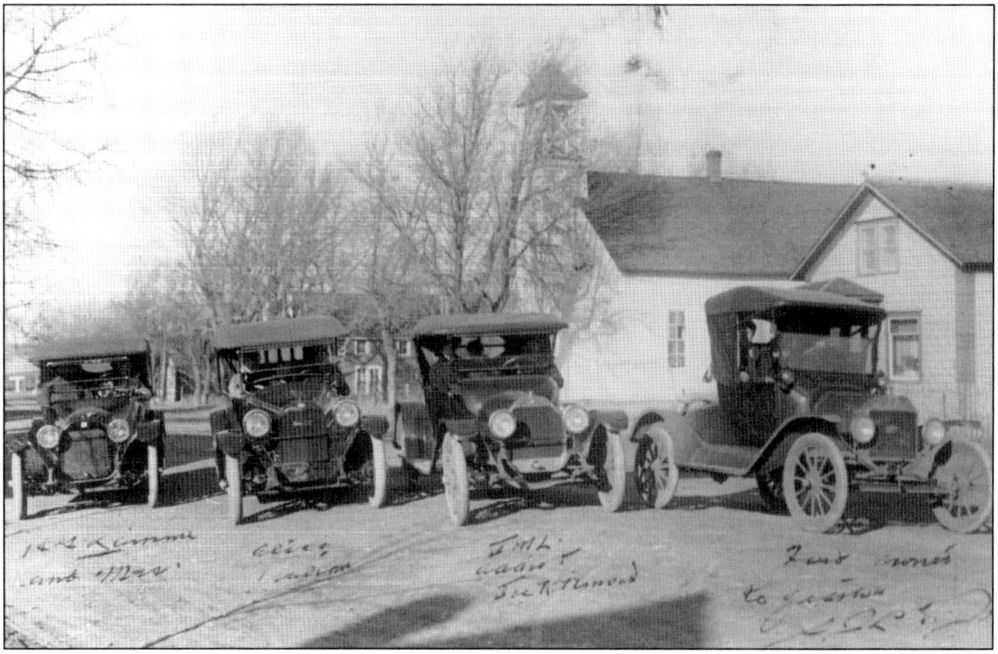

LAMME FAMILY CARS. The Lamme family proudly showed off their automobiles in front of Julian Lamme's home in La Veta in the early 1900s. The church behind the cars is the First Baptist Church. Lamme and his brother S.J. were doctors and had offices in the building across the street, which is shown on page 37. (HCHS.)

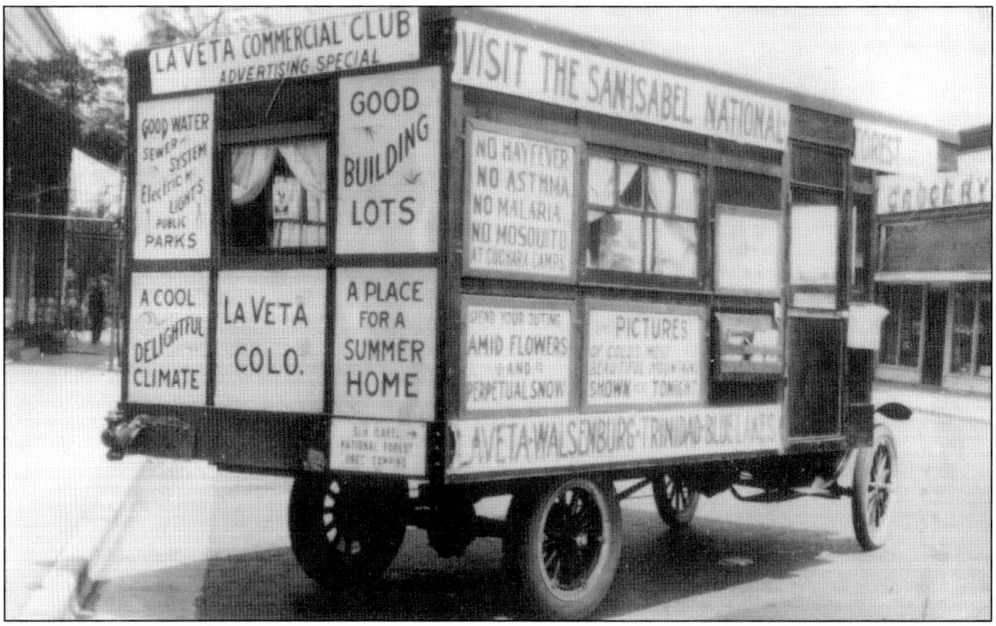

GEORGE MAYES ADVERTISING TRUCK. George Mayes was the founder of the Cuchara Camps (see page 101). To entice tourists to visit La Veta and Cuchara, Mayes drove this truck around Texas and Oklahoma in the 1920s, promoting the "cool delightful climate" of the area. (HCHS.)

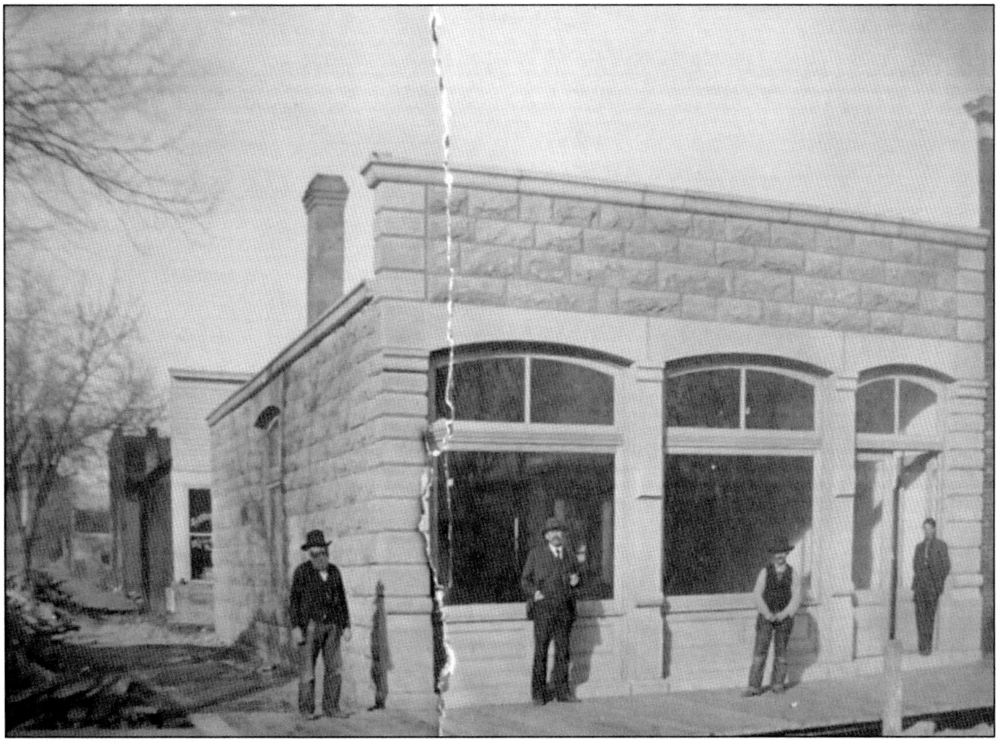

La Veta Bank, 1907. Located at 222 South Main Street, the bank was constructed in 1906 by William Fey, who constructed many of La Veta's stone buildings. There was a 10-foot-by-12-foot brick vault at the back of the building. (FFM.)

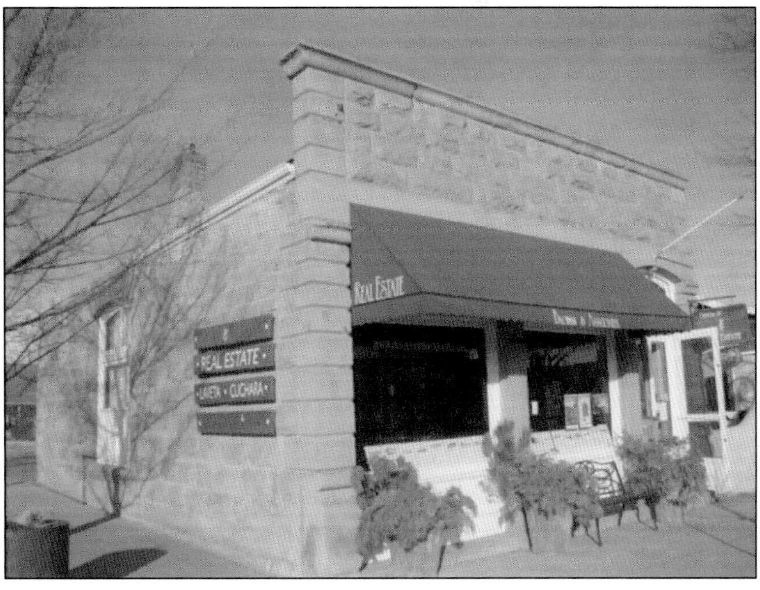

Bank Building, 2011. The old bank building still stands and currently houses a real estate company. The vault is still at the left rear of the building and now serves as a file room for the real estate agents.

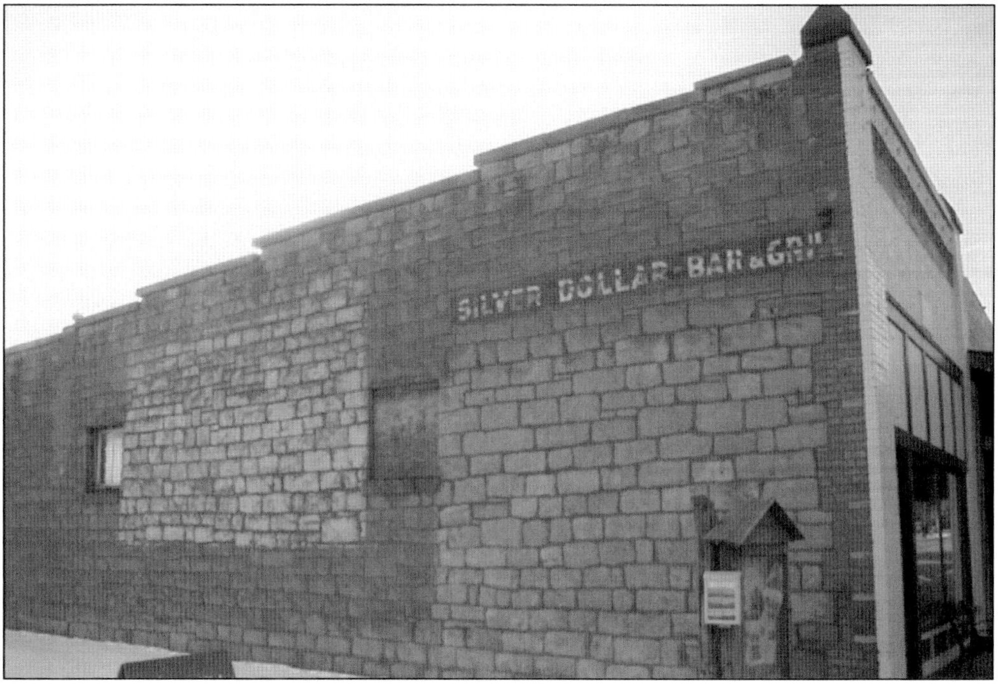

Silver Dollar Building, 203 South Main Street. Built for Giuseppi Micheletti in 1913 by E.R. Coleman, this stone structure housed Micheletti's bar and restaurant. In 1932, it became the Silver Dollar Bar and Grill, and has since been home to a series of retail businesses. An art gallery is currently located in the building.

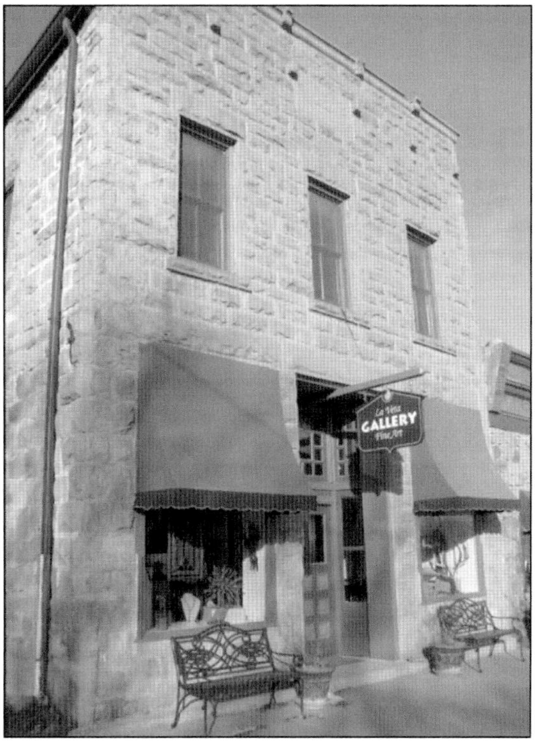

Masonic Hall, 210 South Main Street. This magnificent stone building was constructed in 1889 and sold to Masonic Lodge No. 59 AF&AM in 1893. The Masons held their meetings on the second floor and rented the first floor to businesses until 1927, when they took over the entire building. The Masons moved out in 1998, and the building is now an art gallery with a private residence on the second floor.

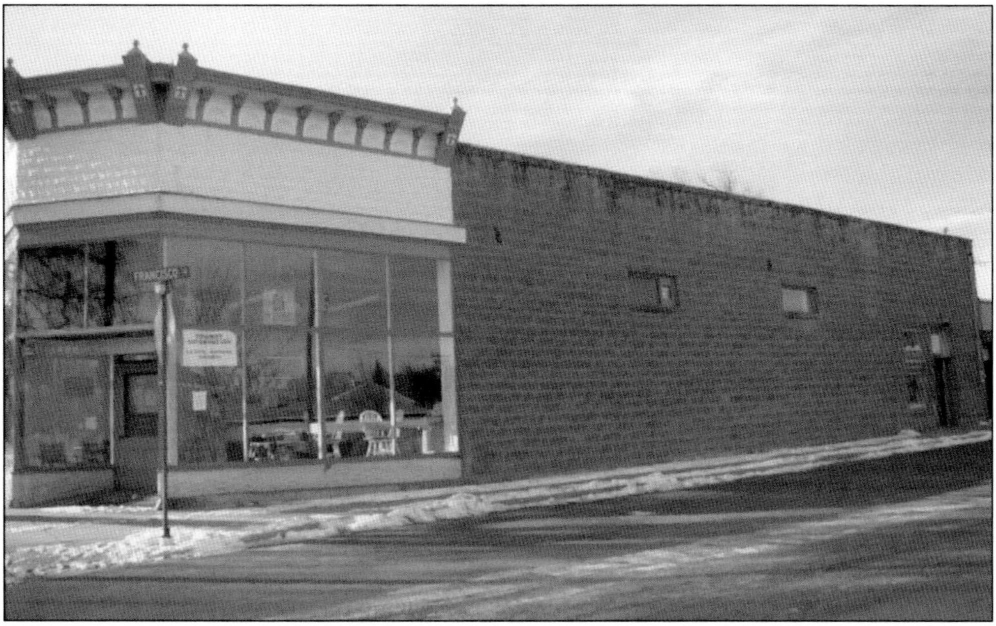

300 South Main Street. This historic stone building, constructed in 1911, sits on the corner of Main and Francisco Streets. The large structure has housed a number of businesses, most recently a gym and coffee shop.

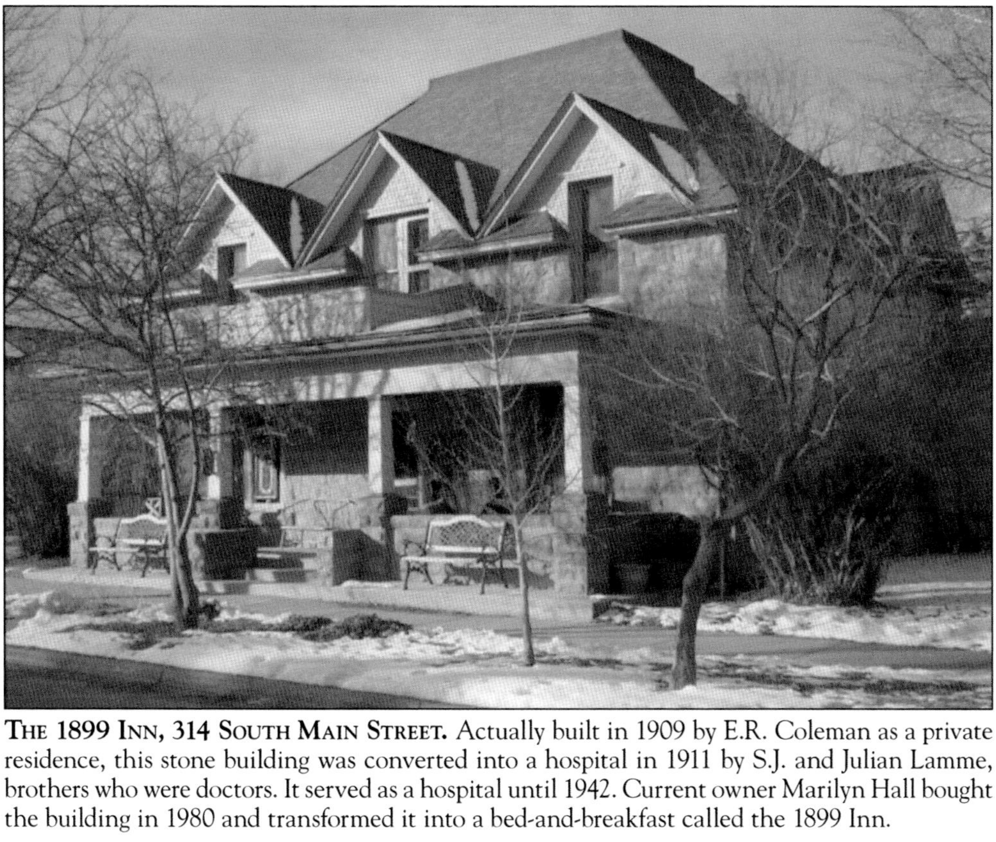

The 1899 Inn, 314 South Main Street. Actually built in 1909 by E.R. Coleman as a private residence, this stone building was converted into a hospital in 1911 by S.J. and Julian Lamme, brothers who were doctors. It served as a hospital until 1942. Current owner Marilyn Hall bought the building in 1980 and transformed it into a bed-and-breakfast called the 1899 Inn.

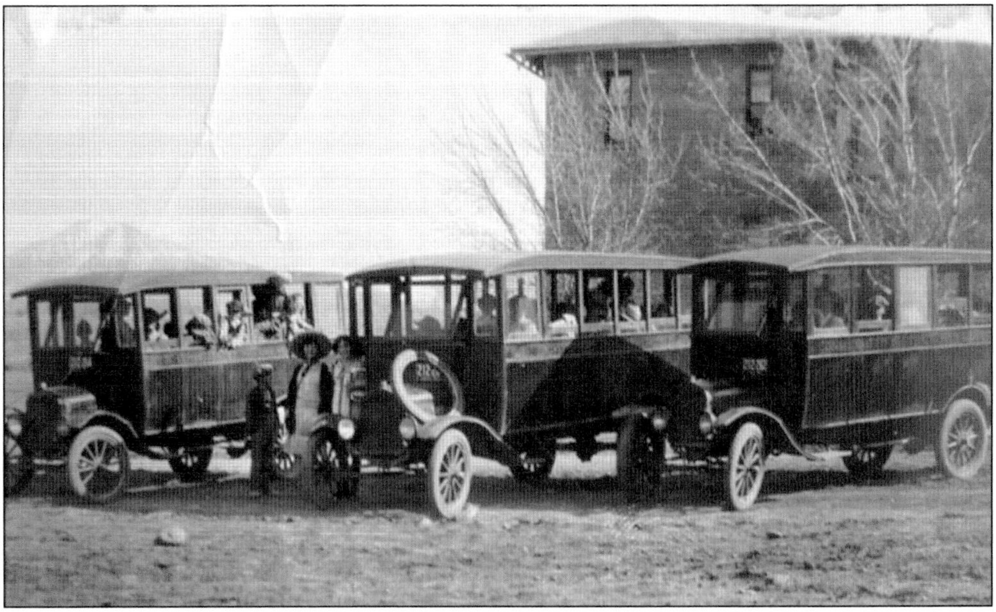

SCHOOL BUSES AT LA VETA HIGH SCHOOL. The La Veta High School building was a sandstone structure erected in 1911, and subsequently added onto in 1924 and 1937. These buses transported students around 1915. The West Spanish Peak is visible in the background at left. (FFM.)

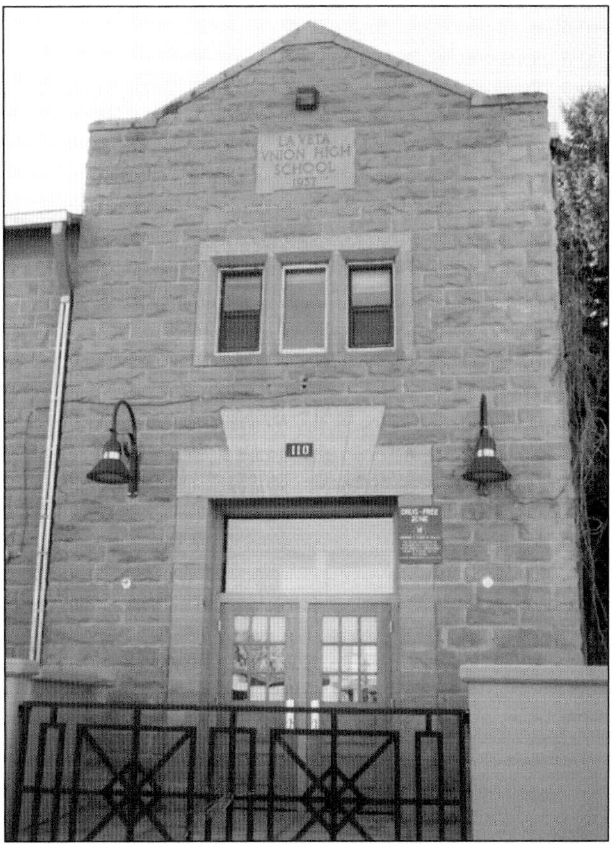

LA VETA HIGH SCHOOL ADDITION. Completed in 1937, this stone addition finished the structure that currently comprises the La Veta High School complex.

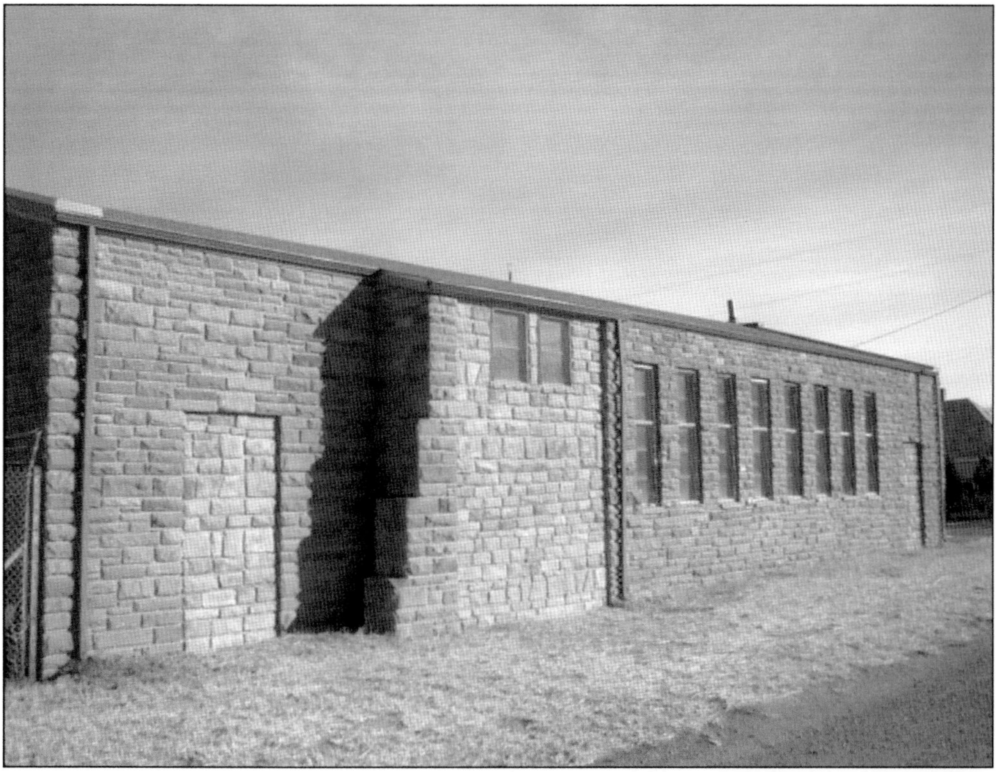

COUNTY MAINTENANCE BUILDING, 316 SOUTH LOCUST STREET. Construction began on this stone building in 1941 by crews of the Work Projects Administration. It was intended to house Huerfano County road equipment. Building was delayed as crew members enlisted in World War II, but the structure was finally finished in 1942.

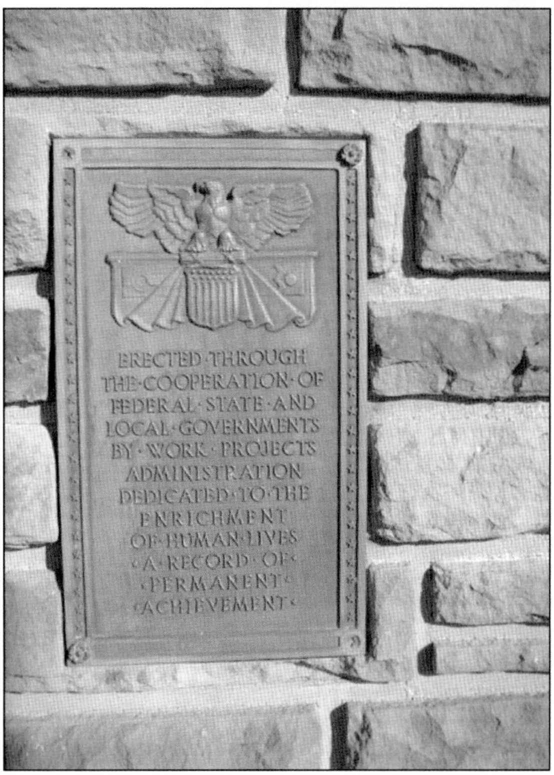

WPA PLAQUE. This plaque on the southeast corner of the county maintenance building commemorates the efforts of the Work Projects Administration crews who constructed the building. The WPA, a holdover from the Depression years of the 1930s, was a federal government program designed to put unemployed men to work.

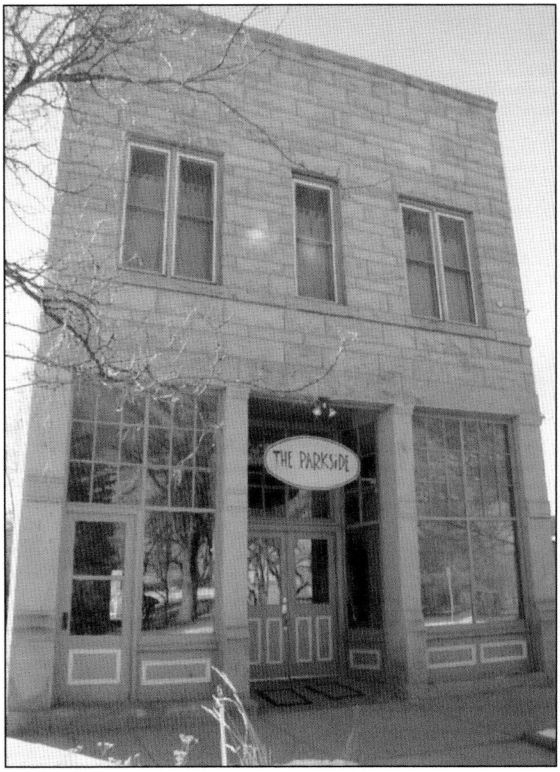

Parkside Building, 127 West Ryus Avenue. Built in 1909 for Peligrino Glassini to house his Olympia Saloon, this beautiful stone building is 25 feet wide and 58 feet long. The structure was later used as a billiard parlor, fruit and vegetable market, automotive garage, and Odd Fellows Hall. Today, concerts and art shows are held here.

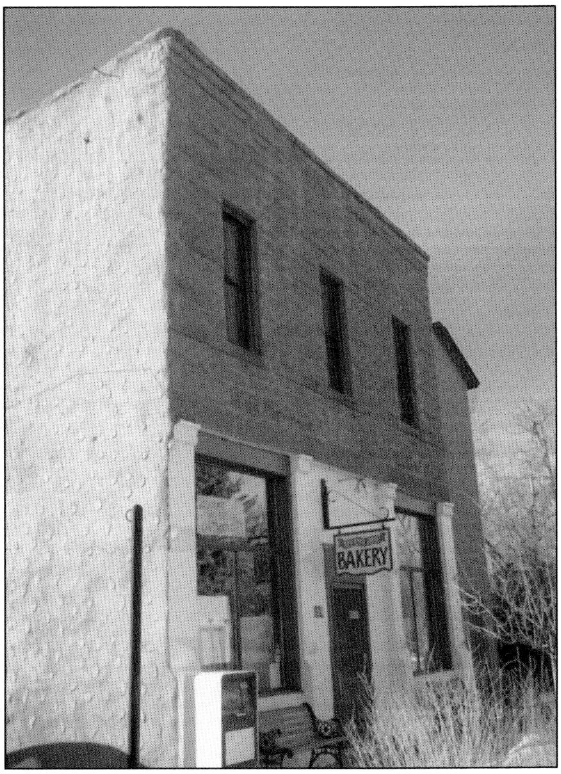

Stranger Building, 129 West Ryus Avenue. At 27 feet wide and 60 feet long, this building is similar in size to its neighbor, the Parkside. It was built in 1904 by the Coleman brothers for John Stranger's businesses. Over the years, it has housed restaurants, saloons, grocery stores, automotive garages, and a meat locker and meat market. It is currently the home of the Ryus Avenue Bakery.

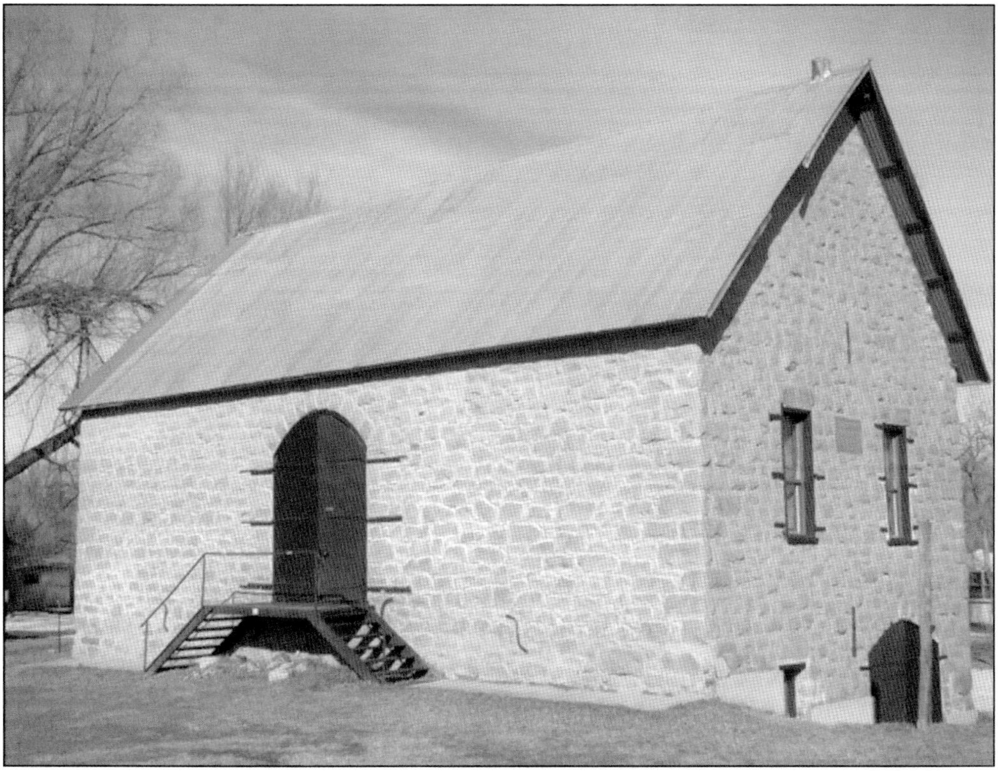

GOEMMER BARN, CORNER OF FIELD AND OAK STREETS. E.R. Coleman built this impressive stone barn in 1895 for John Goemmer. Goemmer used it for hay storage and as a stable. The horses were kept downstairs and farm equipment was stored upstairs.

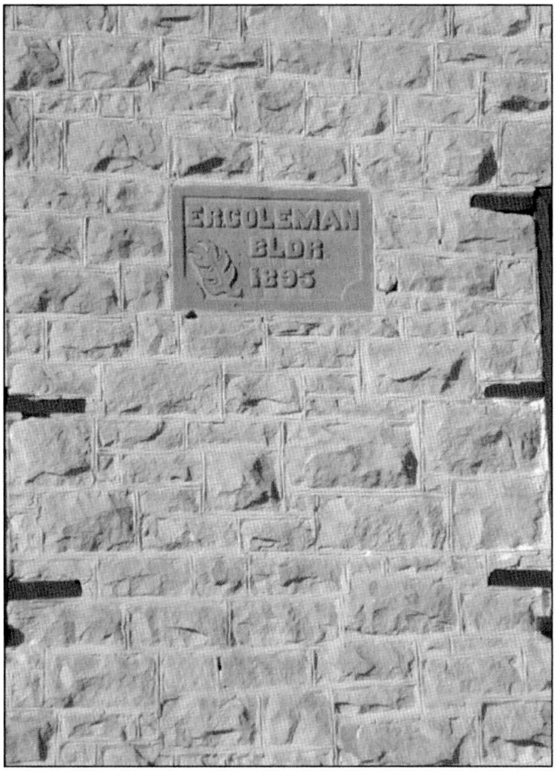

PLAQUE ON GOEMMER BARN. This plaque, on the east side of the Goemmer Barn, identifies E.R. Coleman as the builder. This was Coleman's first stone building in La Veta. Over the years, he and his brother built several other stone structures in La Veta, as noted throughout this chapter.

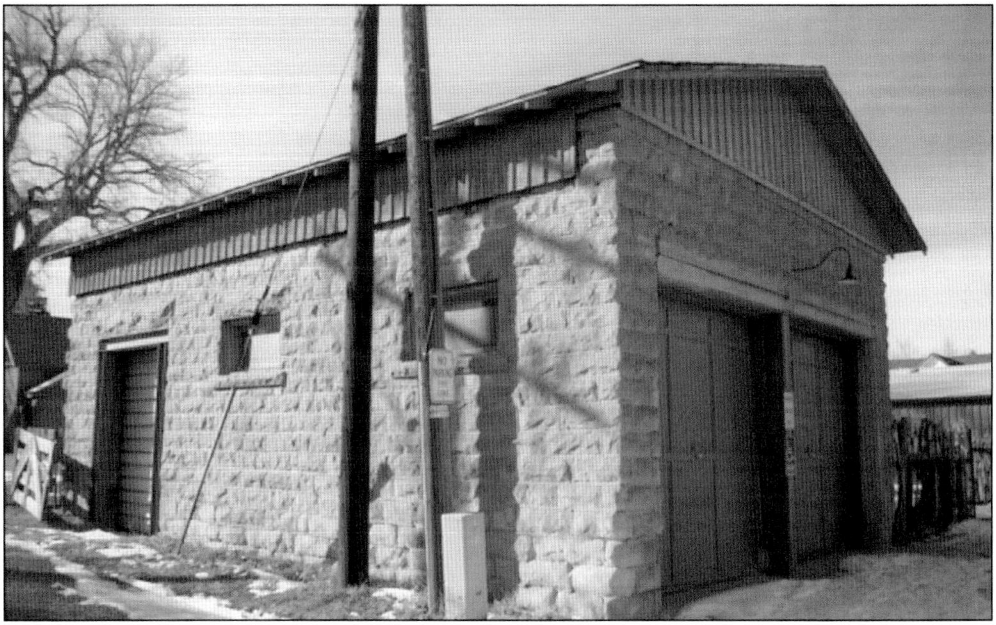

FIREHOUSE ON WEST FRANCISCO STREET. The two-door firehouse was built in 1912. The two fire engines were busy, as La Veta's early frame buildings kept going up in flames. Today, the building is a storage shed for Francisco Fort Museum.

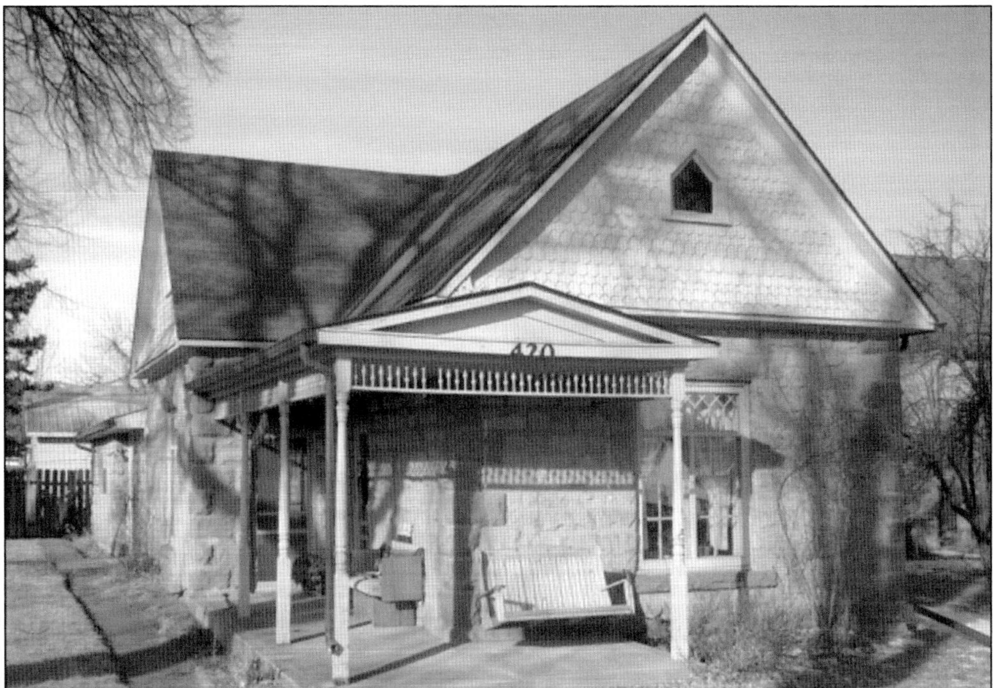

METHODIST PARSONAGE, 420 SOUTH MAIN STREET. This stone home was built by the Coleman brothers in 1905 as a residence for Edwin L. Smith. It has been added to over the years to increase the size from the original four rooms. The house was sold to the La Veta Methodist Church in 1928 for use as a parsonage, as the church is located next door.

116 West Garland Street. Built in 1908, this historic stone home has been restored and remodeled with modern conveniences. It has two bedrooms and two bathrooms, with wood floors and granite countertops.

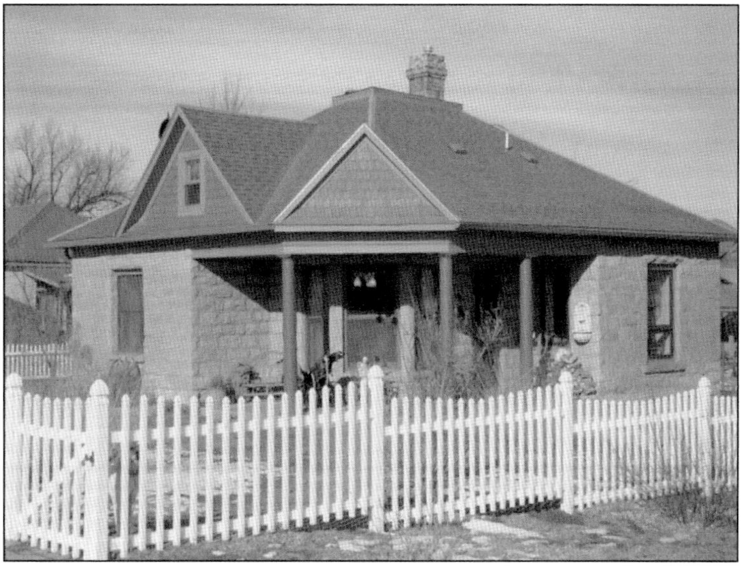

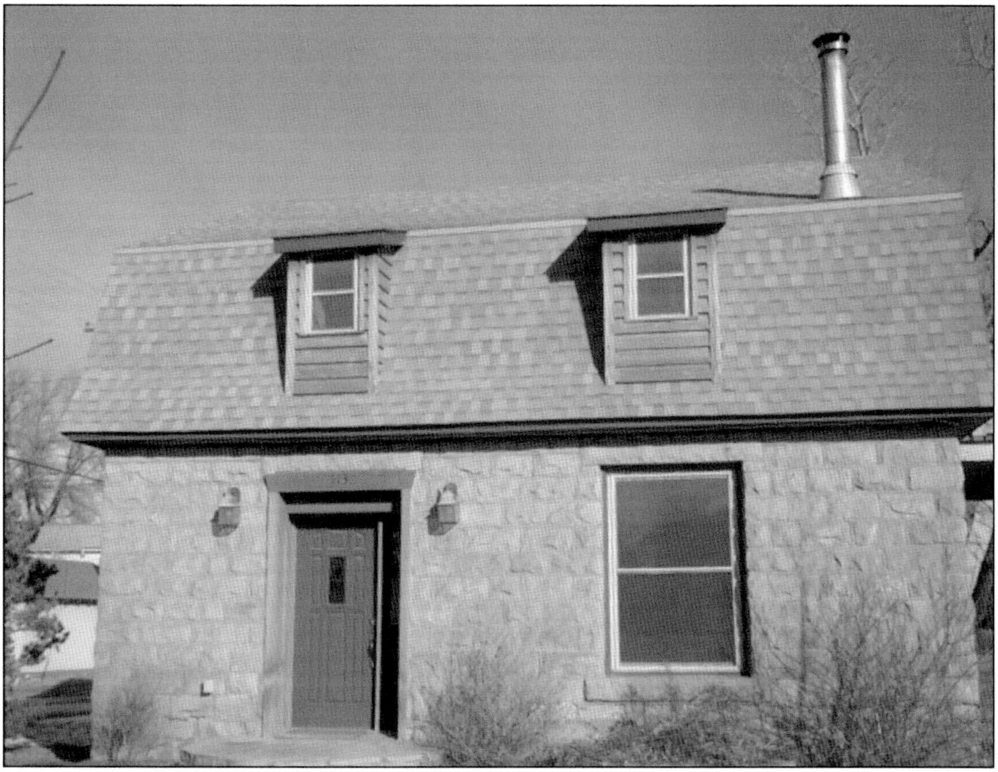

113 East Field Street. This 1914 stone home has been completely remodeled, with a second story added with dormer windows. A patio and deck extend to the right.

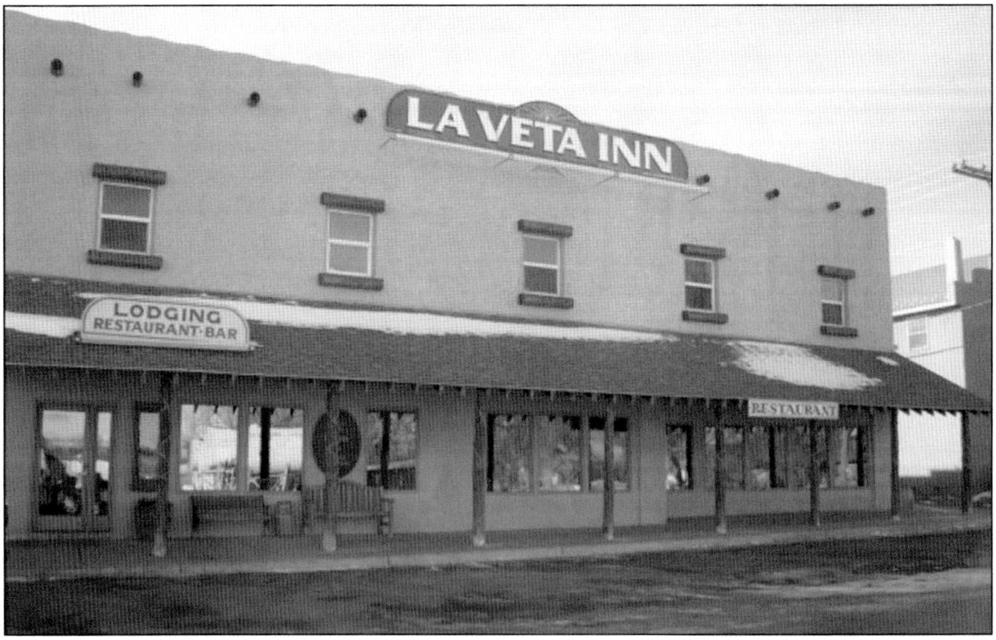

La Veta Inn on West Ryus Avenue. Not all of La Veta's prominent buildings are made of stone. Several, such as the La Veta Inn, are built in the adobe style typical in the Southwest. The La Veta Inn is on the same site as the La Veta Hotel (shown on page 31).

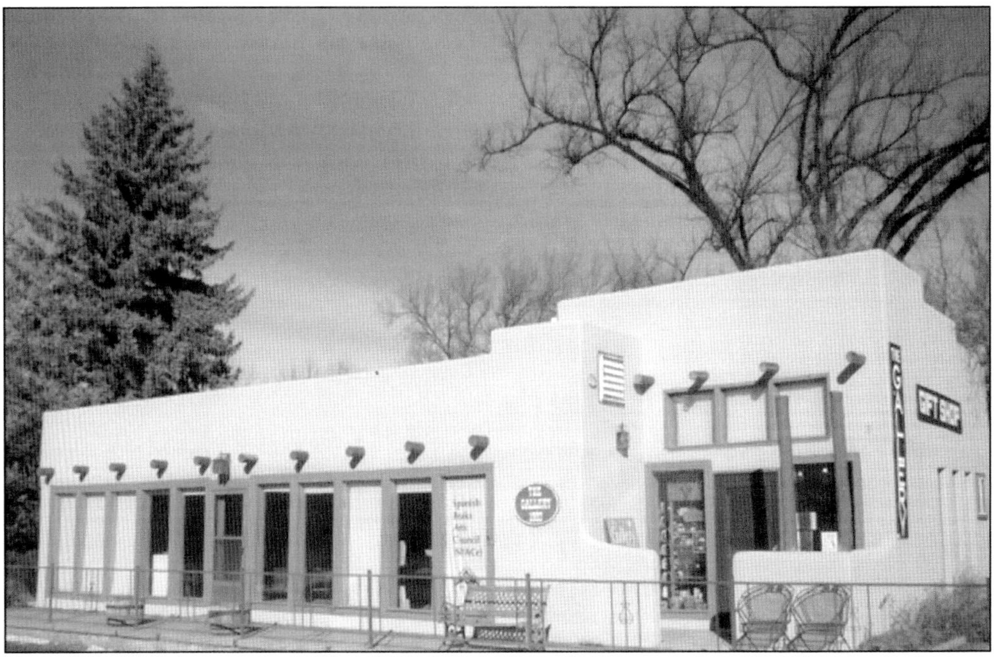

Gallery on West Ryus Avenue. This beautiful adobe building, built in 1980, is the home of the Spanish Peaks Arts Council (SPACe) Gallery. In 2011, SPACe constructed a two-story addition to the right for more gallery and classroom space.

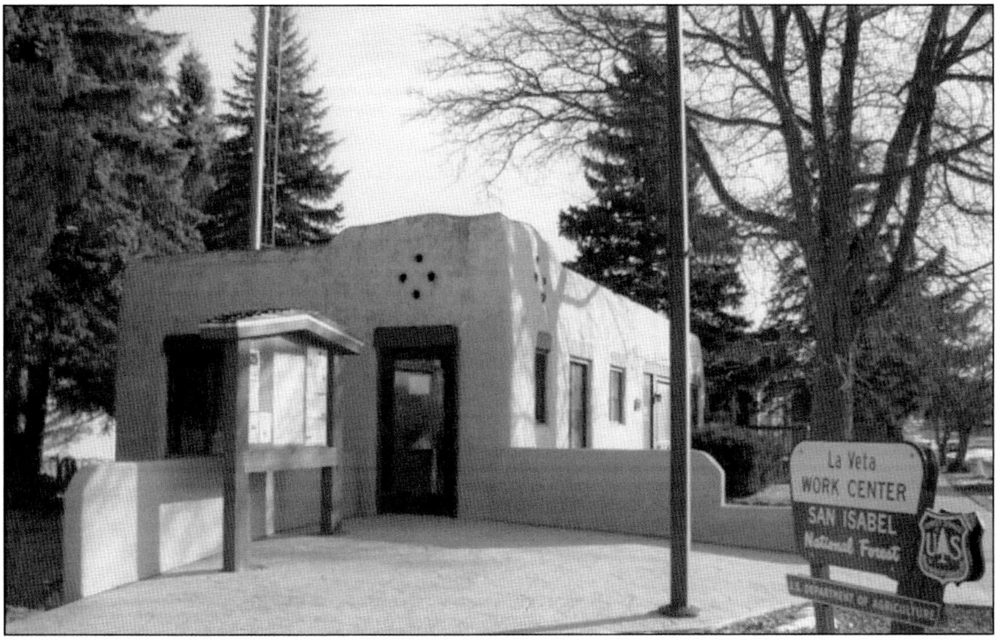

District Ranger Office, Main and Field Streets. Built in 1935 with labor from the Civilian Conservation Corps (CCC), this building still houses offices for the La Veta ranger district of the San Isabel National Forest. Constructed of adobe bricks and stucco, the building is a classic example of the southwest pueblo style employed by the Forest Service for its buildings in southern Colorado.

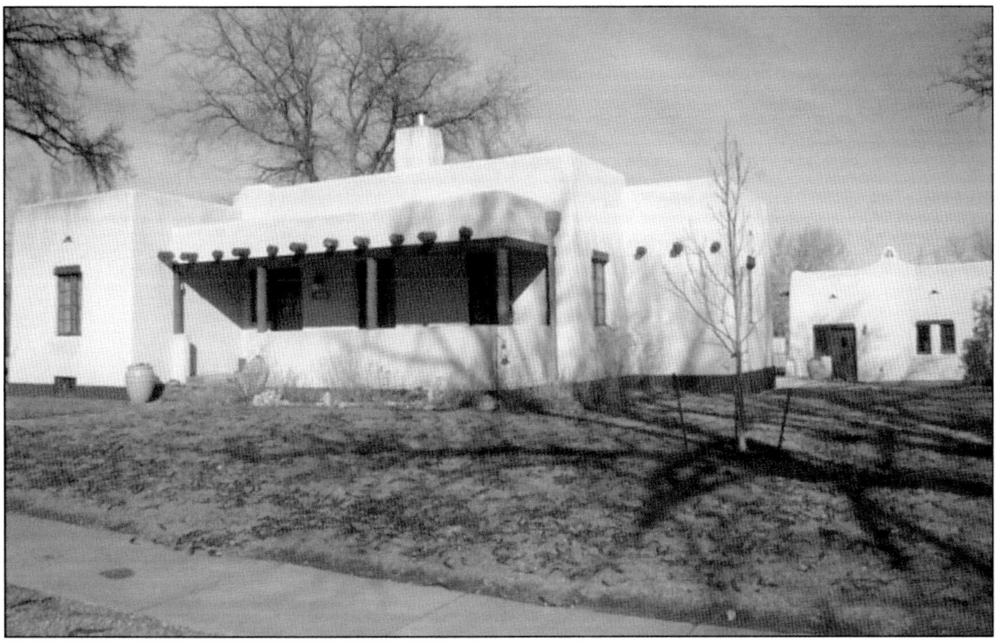

Forest Service Home, 134 West Field Street. Completed in 1937 by the CCC for the US Forest Service, this home was used by the district ranger's family in La Veta. It is a block west of the Forest Service office. It has a three-car garage at the back, which was used to store Forest Service vehicles and equipment. The home was sold to a private owner in 1987.

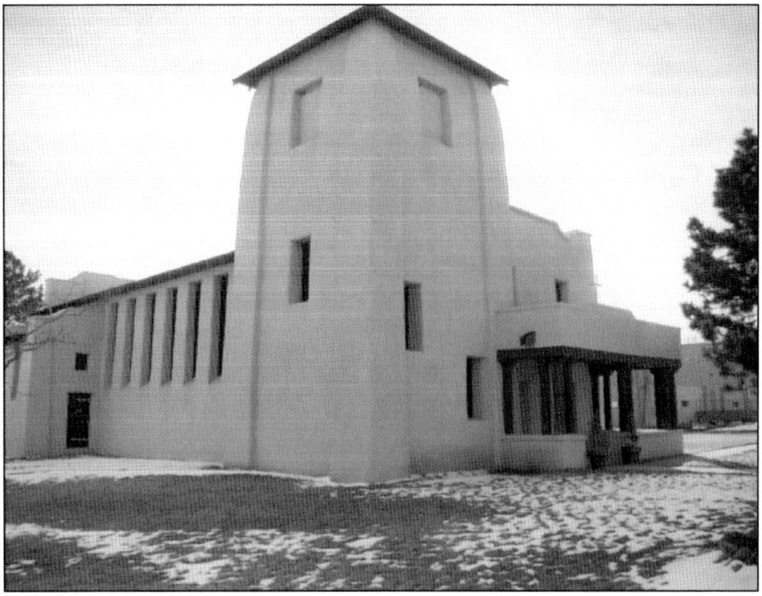

Christ the King Catholic Church. Located on the corner of Virginia and Main Streets, this spectacular adobe church was completed in 1949. It has a tall tower and long narrow windows reminiscent of churches built in New Mexico in the 1700s and 1800s. The portico at right provides a shaded entrance to the church.

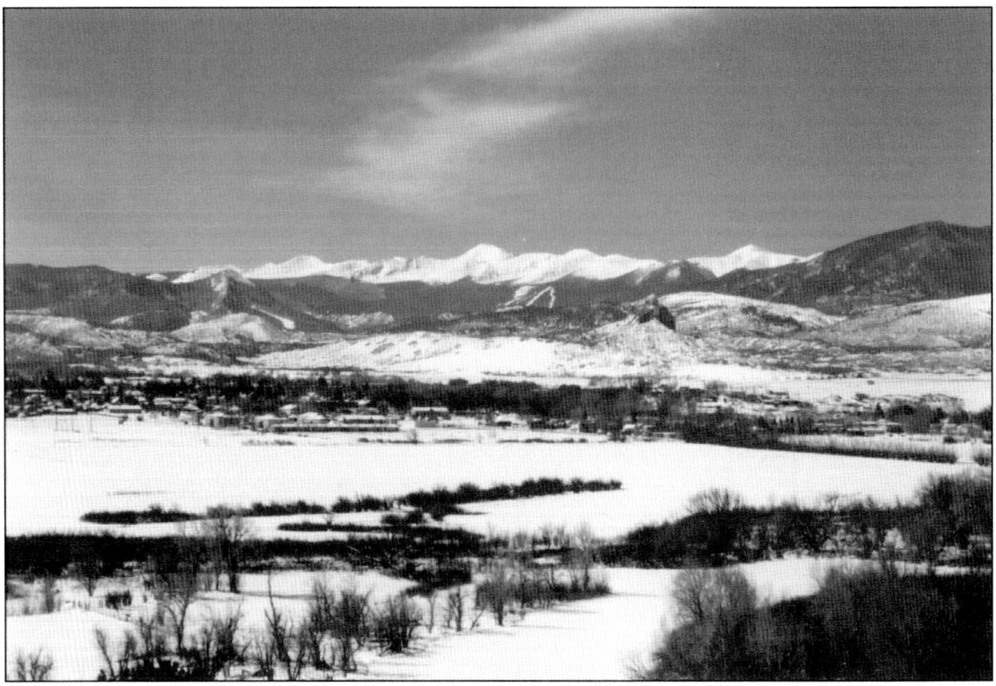

La Veta, March 2005. La Veta's sandstone and adobe buildings, homes, churches, and businesses are blanketed with snow. Trinchera Peak is the highest peak in the center of the photograph, with the Cuchara ski slopes just below it.

Four

Rails over La Veta Pass

February 9, 2006, was a red-letter day in La Veta. School was dismissed, businesses closed, and everyone wore red (La Veta's school color) and gathered downtown at the train station to witness the first arrival of a passenger train in La Veta in 53 years. La Veta had a proud railroad history, and its citizens threw a party honoring its revival. The San Luis & Rio Grande Railroad pulled a passenger car into town from Alamosa over La Veta Pass, heralding the start of its new scenic tourist railroad.

The Denver & Rio Grande Western (D&RGW) Railroad first pulled into La Veta with its narrow gauge line in July 1876, determined to head west over the mountains and on to the silver mines at Creede and Silverton. Construction continued westward toward Veta Pass, gaining altitude over what became the famous Muleshoe Curve. The summit of Veta Pass (approximately 9,300 feet above sea level) was reached in June 1877, and the line was completed west to Fort Garland in November 1877.

The continually growing D&RGW built standard gauge (four feet and eight inches wide) tracks into La Veta in 1890. The narrow gauge line (three feet wide) lasted for 22 years, but by 1899, the D&RGW was hauling so much freight that it was a huge nuisance to continually transfer freight from standard gauge cars to narrow gauge cars in La Veta for the journey over the pass. Railroad surveyors found a route for their standard gauge rails at Middle Creek Pass, just a few miles south of Veta Pass. This new route was named La Veta Pass, while Veta Pass refers to the old pass on the narrow gauge line. The new line had a maximum grade of 3 percent, compared to 4.7 percent on the narrow gauge, and it shaved a mile off the route.

The old route over Veta Pass became a road. Visitors can still drive over it and see the restored depot at the top. Today, US Highway 160 crosses a pass a few miles north, known as North La Veta Pass.

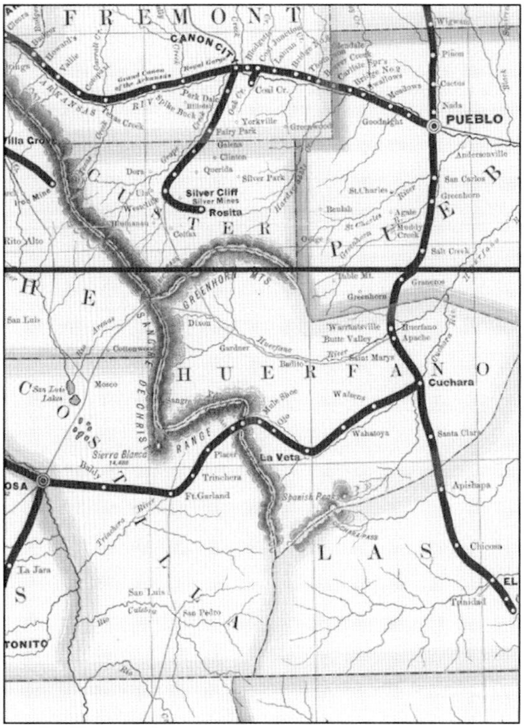

D&RGW Railroad Map, 1881. This map shows the route of the narrow gauge railroad across Huerfano County from Walsenburg (Walsens) west to La Veta, Ojo, Mule Shoe, and over Veta Pass to Fort Garland. (LOC.)

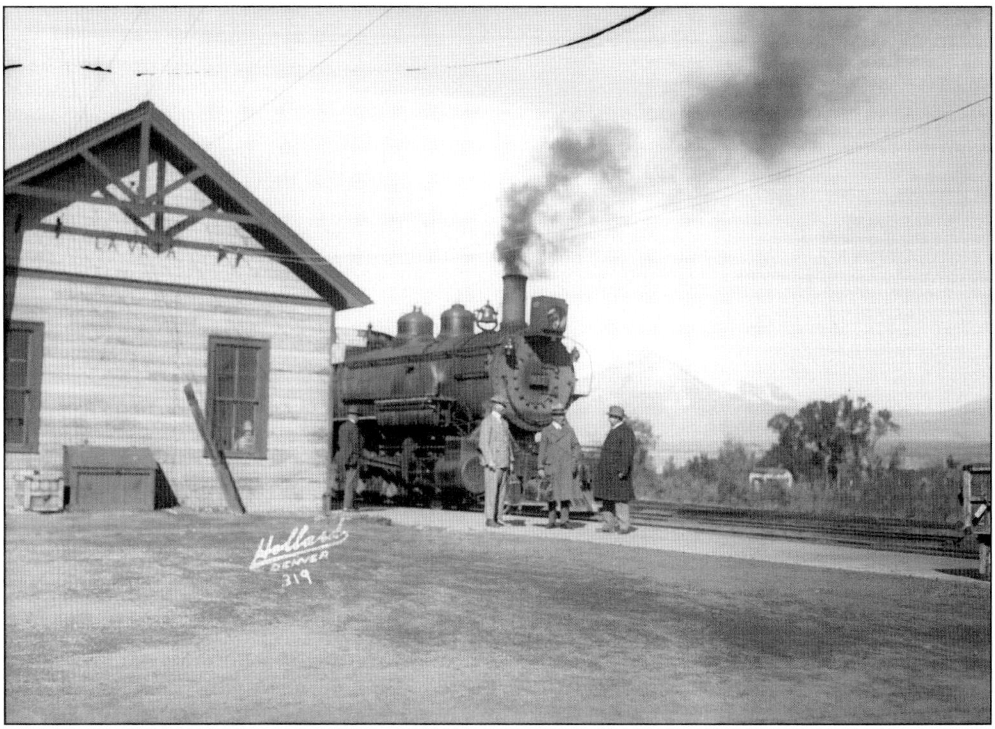

La Veta Depot, 1912. This photograph by Louis Hollard shows an eastbound steam engine at the La Veta depot. The well-dressed men in front of the engine may be railroad officials on an inspection tour. (DPL no. X-11938.)

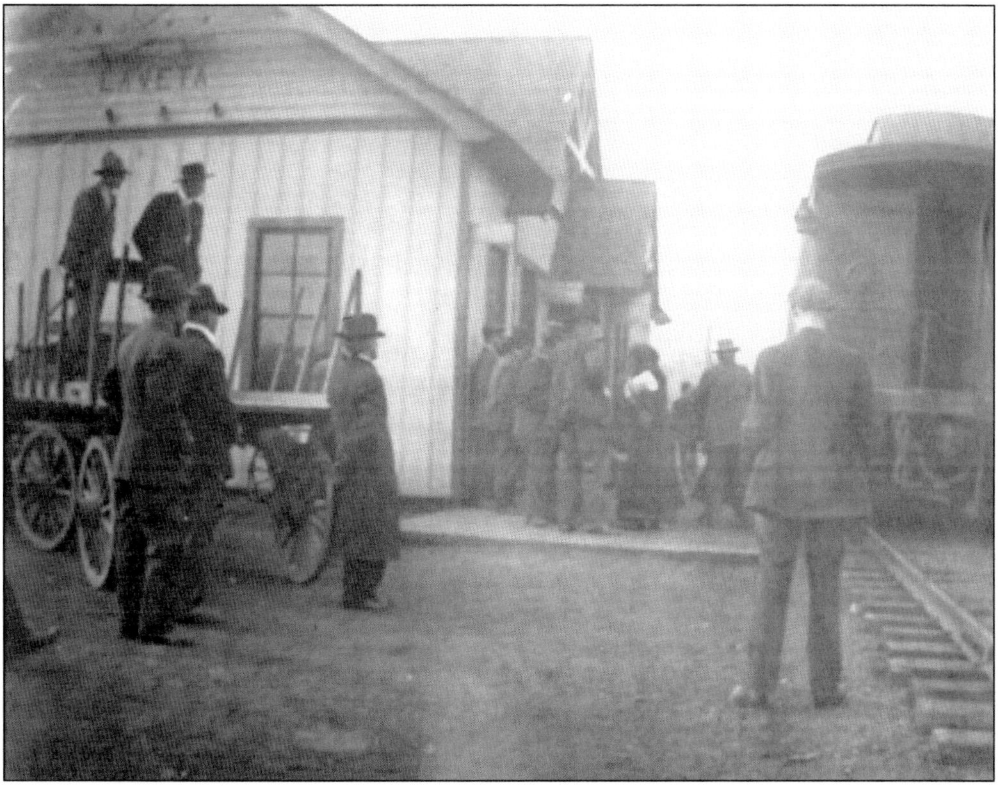

La Veta Depot, 1913. A crowd waits to board a westbound passenger train at the La Veta Depot. Perhaps a celebrity was boarding, and two men jumped onto the wagon for a better view. (FFM.)

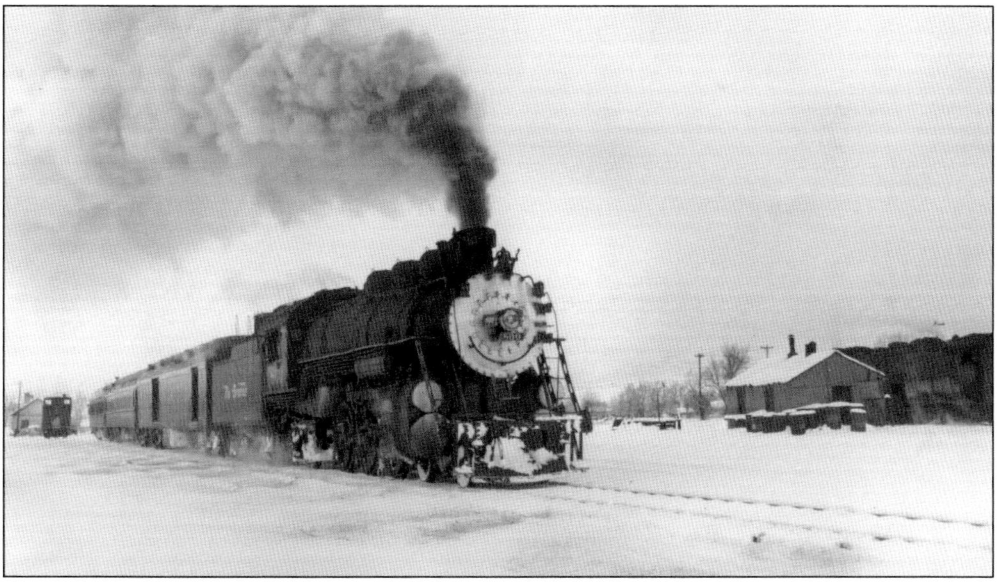

"San Luis" Westbound. Robert W. Richardson photographed the westbound San Luis passenger train in La Veta in December 1951. That day's train consists of a baggage car and two passenger cars. (CRM.)

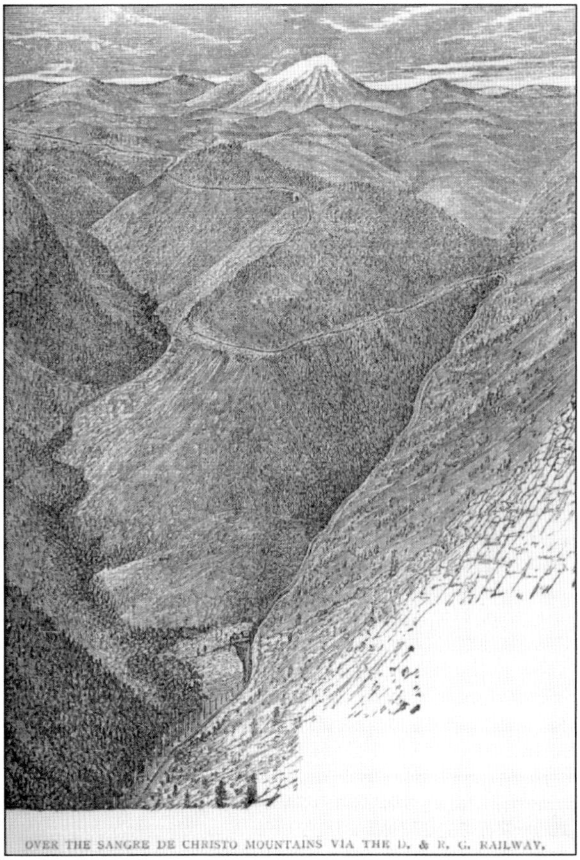

Over the Sangre de Cristo Mountains. An 1880s magazine drawing shows the tortuous route of the D&RGW narrow gauge railroad over Veta Pass. The first curve at the upper right is Muleshoe Curve. The next curve goes around Dump Mountain, with two subsequent curves leading to Veta Pass.

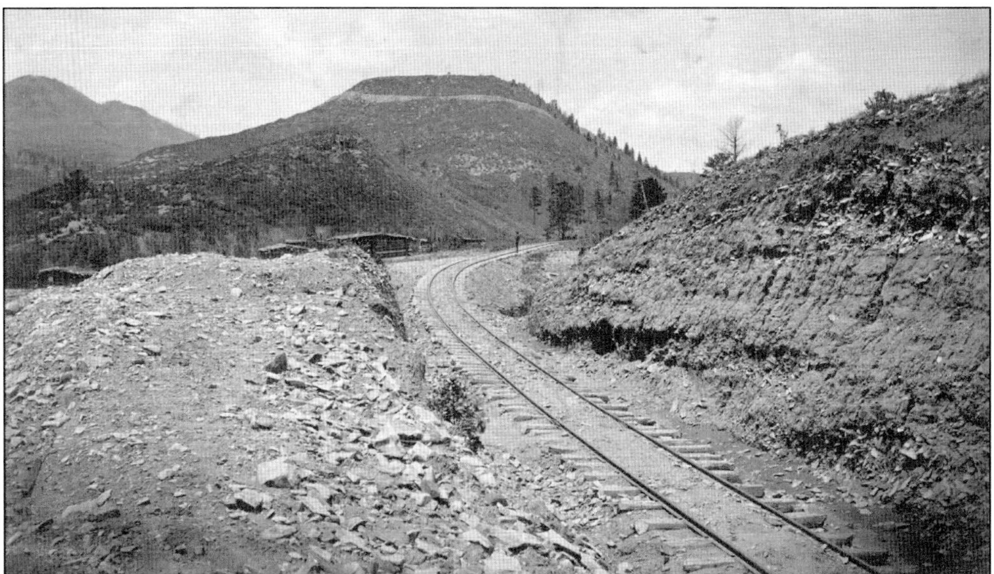

Climbing to Veta Pass. W.G. Chamberlain took this c. 1886 photograph. The narrow gauge twists to the right to reach Muleshoe Curve. Beyond that, the cut for the tracks is visible near the top of Dump Mountain at center. (DPL no. Z-2473.)

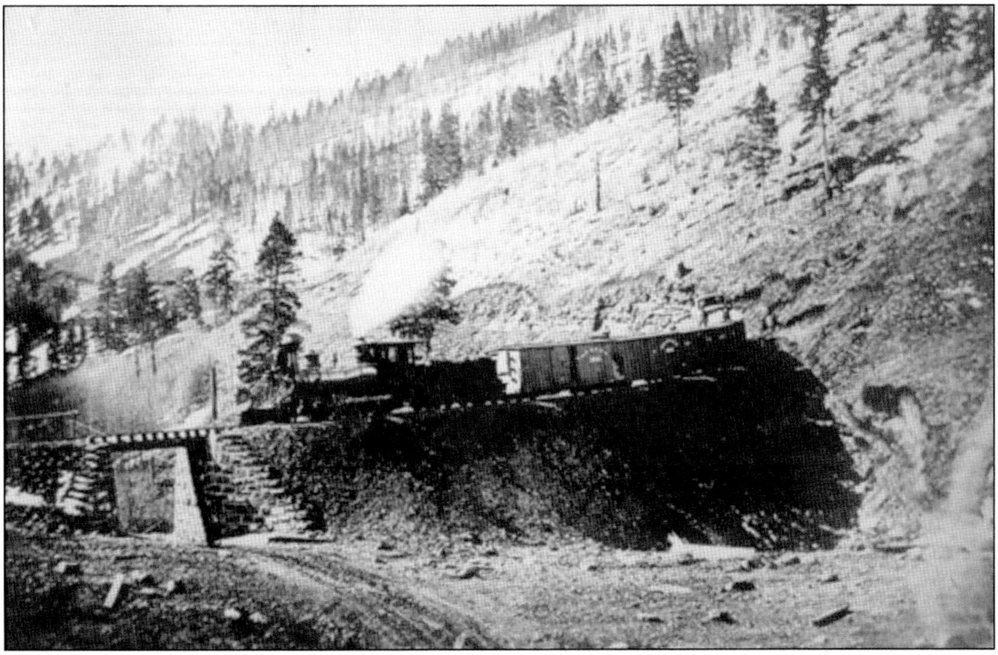

A Pause on Muleshoe Curve. A short freight train (possibly a work train) stops on Muleshoe Curve in the 1880s. The bridge crosses over Baldy Scott's toll road, which went up to Veta Pass. (FFM.)

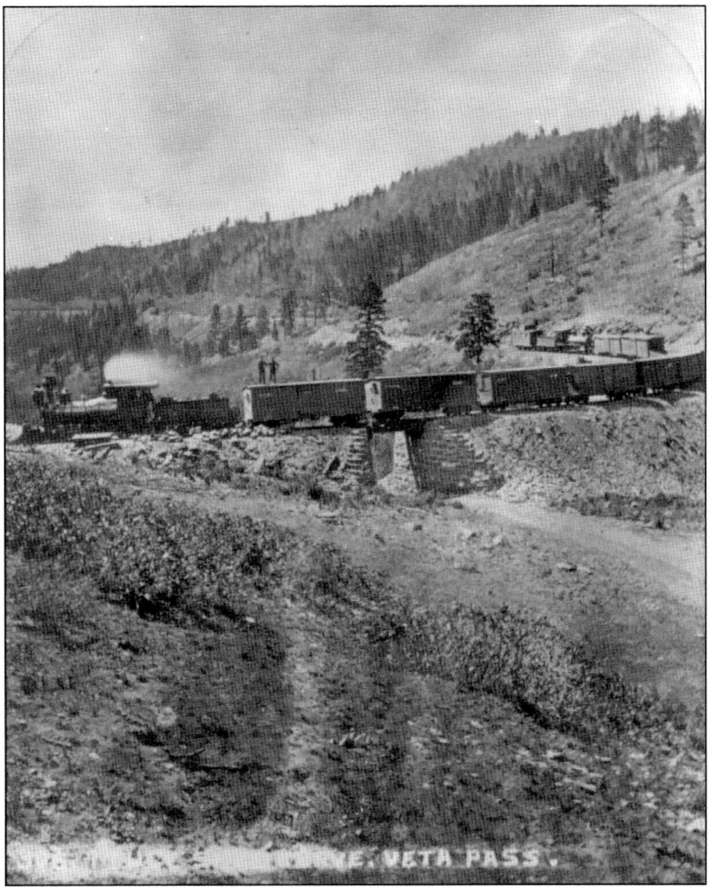

Muleshoe Curve. Men stand on top of freight cars while the train is stopped on Muleshoe Curve. A helper engine is at the back of the train. (CRM.)

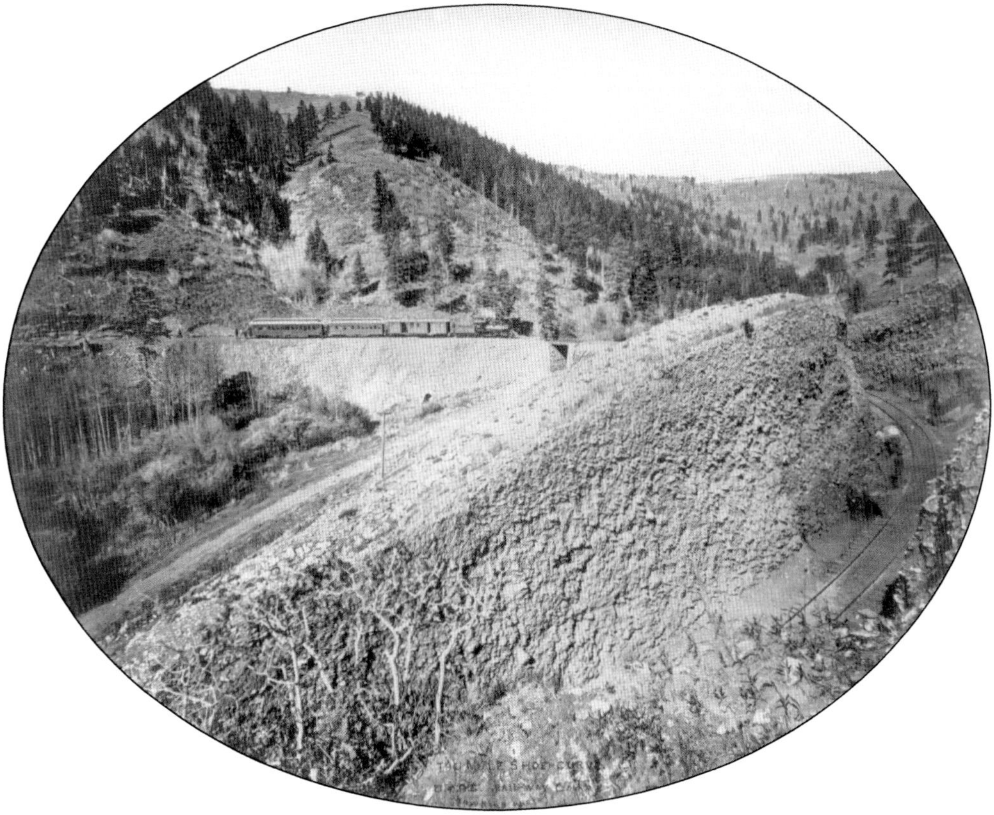

PASSENGER TRAIN ON MULESHOE CURVE. This 1880 Hawkins photograph shows a rarity—a D&RGW passenger train in daylight. Most passenger trains were routed over Veta Pass at night, except for the occasional daylight excursion train. (CRM.)

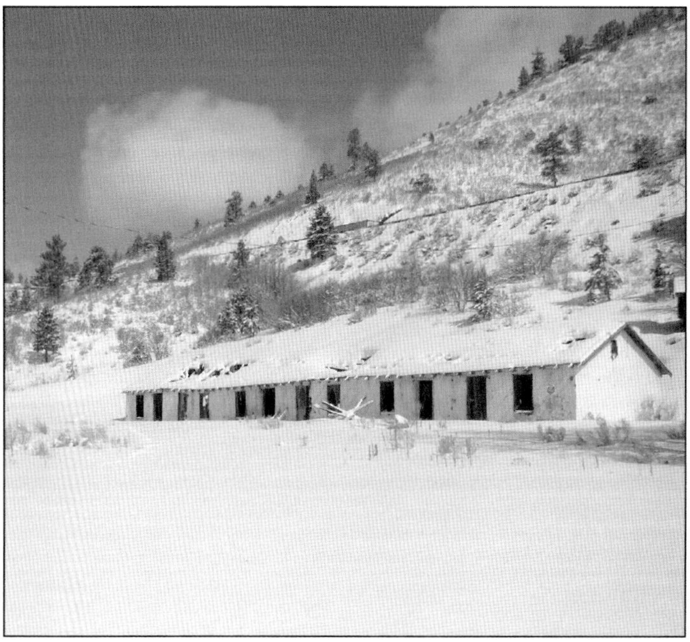

PRESENT-DAY MULESHOE CURVE. This contemporary winter view shows a derelict motel at Muleshoe Curve. When the narrow gauge railroad was abandoned in 1899, the route became a road lined with hotels, motels, and restaurants. The top of a truck traveling on US Highway 160 is barely visible above the motel.

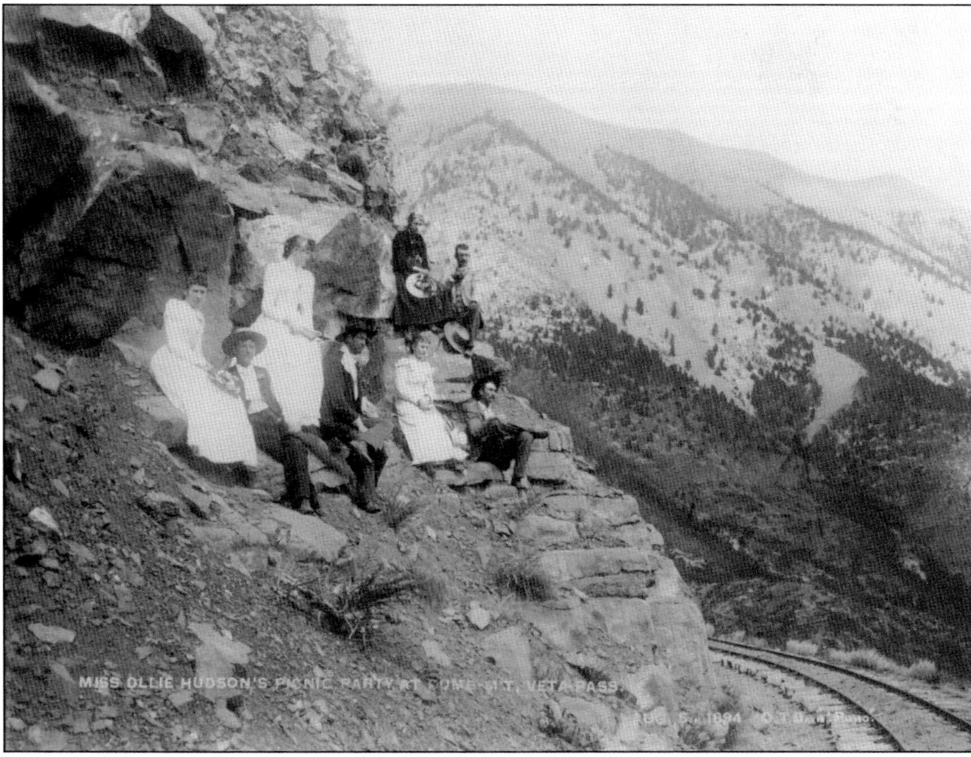

Picnic Party on Dump Mountain. Ollie Hudson's picnic party, held on August 5, 1894, was captured by photographer O.T. Davis. The well-dressed picnickers rode the narrow gauge train to this spot. Mount Mestas is in the background. (Monte Vista Historical Society.)

Picnic Spot on Dump Mountain. Cross-country ski tracks take the place of narrow gauge train tracks in this contemporary photograph. Ollie Hudson and her friends sat on the rocks to the left; Mount Mestas is to the right.

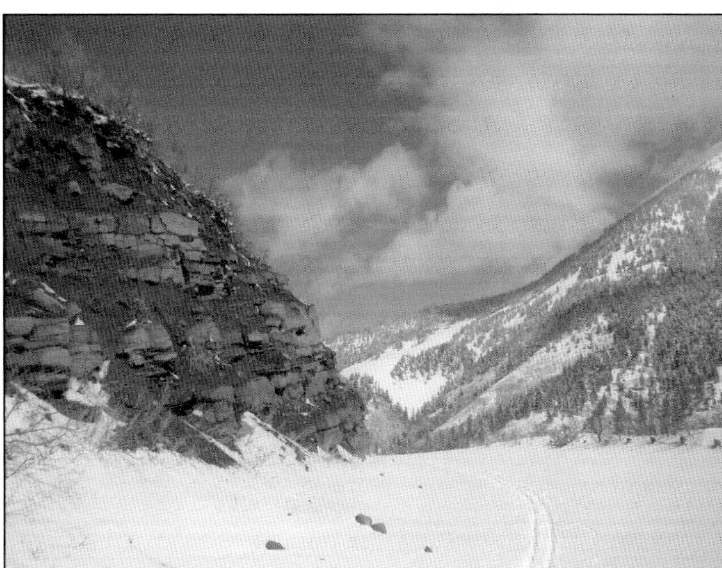

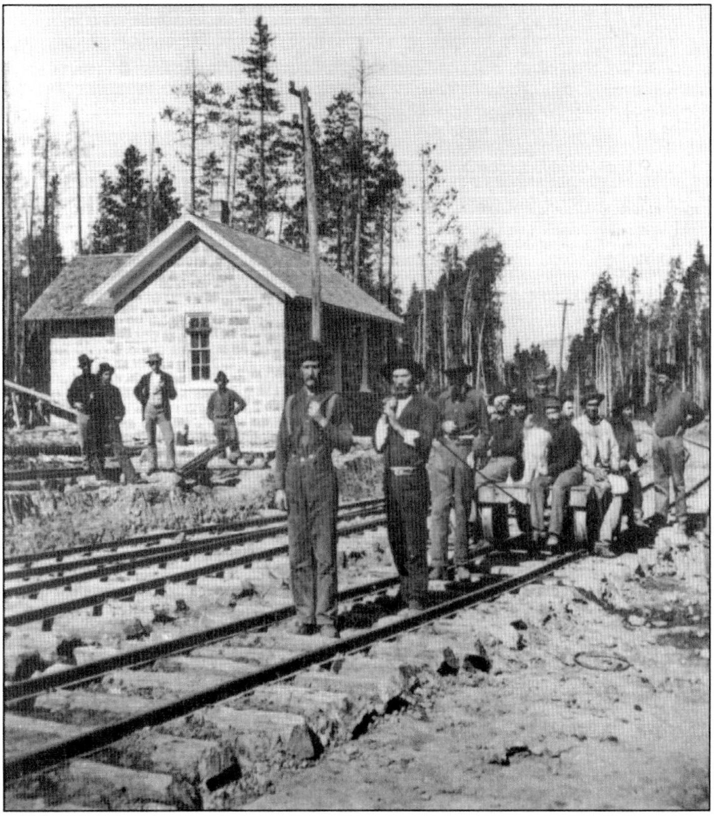

Construction Crew, Summit of Veta Pass. This picture was probably taken around June 1877, when the tracks were completed over the pass. The stone building on the left is the D&RGW depot. (CRM.)

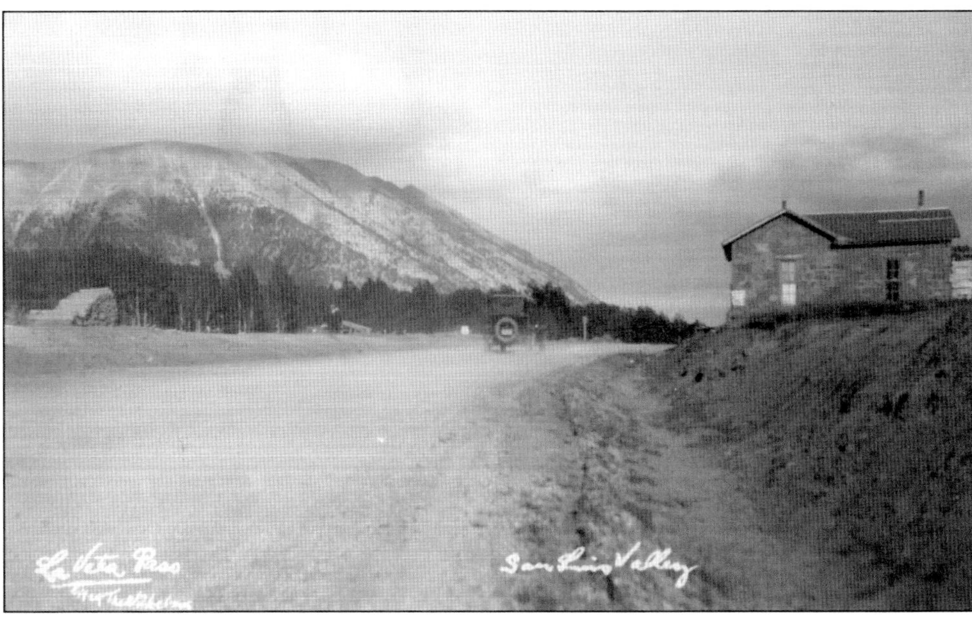

Veta Pass Automobile Road. With the abandonment of the narrow gauge railroad over Veta Pass in 1899, the railroad grade was turned into a road. Here, a car heads east over the pass, with Mount Mestas at left and the railroad depot at right. (CRM.)

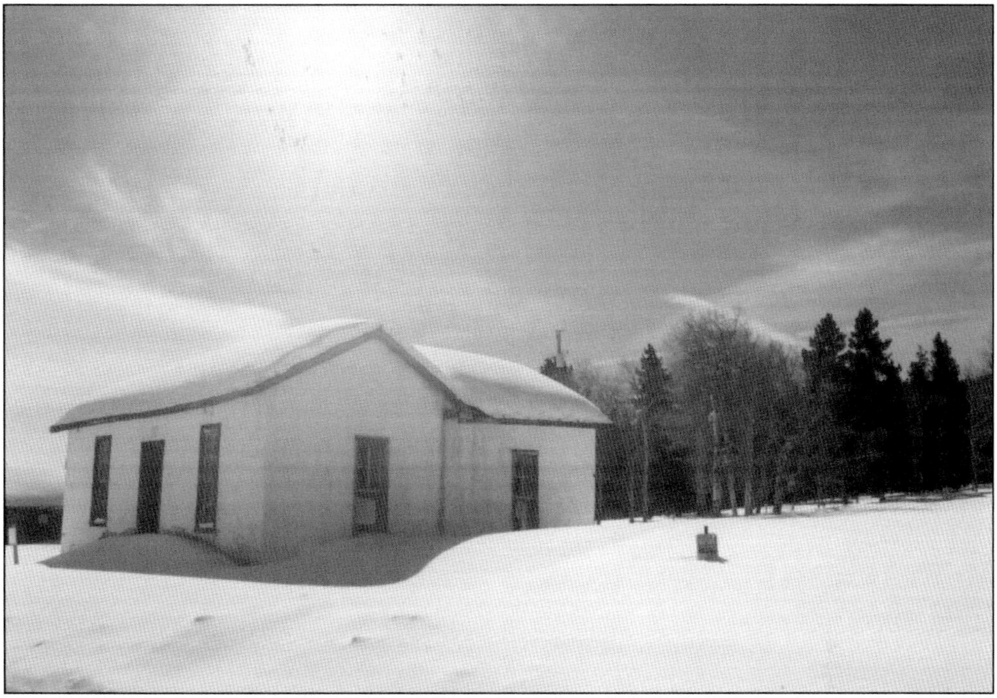

VETA PASS TRAIN DEPOT, 2005. The old depot can be reached on cross-country skis in the winter. The structure, which had been crumbling, has been restored, and the stone walls have been covered over with stucco. This view is facing southeast.

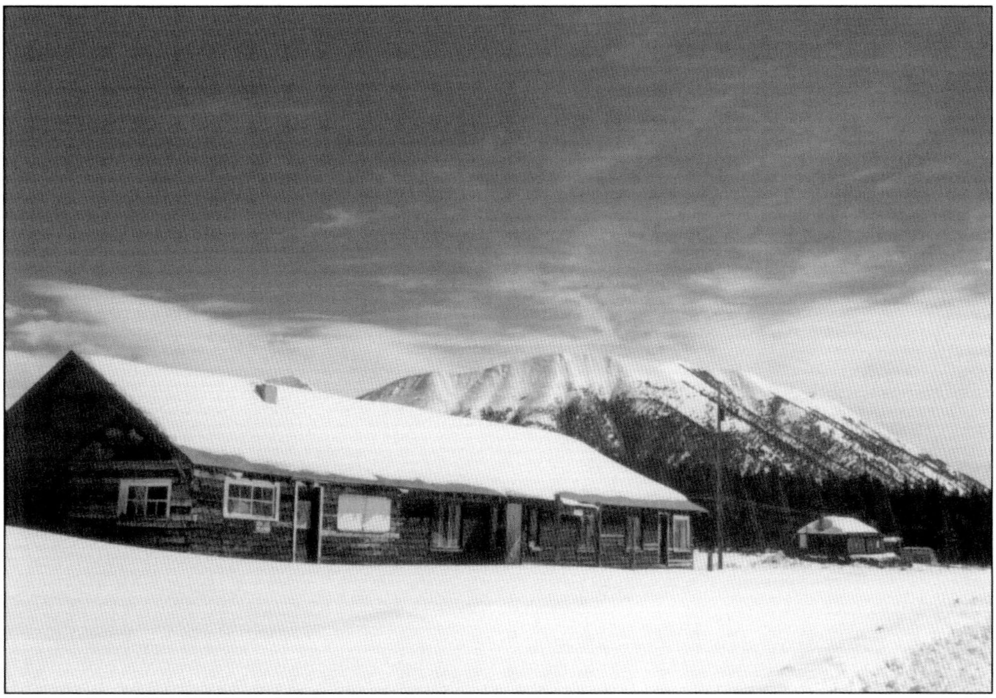

VETA PASS. Across the road from the old depot, these buildings served as a restaurant and a hotel for travelers. Mount Mestas rises in the background. Veta Pass is now called Old La Veta Pass.

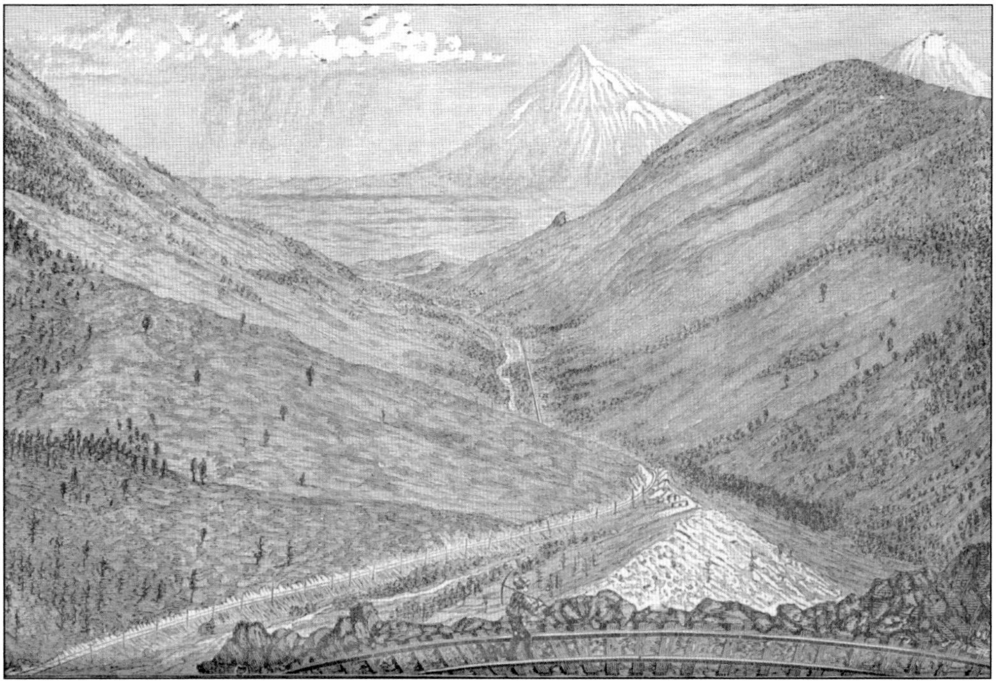

Spanish Peaks from Dump Mountain. This highly stylized drawing from the 1880s looks east from the railroad tracks on Dump Mountain toward La Veta and the Spanish Peaks. Ollie Hudson's picnic party would have occurred on the rocks just above the tracks (below the lower edge of the drawing).

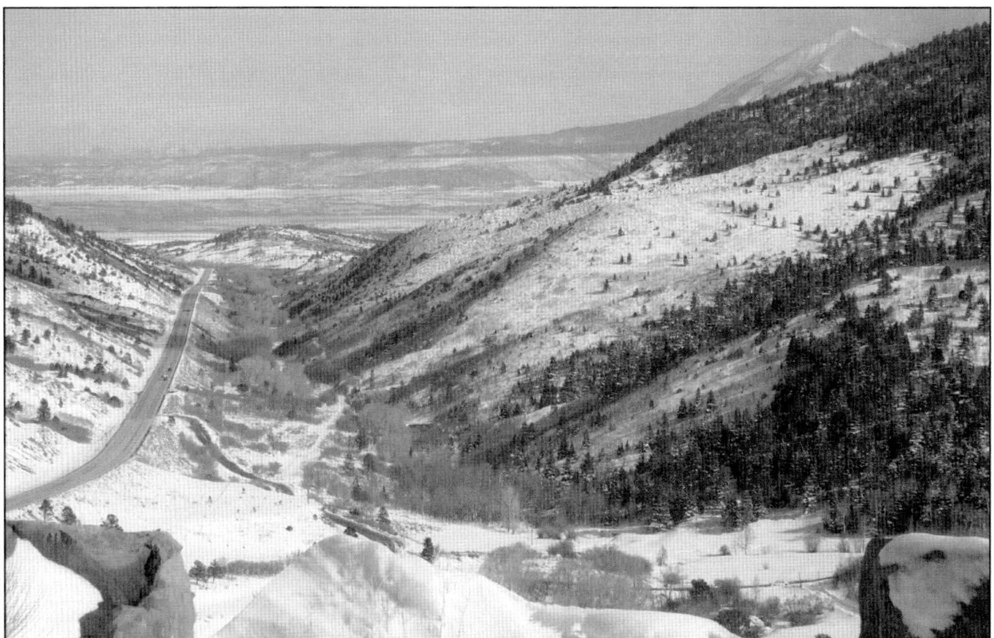

East Spanish Peak from Dump Mountain. A contemporary view shows US Highway 160 extending east down the valley, where the narrow gauge railroad tracks used to be. The East Spanish Peak is seen in the top right background.

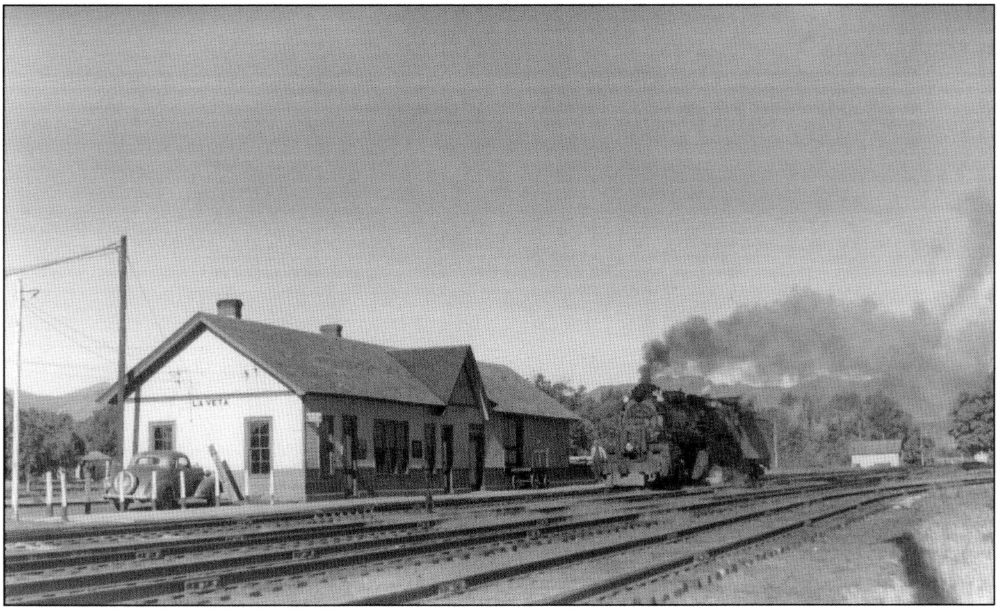

La Veta, 1950. Otto Perry took this photograph of a Denver & Rio Grande (D&RG) steam engine heading into La Veta from the west in 1950. Perry was a premier Colorado railroad photographer, and his images appear in many books. (CRM.)

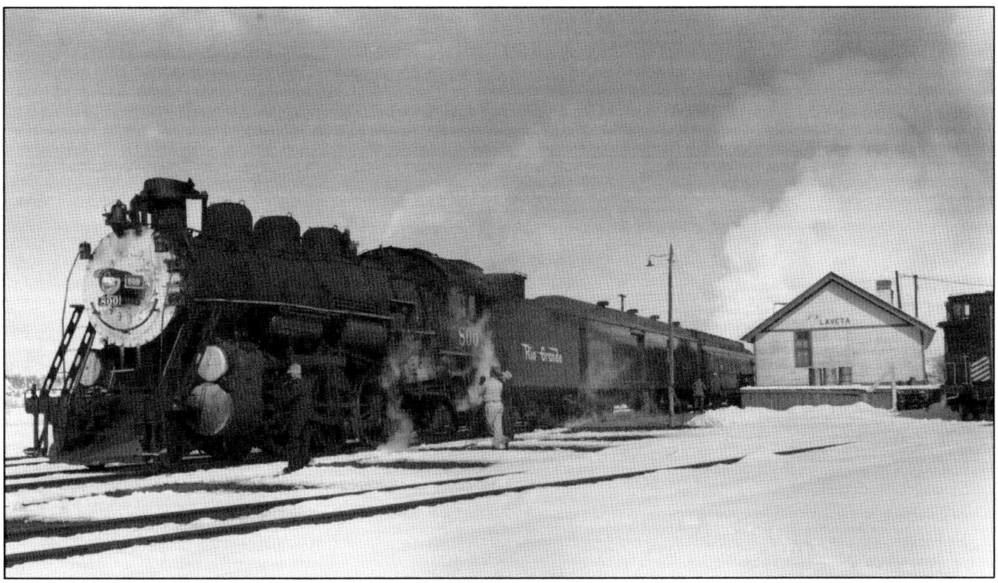

La Veta, December 1951. Robert W. Richardson, founder of the Colorado Railroad Museum, took this photograph of the westbound San Luis passenger train on a snowy December day in 1951. (CRM.)

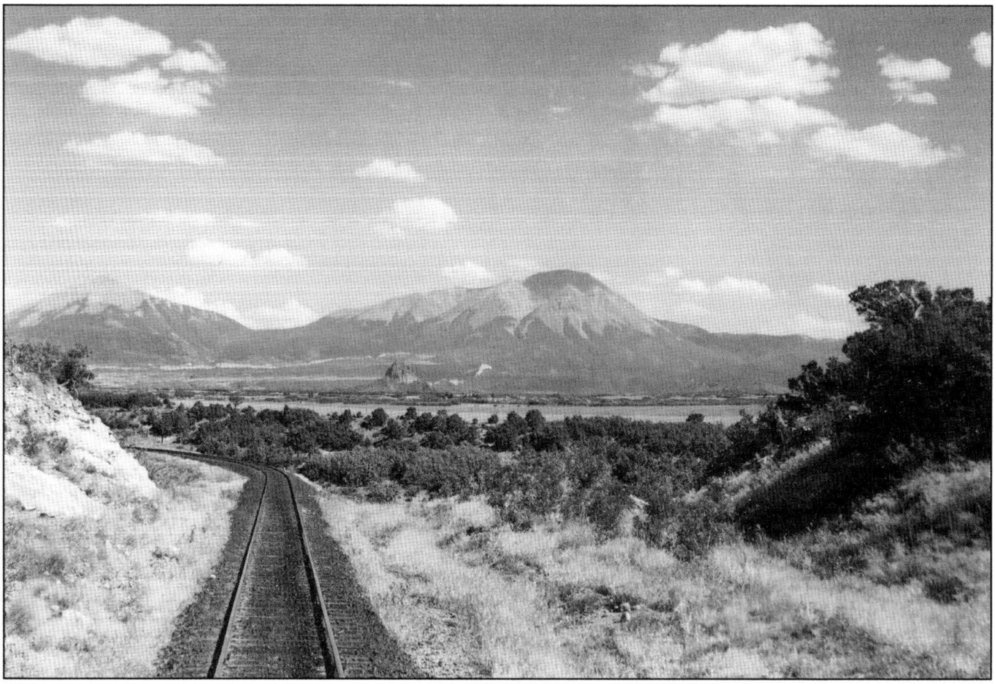

SPANISH PEAKS AND GOEMMER'S BUTTE, 1951. George Trout took this photograph from the D&RGW railroad tracks west of La Veta on July 2, 1951. This route of the standard gauge track was completed over La Veta Pass in 1899 and is still in service today. (DPL no. Z-11008.)

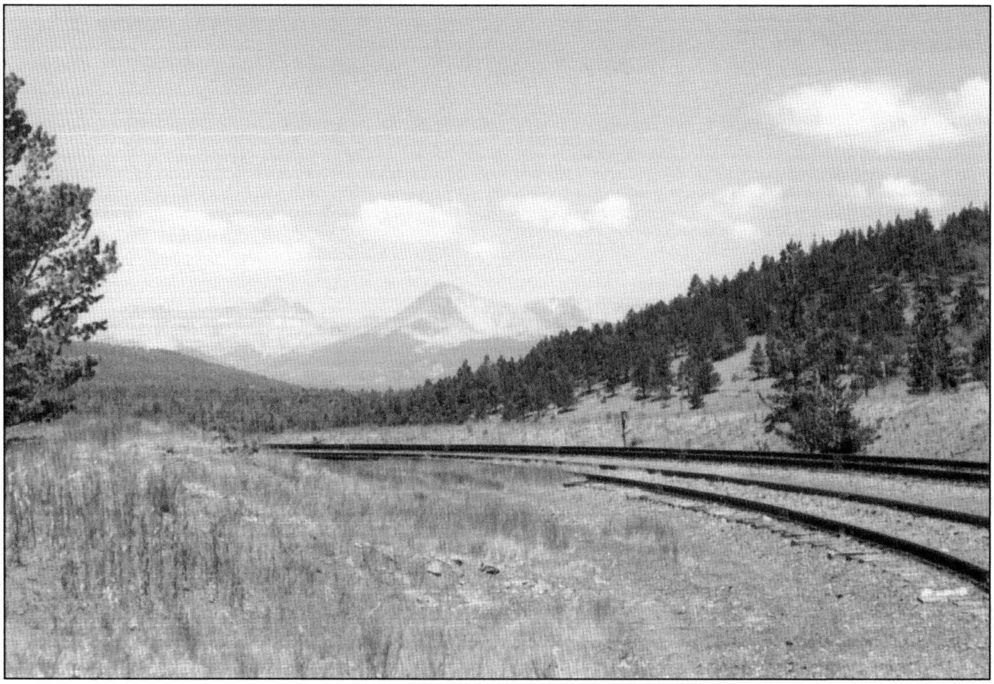

LOOKING WEST FROM LA VETA PASS. As the standard gauge tracks climb La Veta Pass and curve to the west, two of Colorado's 14,000-foot-high peaks come into view. Mount Lindsey (14,042 feet) is to the right, and Blanca Peak (14,345 feet) is to the left.

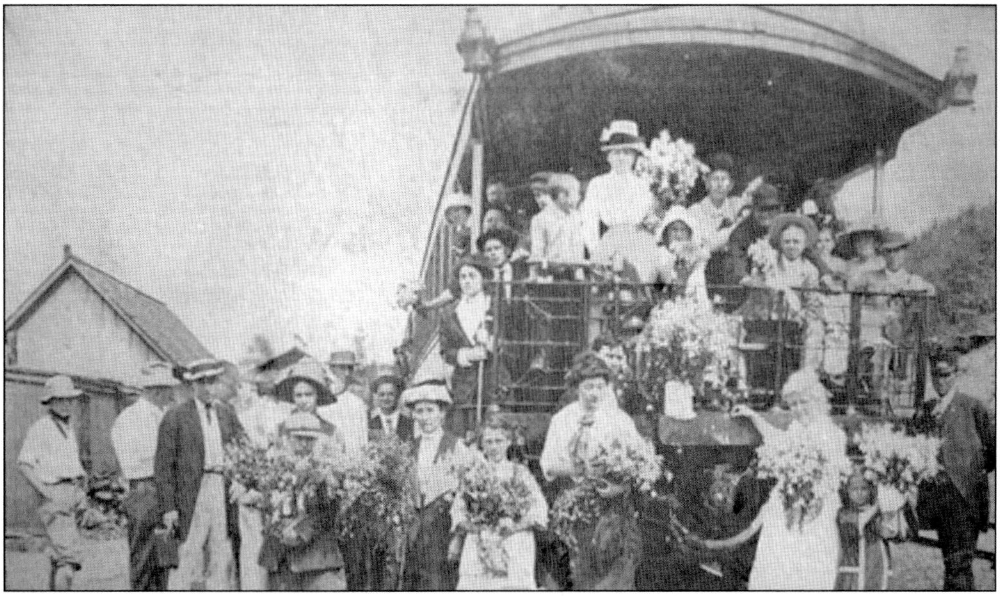

La Veta Pass, July 2, 1916. The D&RGW railroad conducted popular tourist excursions to the top of La Veta Pass in the early 1900s. People came from as far as Denver, Colorado Springs, and Pueblo to ride the train to the pass. The frame building at left is the La Veta Pass depot. (FFM.)

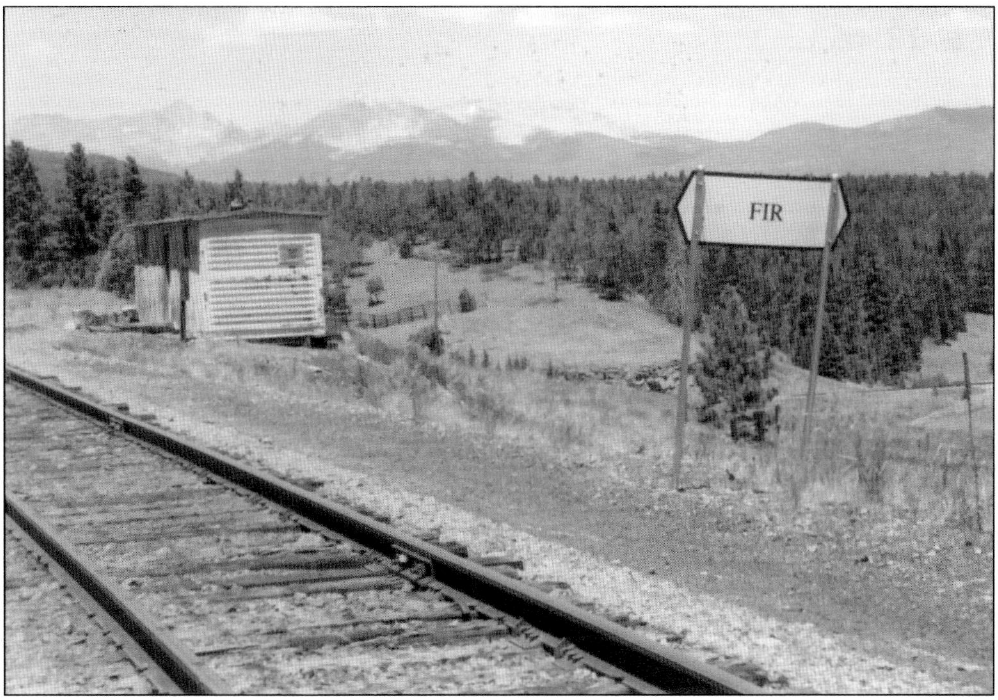

Fir (La Veta Pass), 2006. This old boxcar, used for storage, stands approximately where the La Veta Pass depot stood. The current owners of the Rio Grande Scenic Railroad have since removed it, and the railroad has built an amphitheater for concerts in the meadow below the boxcar.

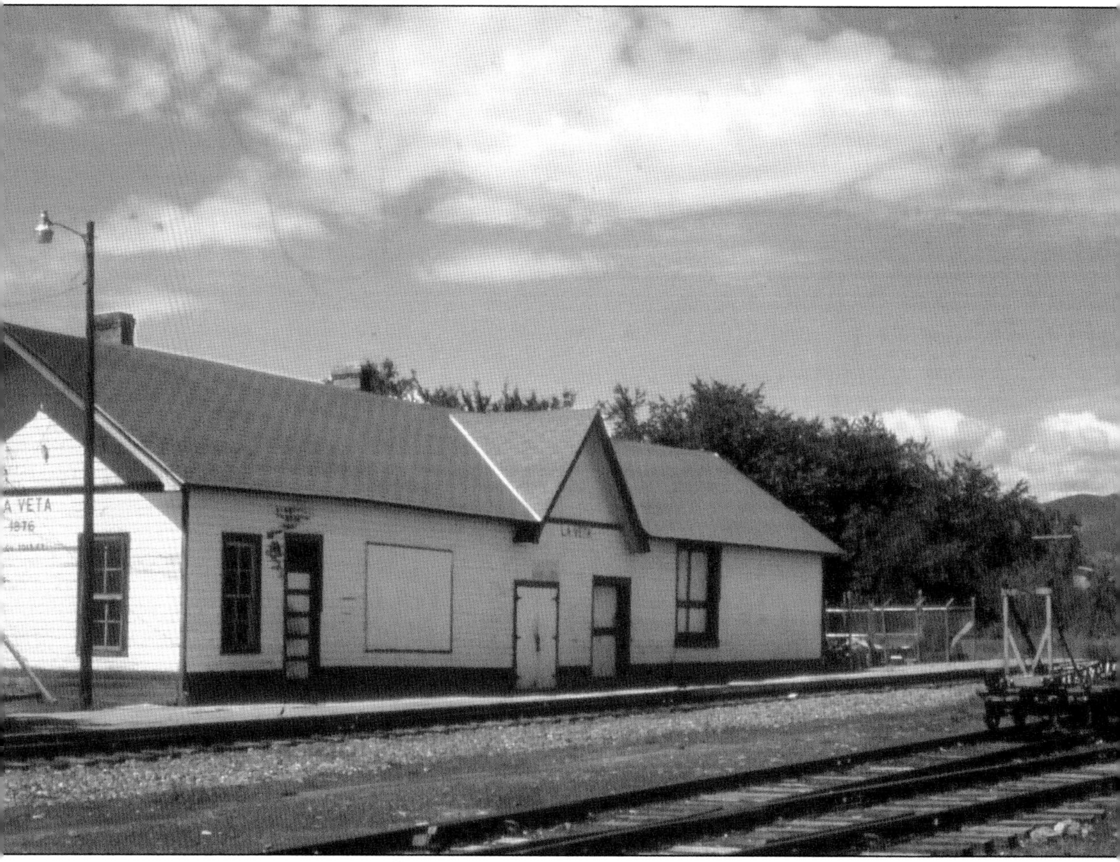

LA VETA DEPOT, 1988. Built in 1876 by the D&RGW, the La Veta depot was still standing in August 1988. Note the track running directly in front of the depot's concrete platform. When the depot was restored in 2003, it was moved several hundred feet south into the town park, away from the tracks.

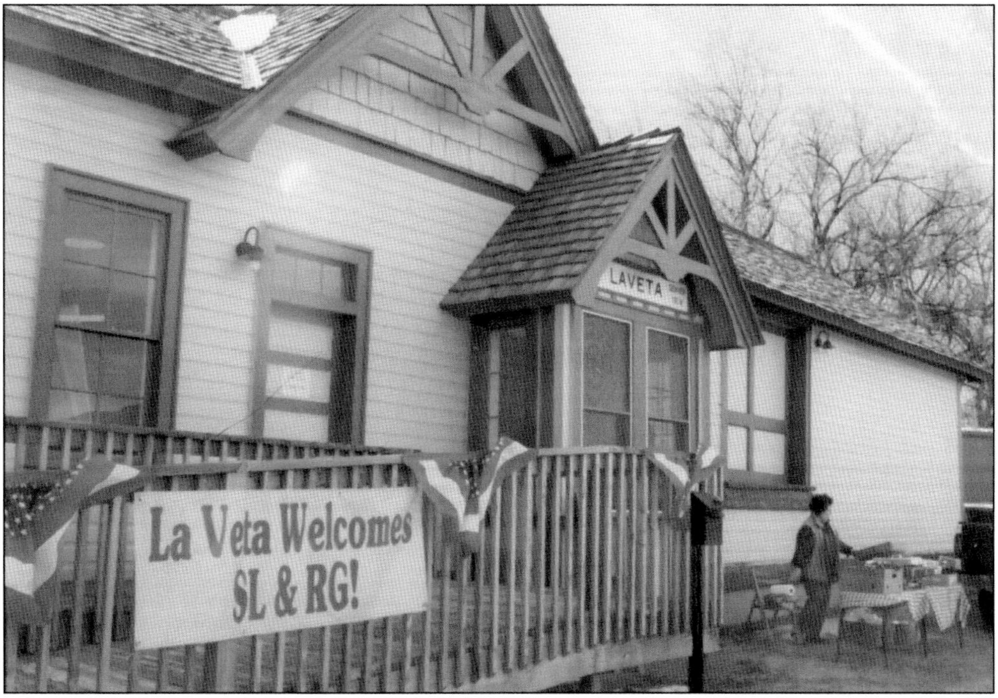

Restored La Veta Depot, February 9, 2006. Now in use as town government offices, the station was all decked out on for the arrival of the first passenger train in 53 years. The San Luis & Rio Grande Railroad (SL&RG) reestablished tourist train service between La Veta and Alamosa over La Veta Pass.

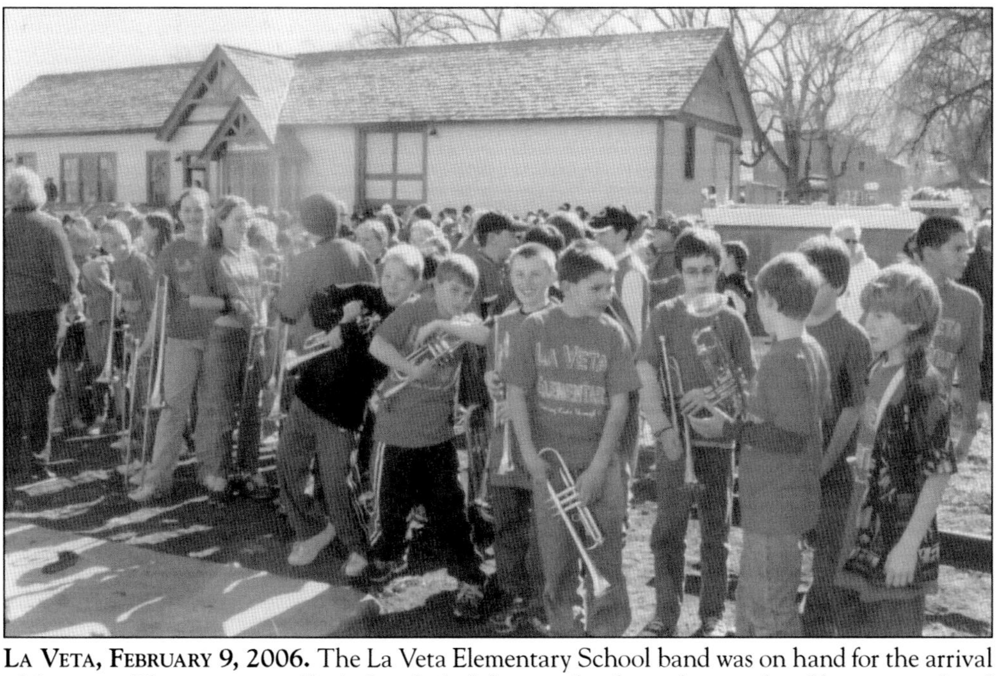

La Veta, February 9, 2006. The La Veta Elementary School band was on hand for the arrival of the train. The town virtually declared a holiday, as school was dismissed and businesses closed so that everyone could witness the coming of the SL&RG train.

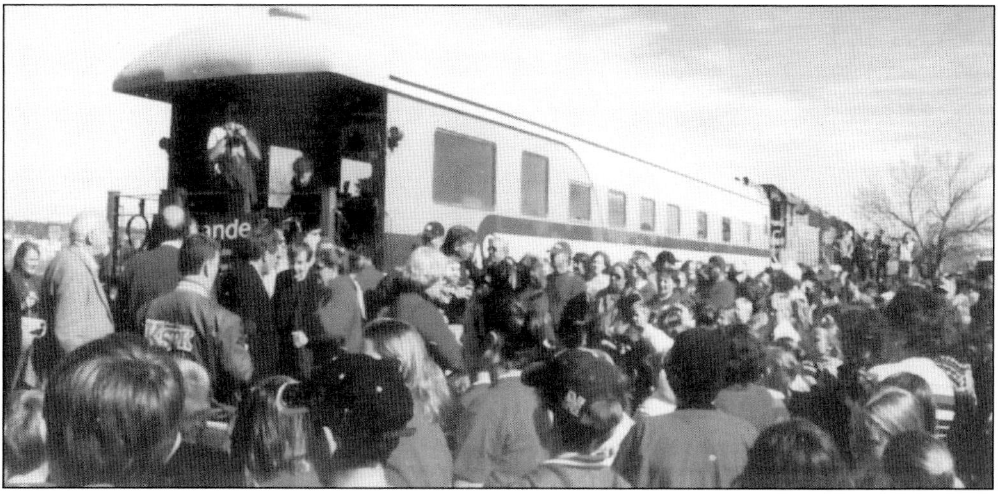

La Veta Celebrates. Hundreds of people greeted the single-car passenger train. Dignitaries from both La Veta and Alamosa were on board. Bands played, speeches were made, and refreshments were enjoyed by all.

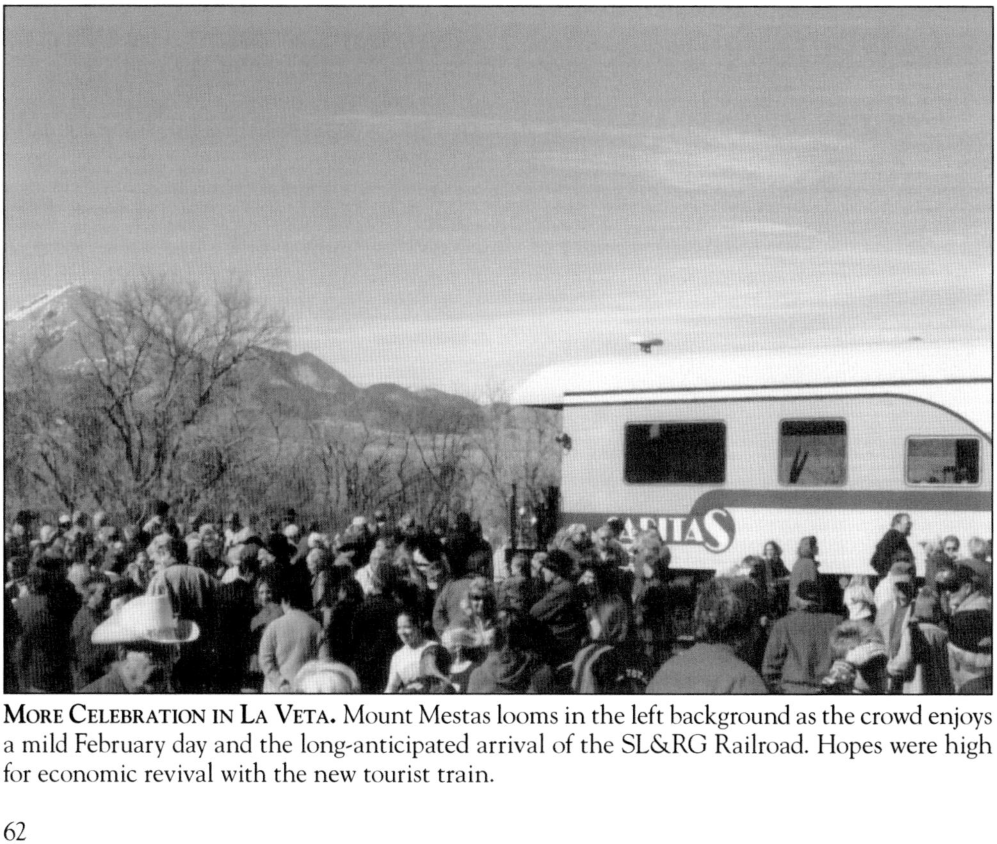

More Celebration in La Veta. Mount Mestas looms in the left background as the crowd enjoys a mild February day and the long-anticipated arrival of the SL&RG Railroad. Hopes were high for economic revival with the new tourist train.

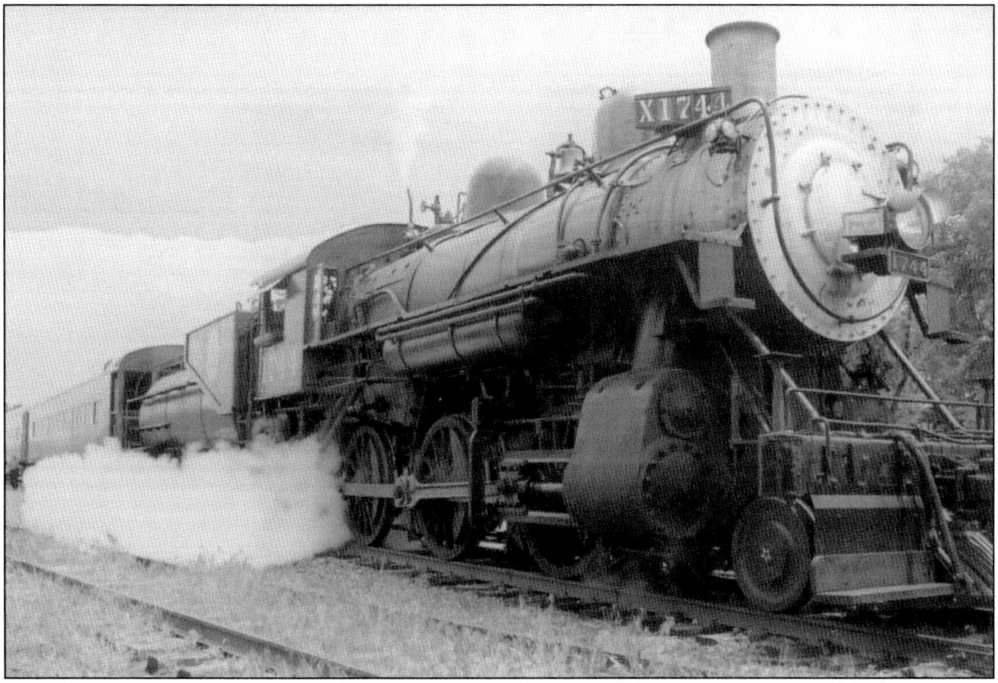

STEAM POWER RETURNS TO LA VETA. Steam engine No. 1744 pulls the SL&RG passenger train into La Veta in July 2007. The railroad ran steam engines on Saturdays and Sundays and diesel engines on weekdays.

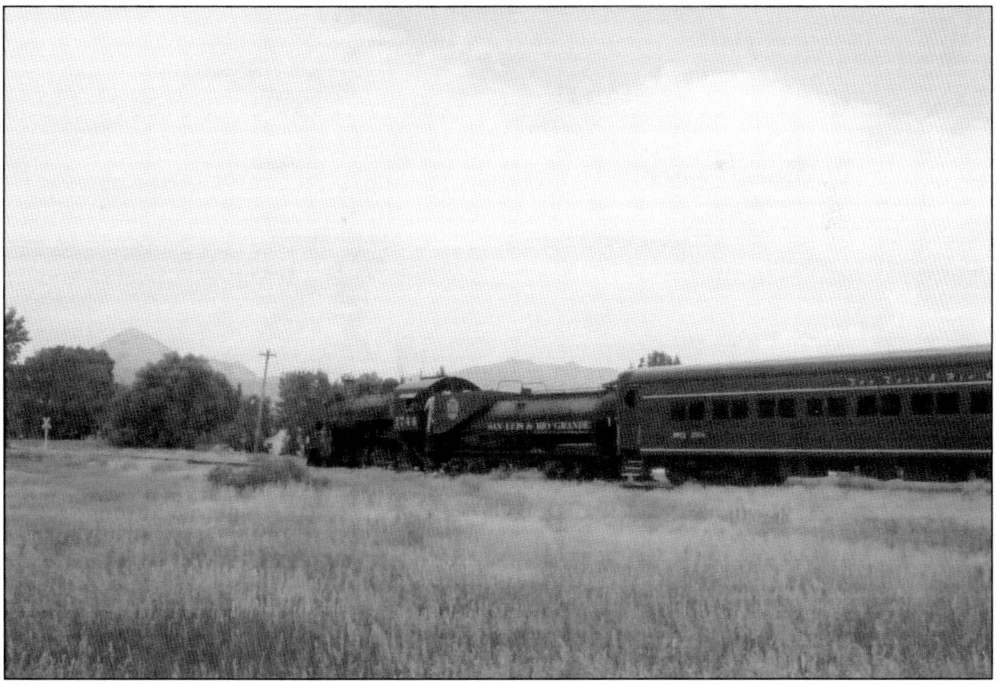

HEADING BACK TO ALAMOSA, JULY 2007. Steam engine No. 1744 pulls the SL&RG train west out of La Veta, with Mount Mestas in the distance at left.

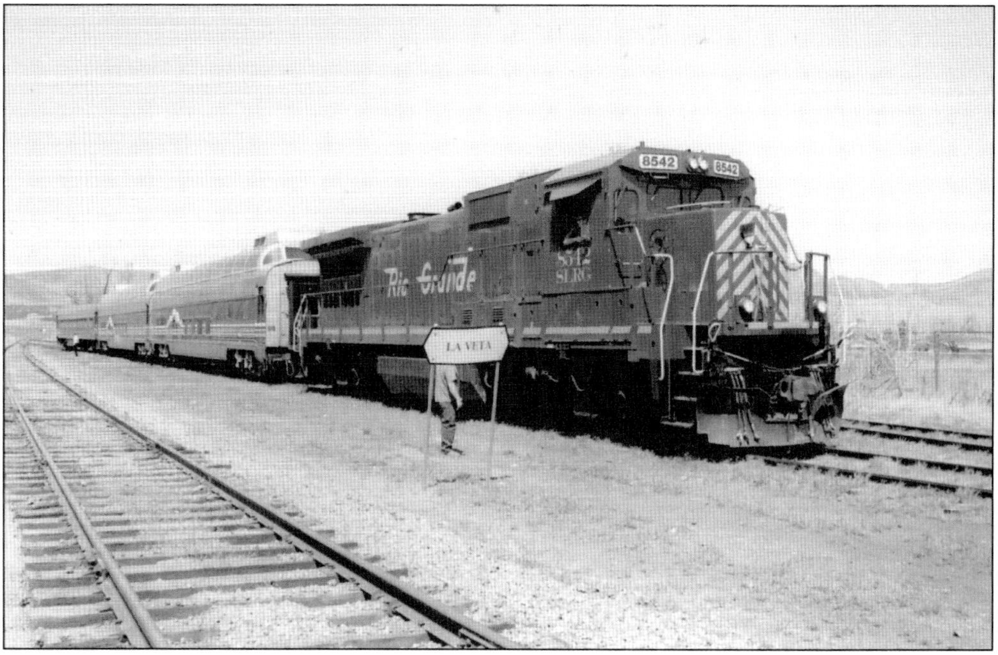

LA VETA, MAY 2008. By 2008, the SL&RG had purchased domed excursion cars from the Alaska Railroad for use on its La Veta Pass line, allowing passengers spectacular views of the scenery. Also, the railroad's name was changed to Rio Grande Scenic Railroad.

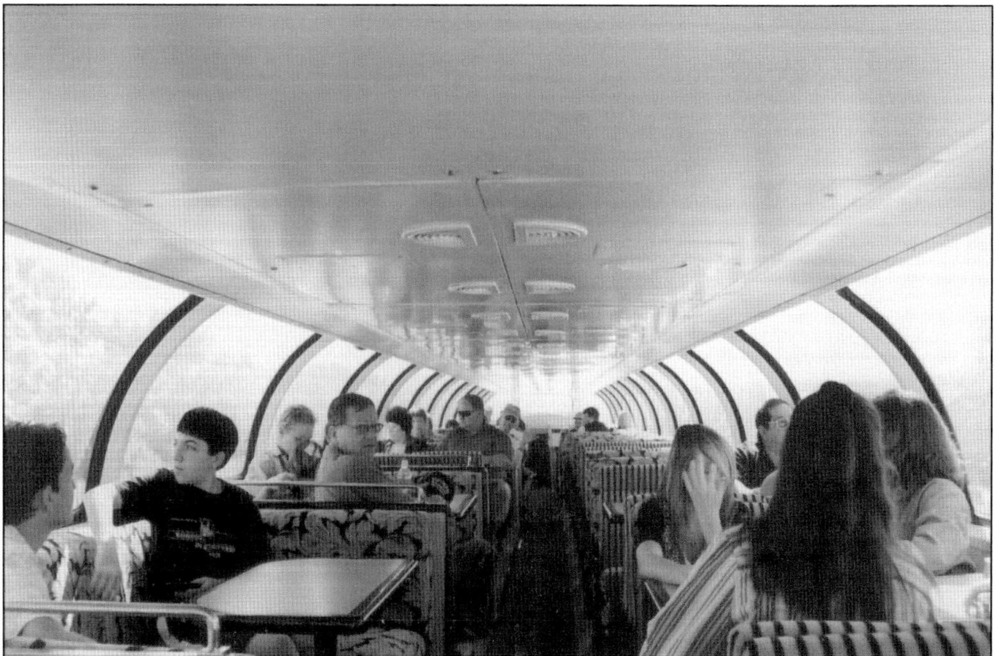

INSIDE THE DOME CAR. Passengers enjoy fantastic views of Mount Mestas, La Veta Pass, Mount Lindsey, and Blanca Peak from the comfort of the dome car on a trip over La Veta Pass in May 2008. The tradition of passenger service over the Sangre de Cristo Mountains, begun in 1877 by the D&RGW, continues today.

Five

When Coal Was King in Walsenburg

On the banks of the Cuchara River, in view of the mighty Spanish Peaks, Don Miguel Antonio Leon established La Plaza de Los Leones in 1858. German immigrant Fred Walsen arrived at the plaza with his bride, Emilie Sporleder, in 1870. Walsen established a trading post and purchased land around the settlement. He became the first mayor, and the town's name was changed to Walsenburg; it became the seat of Huerfano County in 1872.

The first coal mine in Huerfano County was established in March 1876, when Walsen leased some of his land west of Walsenburg to the predecessors of the Colorado Fuel & Iron Company (CF&I). Thus, the Walsen Mine was born, and the Denver & Rio Grande Western (D&RGW) Railroad arrived from Denver in the summer of 1876 to begin hauling out the coal. The railroad purchased much of the coal for its locomotive operations, and it also hauled coal to the CF&I steel mill in Pueblo.

Working in the coal mines was very difficult for the early miners. There was little ventilation, timbering was slipshod, and there were frequent cave-ins and floods. Hundreds of miners lost their lives. Poor working conditions led to frequent strikes by the miners. The strike of April 1914 became violent, with shots fired between miners and guards. Fighting proceeded into Walsenburg, and several people were killed.

When the strikes and violence of 1914 subsided, a shaky peace came to the Walsen Mine as CF&I recognized the existence of the United Mine Workers union and gradually improved conditions in and around the mine. Miners' pay was increased, new homes were built in the company town, and CF&I even constructed a new YMCA building at the Walsen camp in 1916.

The Walsen Mine was permanently closed in 1931 due to extensive flooding, and Walsenburg lost one of its major sources of income—a blow from which it has never recovered.

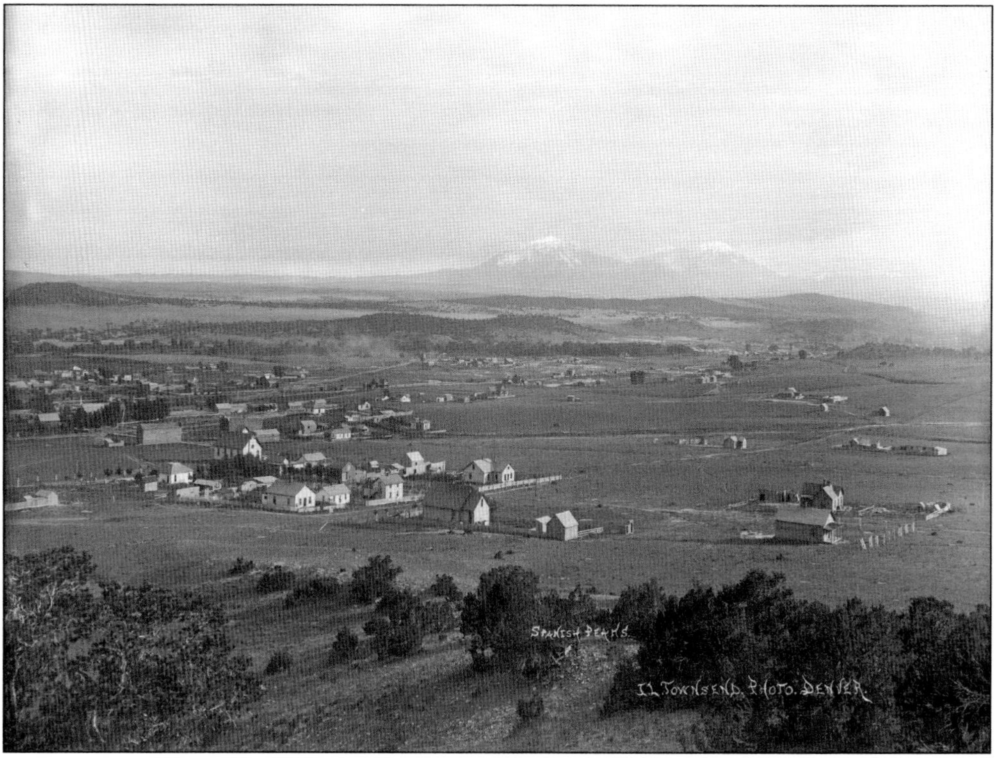

WALSENBURG, 1895. I.L. Townsend photographed this magnificent view of Walsenburg and the Spanish Peaks. Walsenburg became the seat of Huerfano County in 1872, and showed significant growth 23 years later, with many prosperous-looking homes on the north end of town. (DPL no. X-14009.)

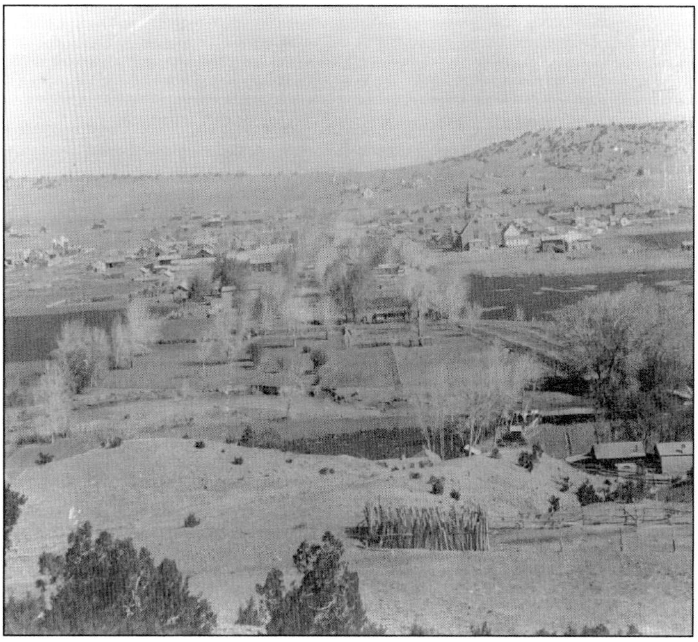

WALSENBURG, C. LATE 1890S. In this northward view of Main Street, St. Mary's Catholic Church dominates the photograph. Construction on the church began in 1892 and was almost completed when the financial Panic of 1893 interrupted work. The church was finally finished in 1900. (HCHS.)

TWELVE "APOSTLES" OF WALSENBURG. Pictured in 1875, these men are the leading citizens and founders of Walsenburg. Standing are, from left to right, James Thompson, John Chapell, John Albert, Fred Walsen, and T.L. Creesy. Seated are, from left to right, A.R. Campbell, Charles Mazzone, Isaac Dailey, Henry Strange, Frank Duhme, John H. Brown, and August Sporleder. (HCHS.)

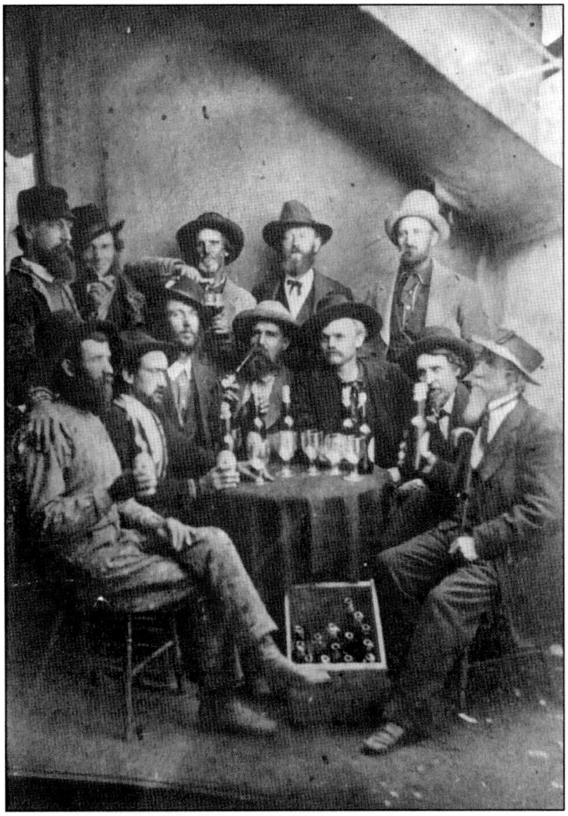

FRED WALSEN'S HOME, C. 1876. Walsen was founder, mayor, and chief businessman of Walsenburg. His home was at the well-to-do north end of town. In this photograph, his wife, Millie Sporleder, is on the left, a child is in the center, and Fred is on the right. (DPL no. X-13996.)

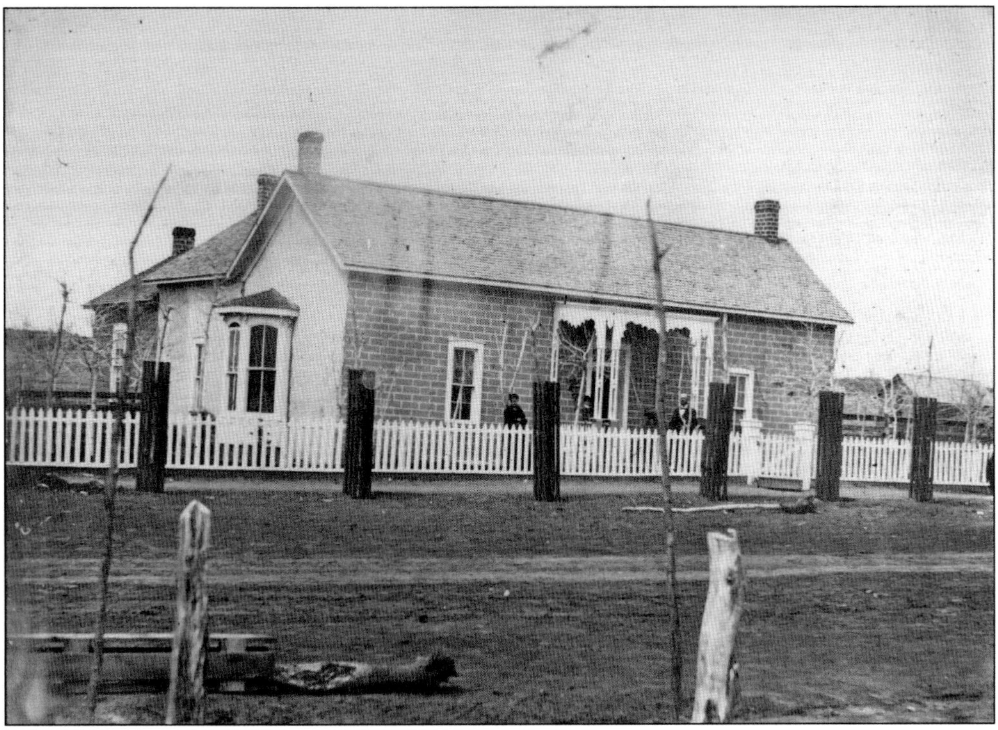

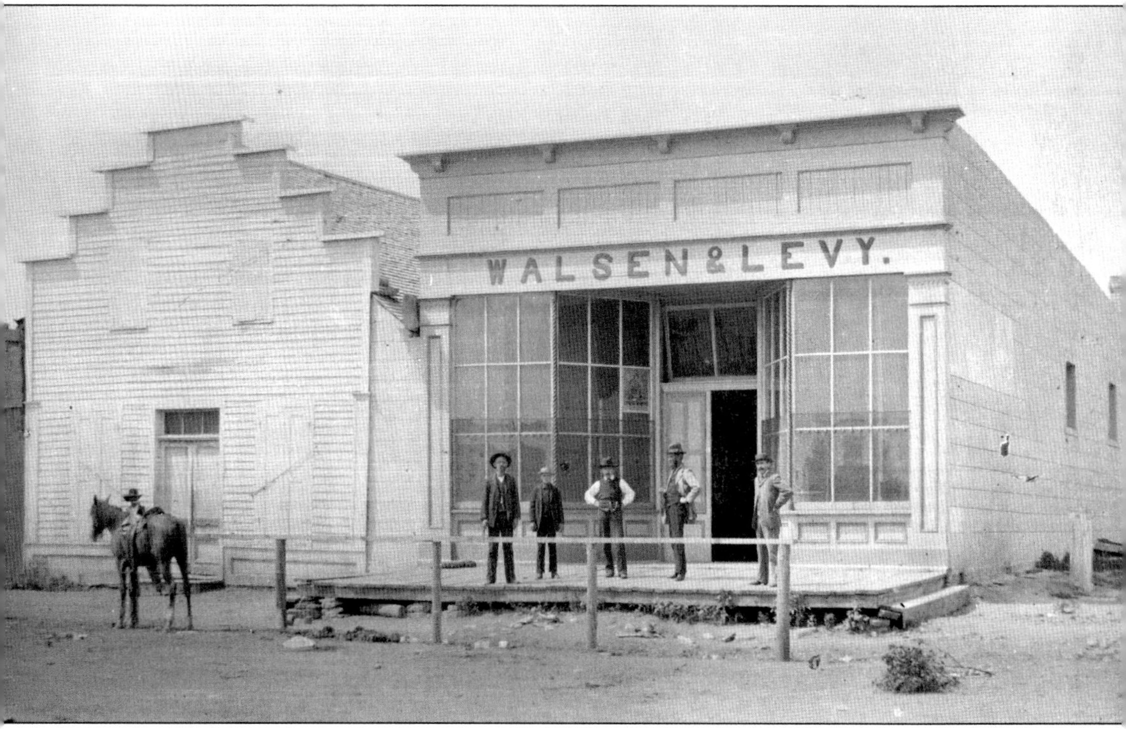

Walsen and Levy Store, 1880s. Alexander Levy started his first store in Walsenburg in 1871. Levy soon joined forces in business with Fred Walsen, who was his brother-in-law. Both men married daughters of August Sporleder (Walsen married Millie, and Levy married Lillian). Pictured in front of the store are Fred Walsen (left), Albert Singer (center), and Fred Unfug (right). The other men are unidentified. (DPL no. X-14007.)

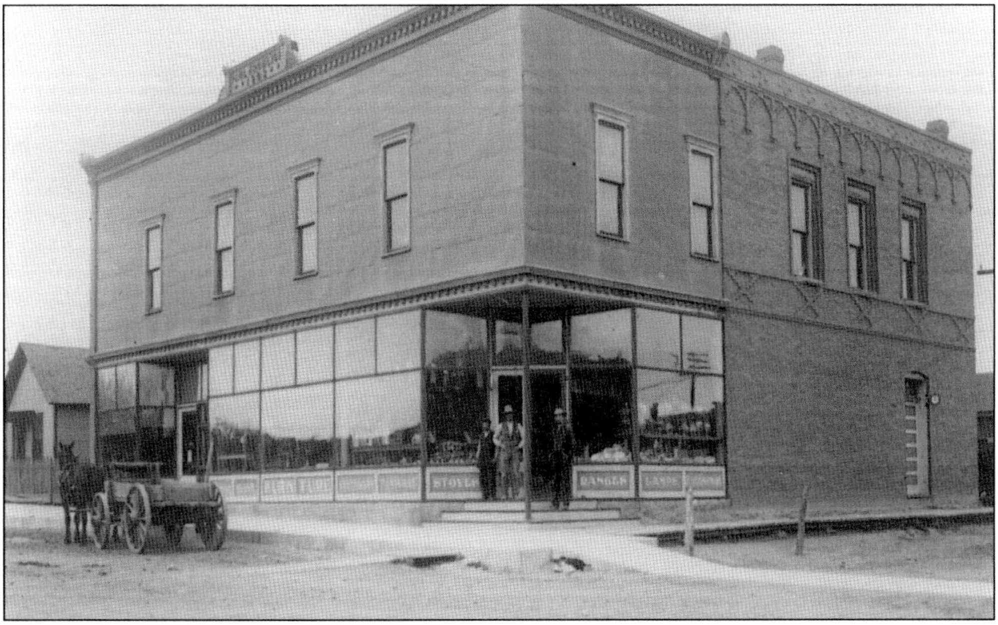

UNFUG HARDWARE, 1880s. The Unfug brothers were hardware merchants in Walsenburg who sold furniture, stoves, ranges, and lamps, among other items. Louis B. Sporleder, nephew of August Sporleder, married Louise Unfug and then joined the Unfug brothers in business. Louis Sporleder went on to become a well-known merchant in his own right (see page 81). (HCHS.)

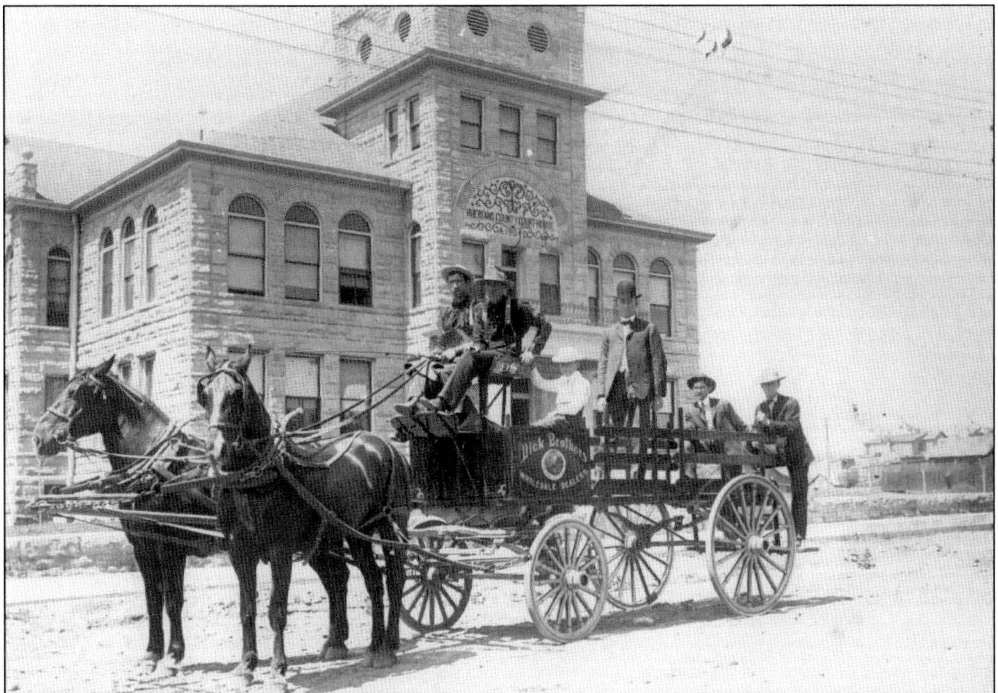

DICK BROTHERS WAGON. The Dick brothers, wholesale liquor dealers, pose on their wagon in front of the Huerfano County Courthouse in Walsenburg. The courthouse, designed by C.A. Henderson, of Pueblo, was built from local sandstone and completed in 1904. (HCHS.)

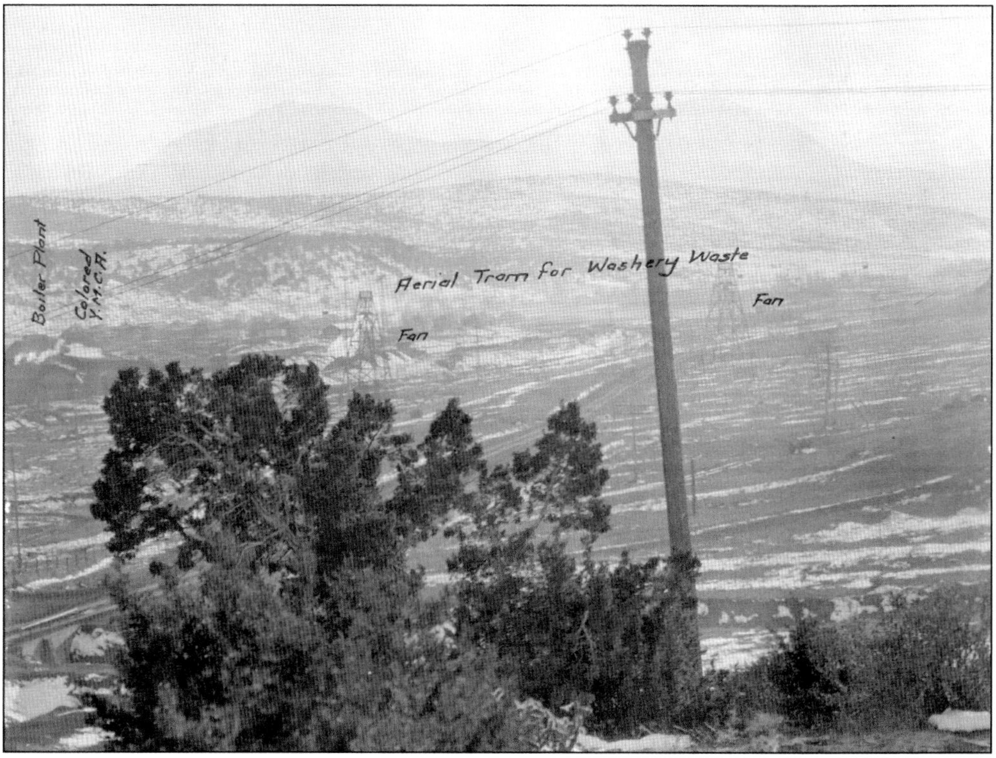

WALSEN MINE AND SPANISH PEAKS, 1922. In 1876, Fred Walsen leased his land west of town for coal mining operations. The Colorado Fuel & Iron Company (CF&I) took over operations in 1892. Thirty years later, this area had developed into a massive complex of structures and buildings, as shown in this and the following three photographs. (BHS/CFI.)

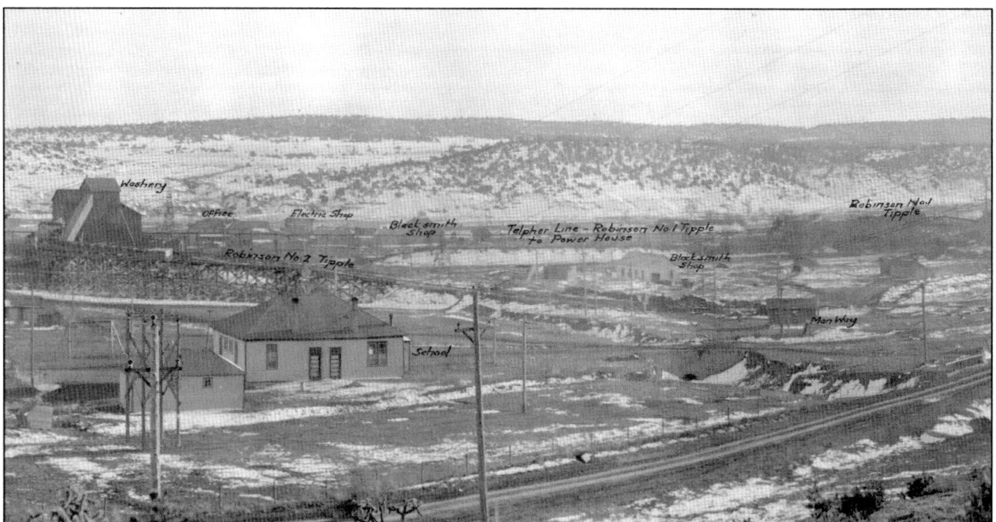

WALSEN MINE COMPLEX, 1922. Proceeding east from the view in the previous photograph, more features of the Walsen Mine complex are revealed. Several coal tipples are shown, along with the blacksmith shop, electric shop, washery, and the camp school. (BHS/CFI.)

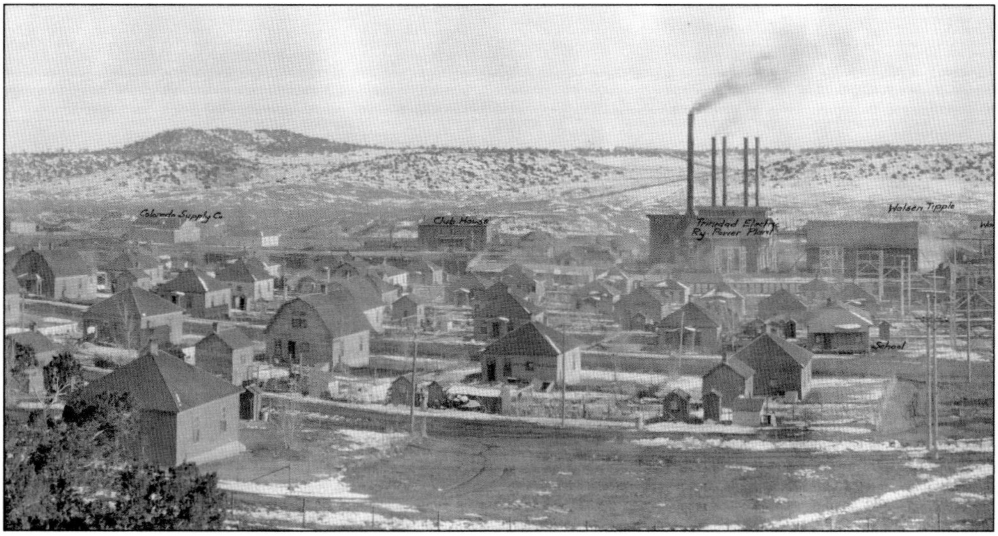

WALSEN MINE POWER PLANT, 1922. Farther east in the Walsen Mine complex, the main tipple is visible, as are the power plant (with five smokestacks), the clubhouse, and the Colorado Supply Company Store (see page 72). Miners' homes were located toward the eastern edge of the complex. (BHS/CFI.)

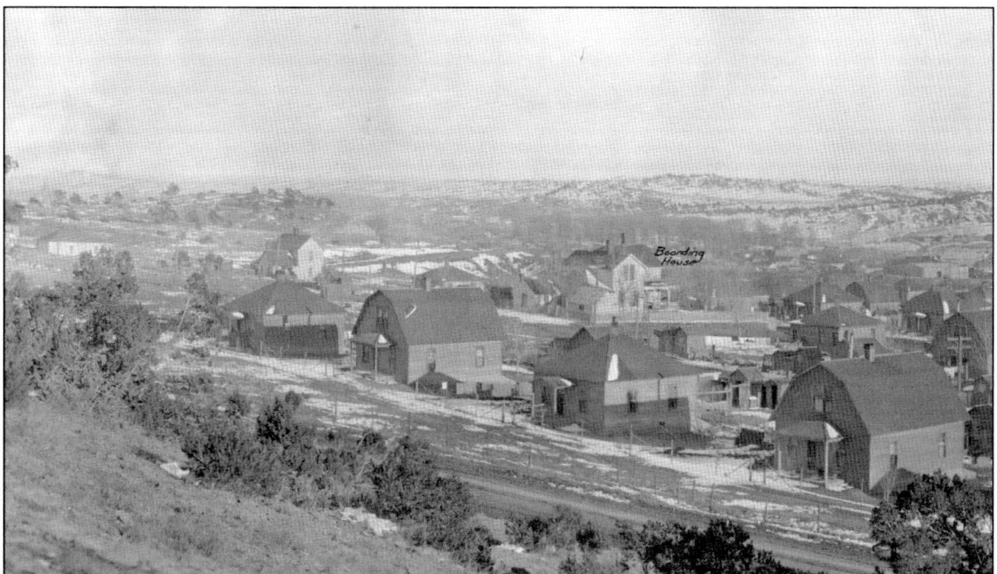

WALSEN MINE, 1922. Toward the farthest eastern end of the mine complex, the single men's boardinghouse (the two-story structure to the right of center) is mixed in with family dwellings. According to CF&I records, the Walsen Mine produced 12,097,891 tones of coal over its lifetime—the most of any mine in Huerfano County. (BHS/CFI.)

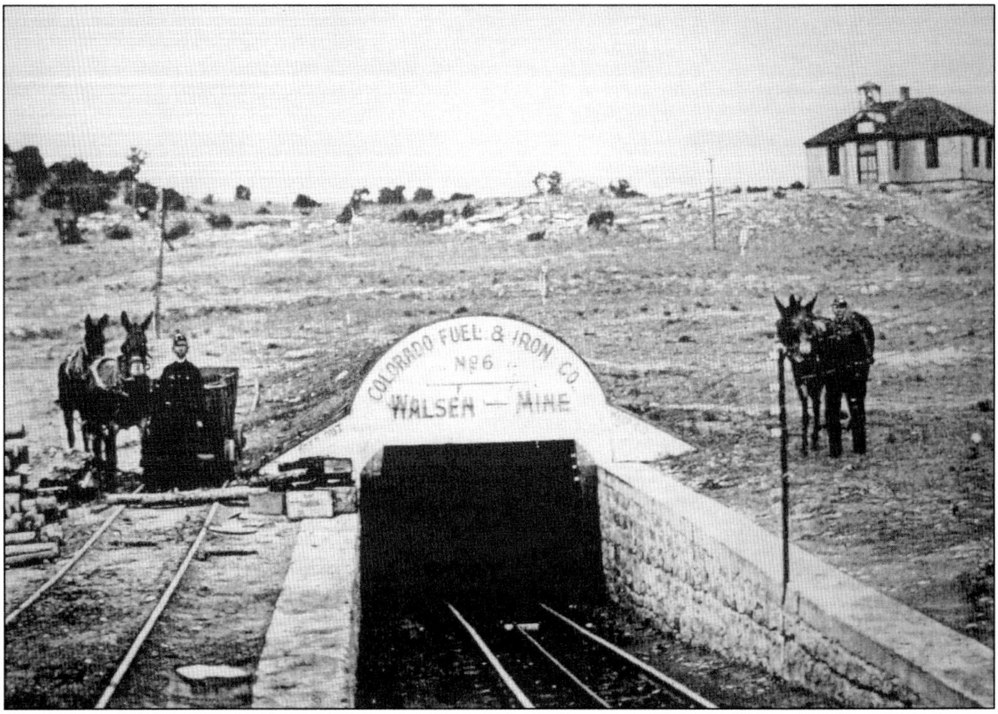

WALSEN MINE ENTRANCE. Guards standing at the entrance to the mine indicate that this photograph may have been taken in 1914, during the times of severe labor unrest and violent strikes. The camp school is on the hill above the mine. (HCHS.)

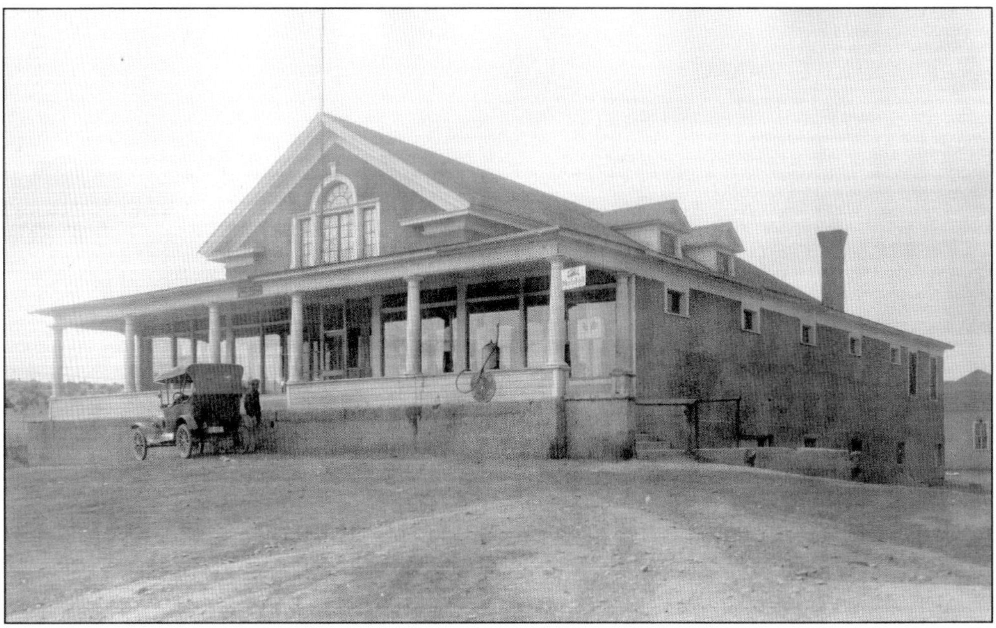

COLORADO SUPPLY COMPANY STORE. A subsidiary of CF&I, the Colorado Supply Company sold every type of good imaginable to miners at the Walsen camp. At some coal camps, miners were paid in scrip (not cash), and the scrip could only be spent in the company store. (BHS/CFI.)

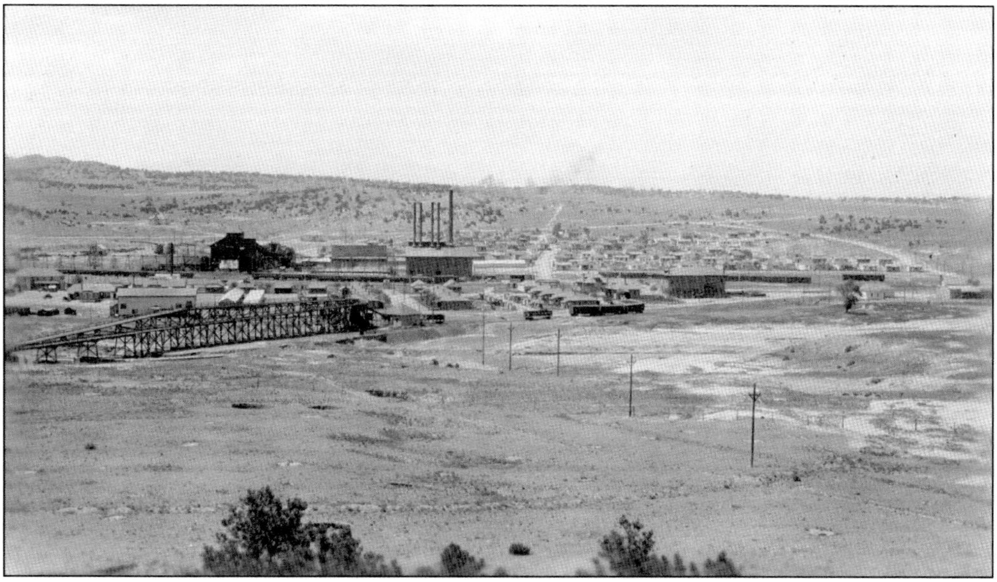

North View of Walsen Mine. The elevated tracks at left form the main Walsen coal tipple. Ore cars were hauled from the mine up the tipple and then dumped into the larger railroad cars waiting below; the cars are visible at right. Also pictured are the washery (black building) and power plant. (BHS/CFI.)

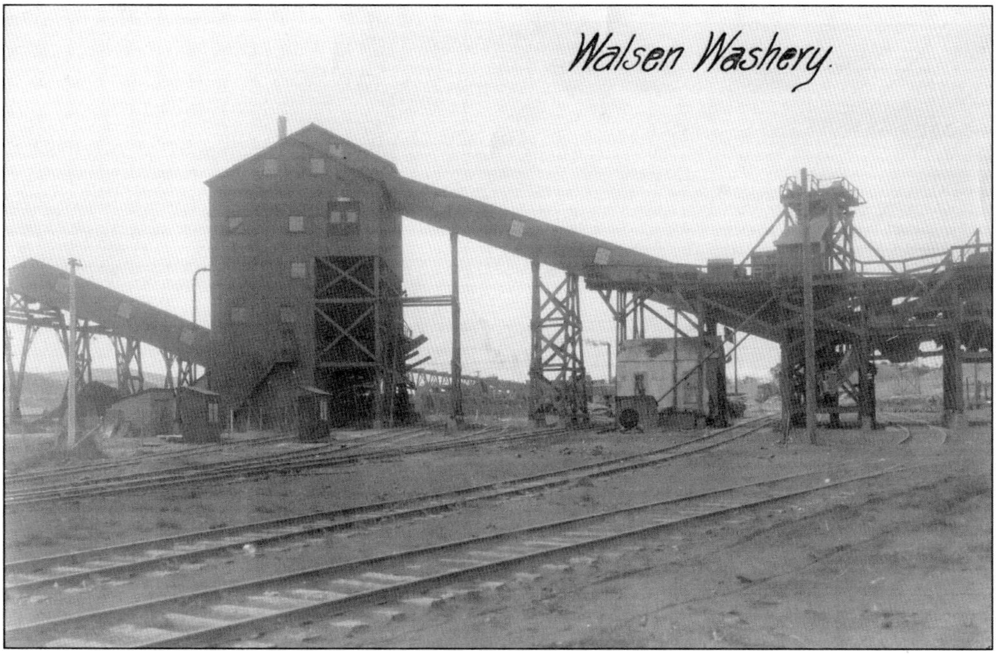

Walsen Washery. Coal was run through the washery to remove impurities, such as sulfur and ash. In the washing process, coal was ground and washed with water, with the heavier impurities sinking to the bottom and the lighter coal rising to the top. Washed coal was much better for coking than unwashed coal. (BHS/CFI.)

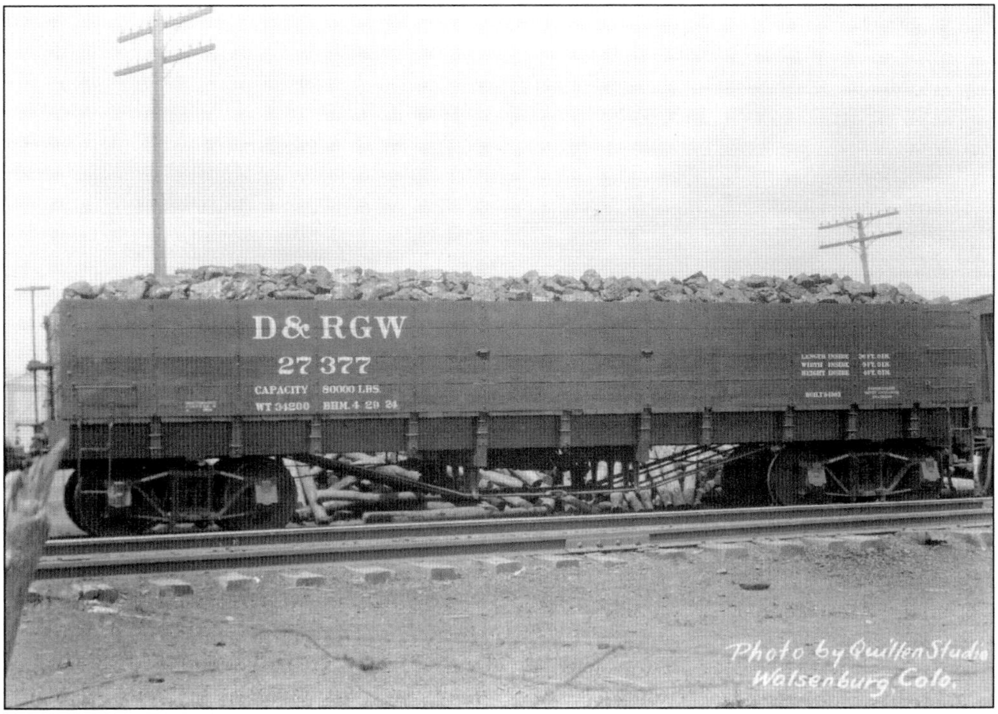

LOADED COAL CAR AT WALSEN. This coal car was loaded under the tipple at Walsen and is ready for its journey north, via the D&RGW railroad, to the CF&I steel mill at Pueblo. (BHS/CFI.)

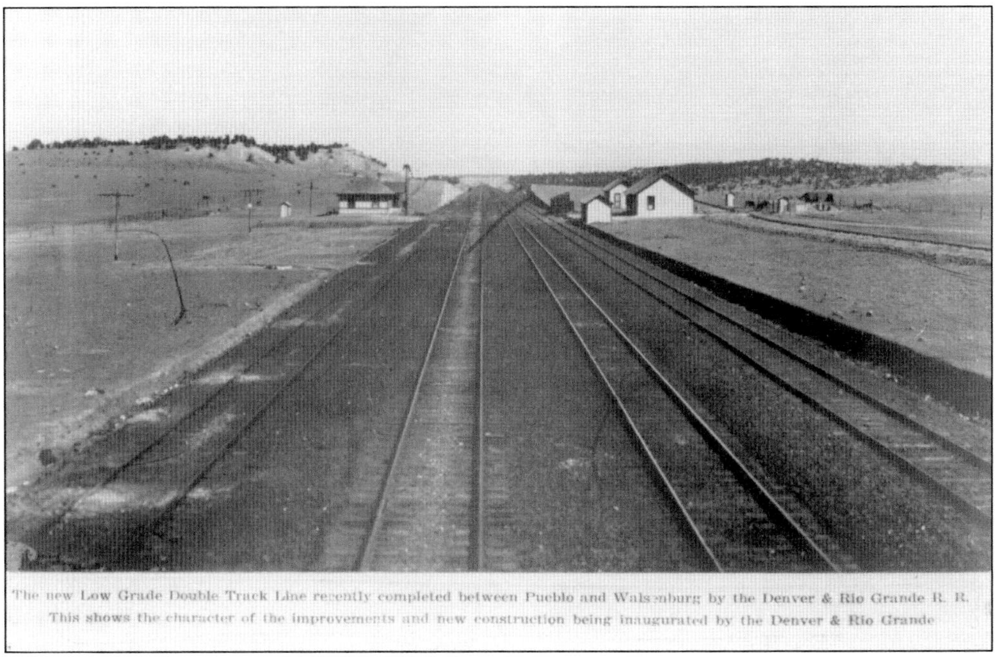

DOUBLE TRACK MAINLINE ON THE D&RGW. To handle the large amount of coal-train traffic between Walsenburg and Pueblo, the D&RGW found it necessary to build two main tracks between the cities, a distance of about 45 miles. (CRM.)

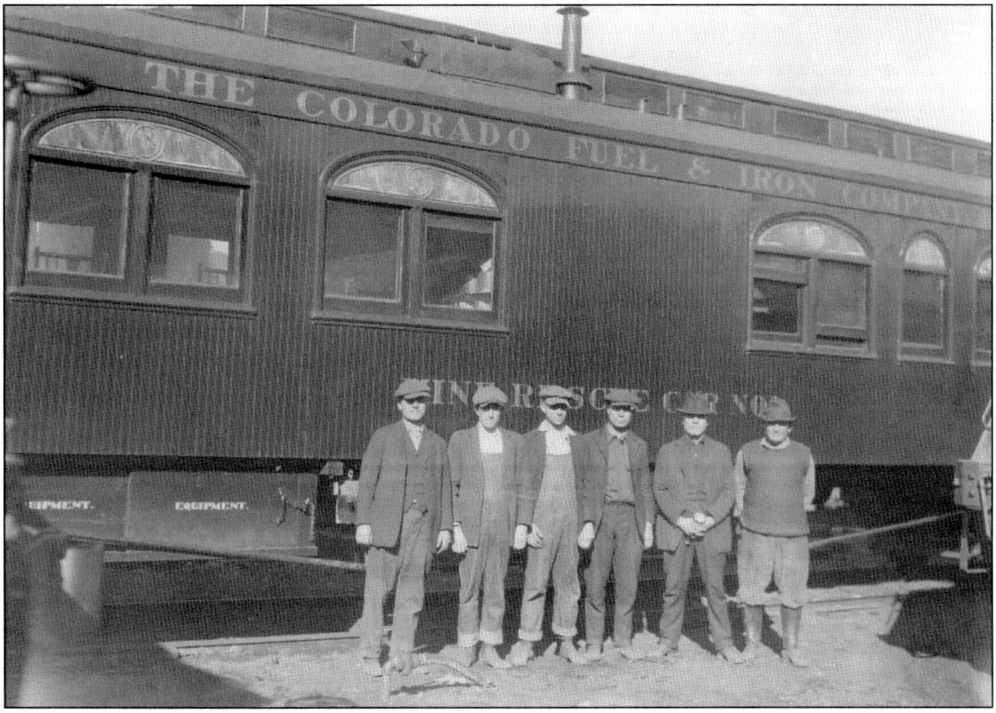

CF&I Mine Rescue Car No. 1. First-aid trainers stand next to the mine rescue car. This car traveled the rails between CF&I mining camps from 1923 to 1941. With the car parked at a camp, the trainers would conduct classes inside, teaching the miners and their families first-aid, triage techniques, and emergency procedures. (CRM.)

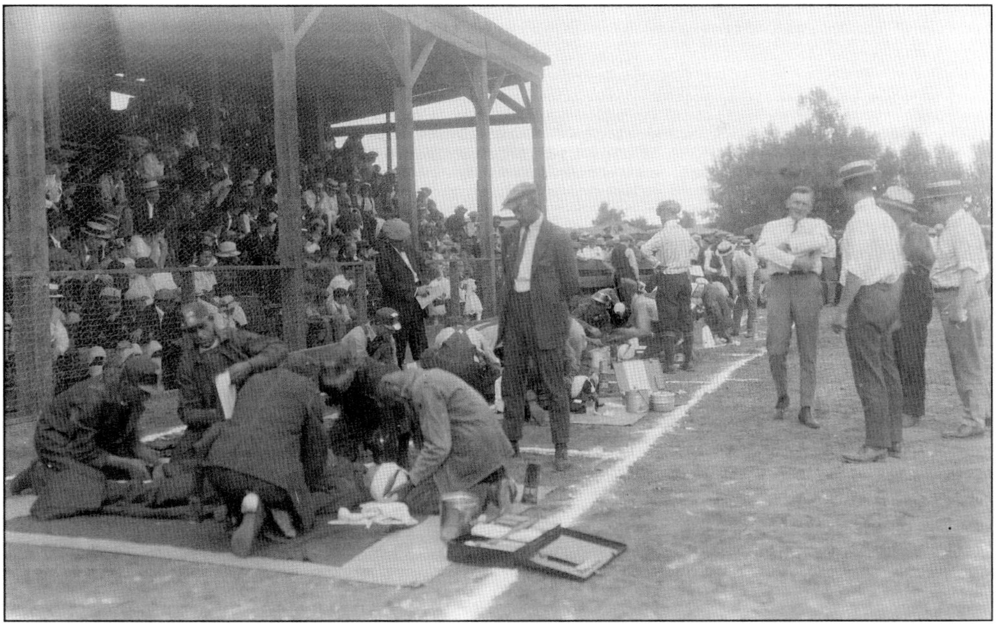

Walsen First-Aid Meet, 1923. First-aid crews from area mining camps occasionally held meets, with teams competing for prizes. Here, well-dressed spectators view the action from the grandstand in Walsenburg. (BHS/CFI.)

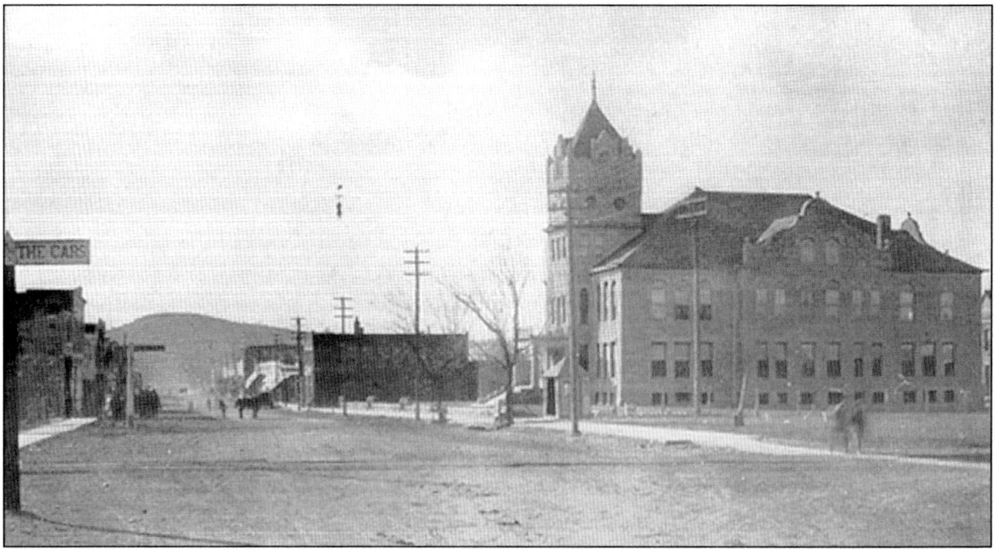

Main Street, Early 1900s. Automobiles were a rarity on Walsenburg's wide Main Street in the early 1900s, but trains were frequent. The railroad tracks cross Main Street just north of the courthouse, and the sign at left warns pedestrians to "Lookout for the Cars." (Colorado State Archives.)

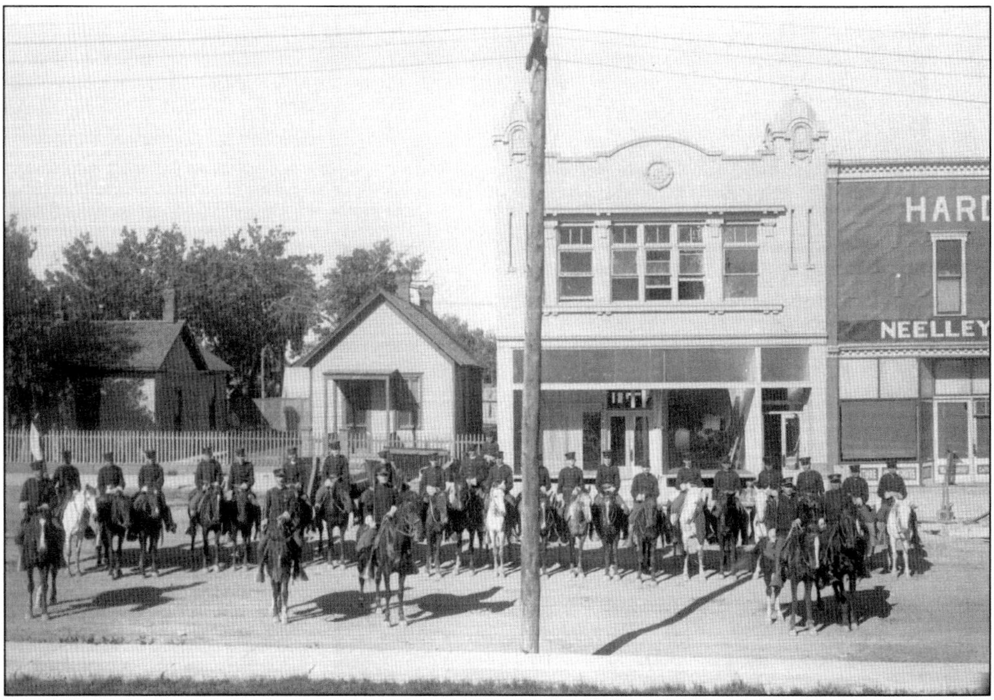

State Militia in Walsenburg, 1913. This militia, out in full force across from the Huerfano County Courthouse on Main Street, is prepared to quell any violence that might spill over to Walsenburg from strikes at the Walsen Mine. (HCHS.)

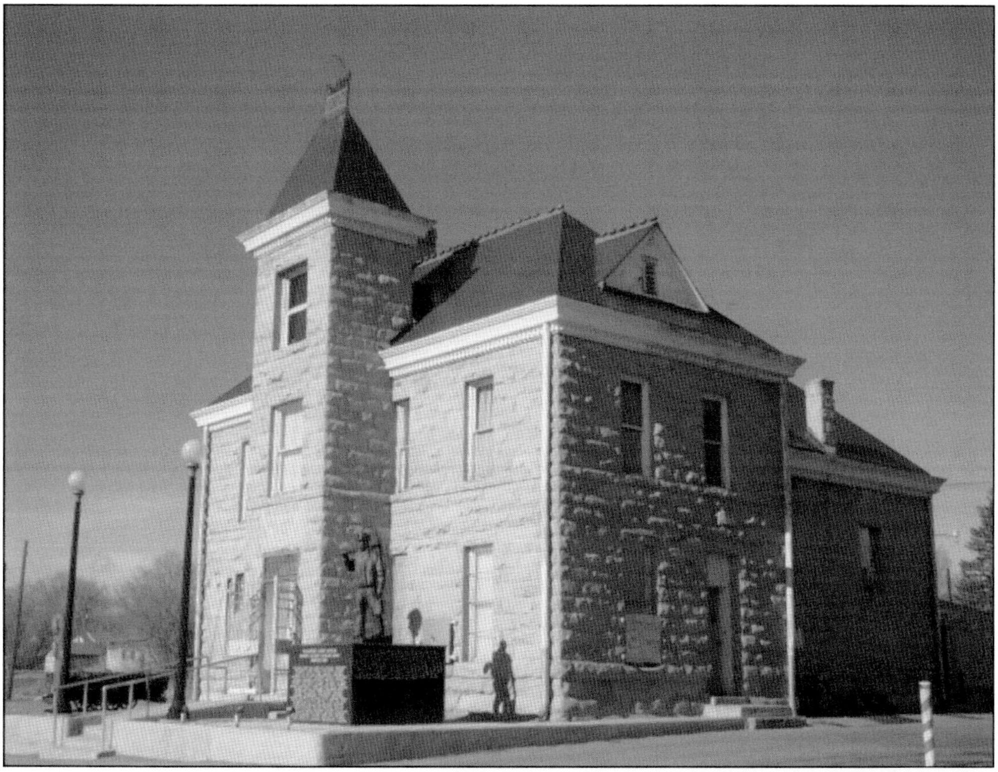

Huerfano County Jail. Constructed in 1896 from locally quarried sandstone, the jail is just west of the county courthouse. Some of the cell bars and steel beds are still in the building, which became the Walsenburg Mining Museum in 1994.

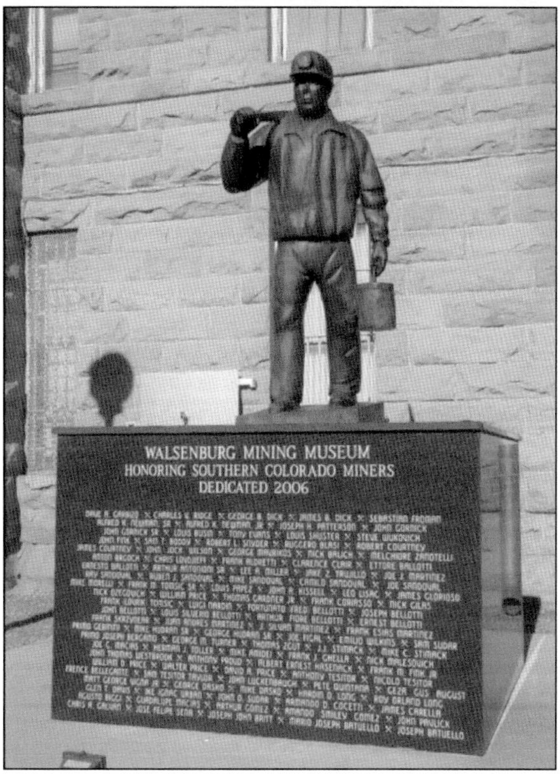

Walsenburg Mining Museum. This statue of a coal miner was dedicated in 2006 in honor of southern Colorado coal miners. Coal mines were very dangerous places in the late 1800s and early 1900s; miners could be killed by explosions, rock falls, floods, or a myriad of other catastrophes.

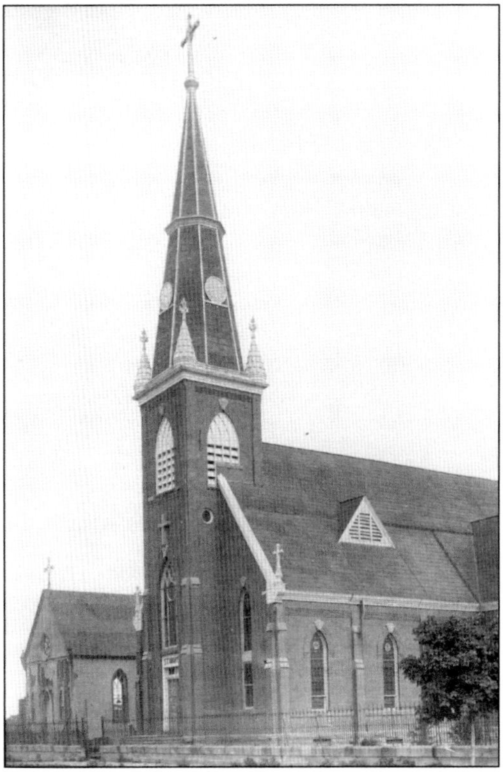

St. Mary's Catholic Church, Walsenburg. Completed in 1900, this beautiful church was constructed of local brick and had a very tall steeple. A windstorm in January 1932 blew off the steeple. (HCHS.)

St. Mary's Catholic Church in 2011. The tall steeple is long gone, and only a small tower with a cross stands above the bell tower. The original brick has been plastered over in an adobe style.

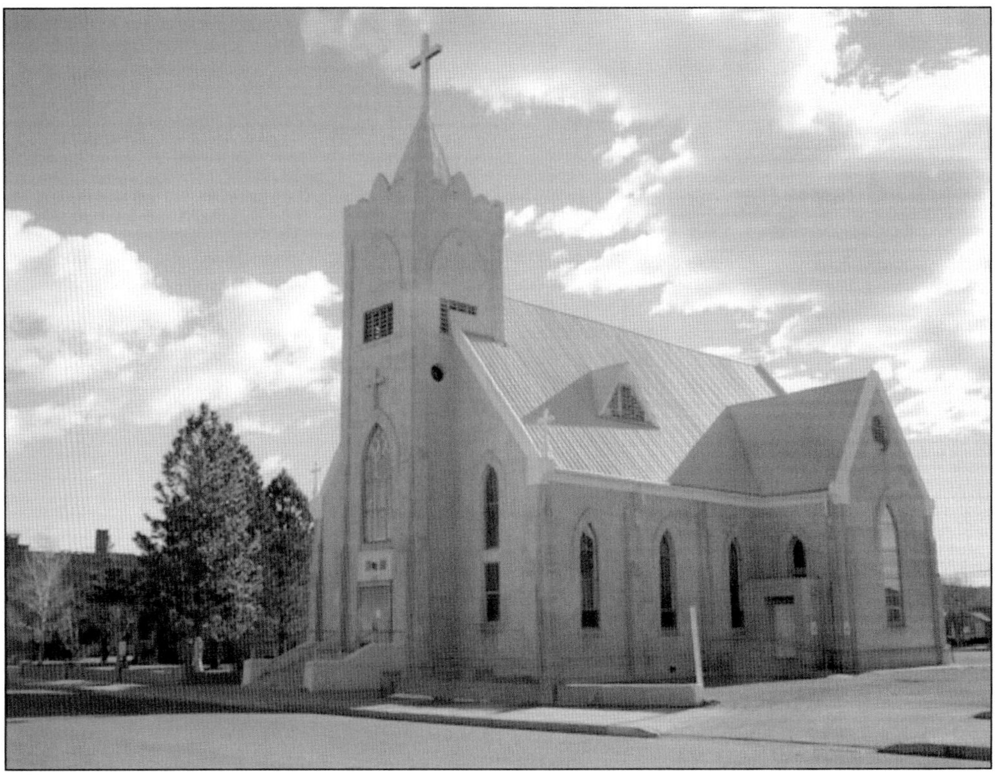

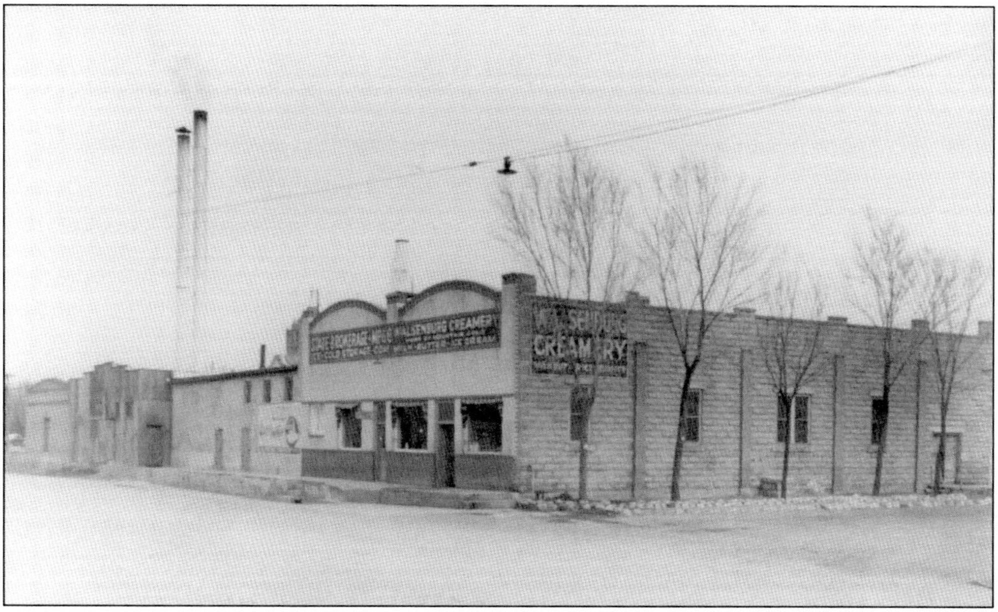

Walsenburg Creamery, 1925. The creamery produced milk, butter, cream, and ice cream at this site in Walsenburg. (HCHS.)

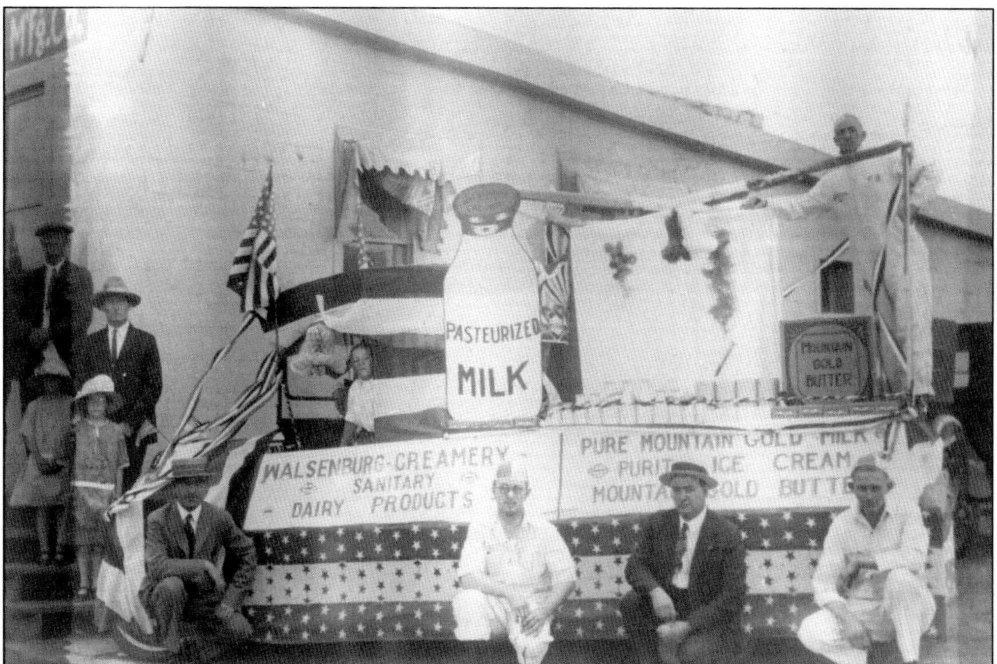

July 4, 1925. Folks in Walsenburg enjoyed a Fourth of July parade as much as the citizens of La Veta (see page 32), and this highly decorated float from the Walsenburg Creamery graced the parade. (HCHS.)

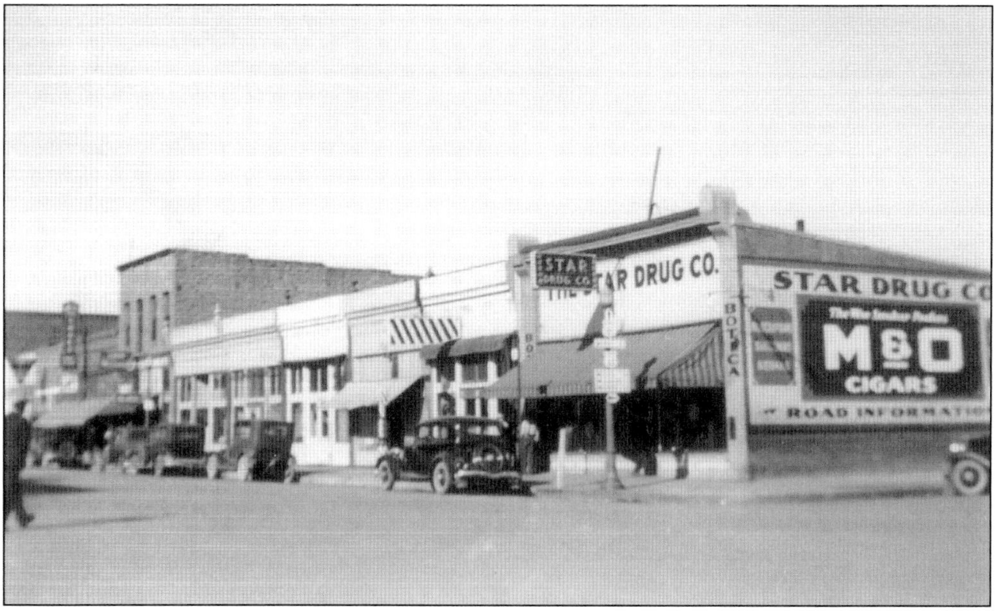

Star Drug Co. Star Drug has dominated the corner of Main and Seventh Streets in Walsenburg since the 1930s. (HCHS.)

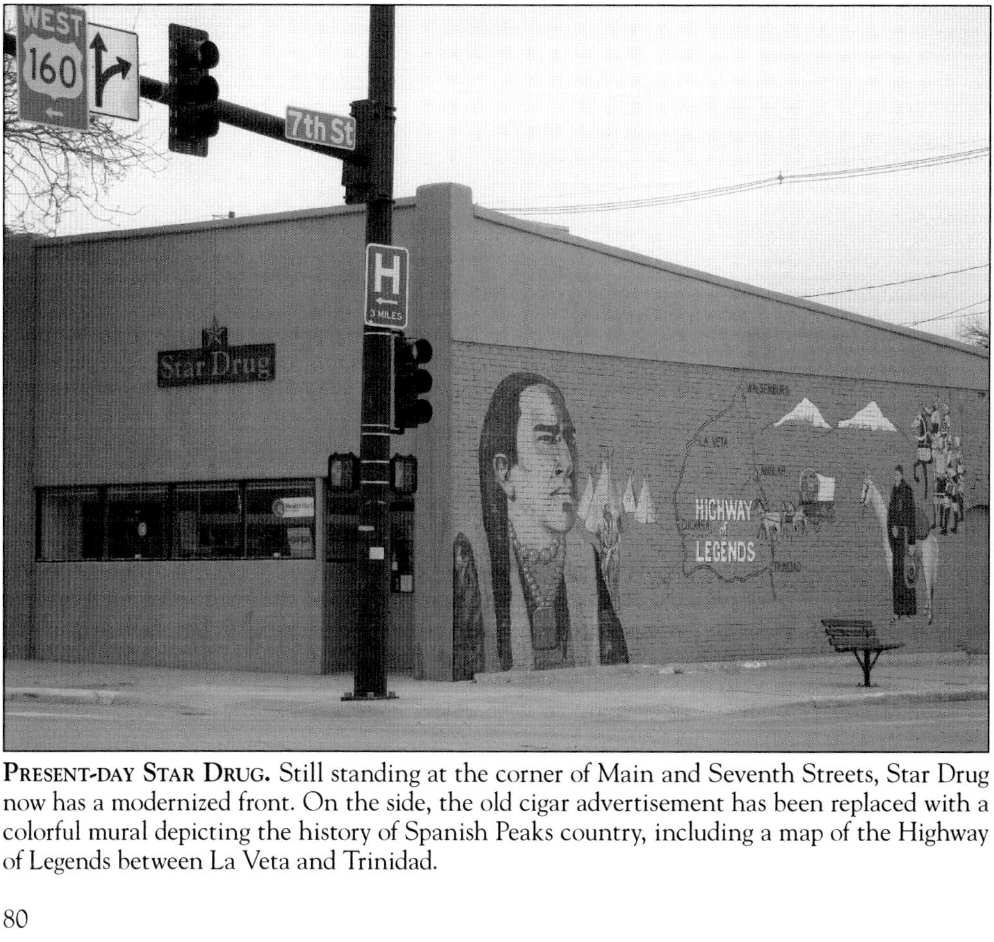

Present-day Star Drug. Still standing at the corner of Main and Seventh Streets, Star Drug now has a modernized front. On the side, the old cigar advertisement has been replaced with a colorful mural depicting the history of Spanish Peaks country, including a map of the Highway of Legends between La Veta and Trinidad.

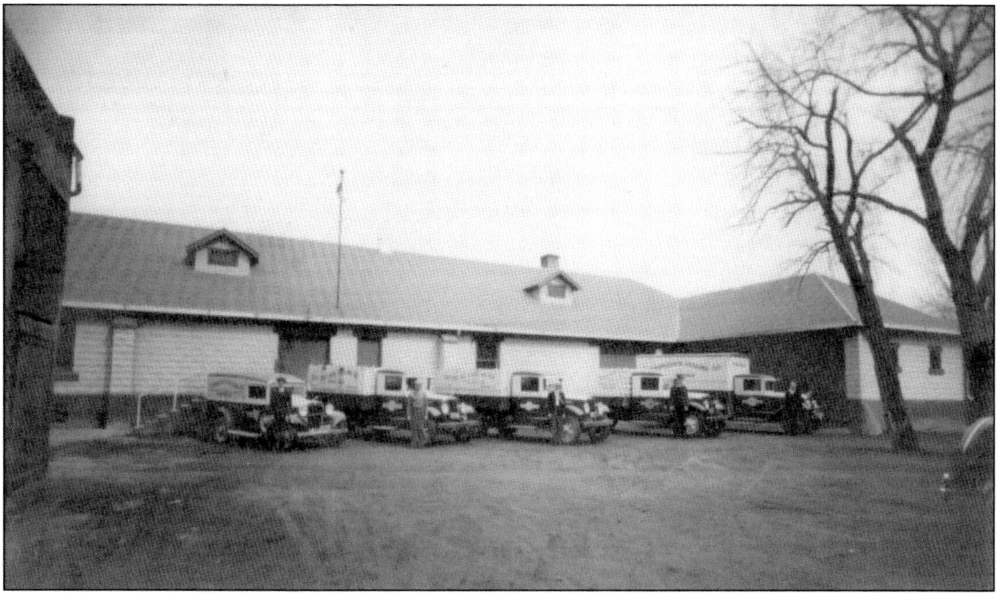

Sporleder Delivery Trucks. Shown at the Sporleder Selling Company warehouse at 217 East Fourth Street in Walsenburg on July 2, 1935, these trucks delivered wholesale groceries to retail stores throughout southern Colorado. The company also had warehouses in Alamosa and Trinidad. (Gretchen Sporleder Orr.)

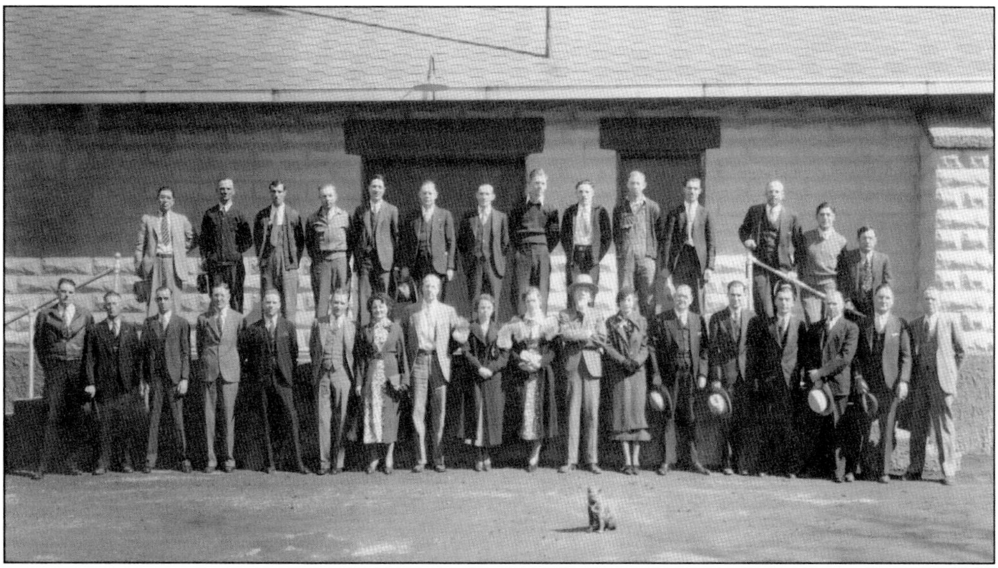

Sporleder Selling Company Employees. Sporleder employees pose in front of the Walsenburg warehouse on July 2, 1935. Company president Louis B. Sporleder Sr. is in the first row, eighth from the right. He was the nephew of August Sporleder, one of the original "Twelve Apostles of Walsenburg" (see page 67). (Gretchen Sporleder Orr.)

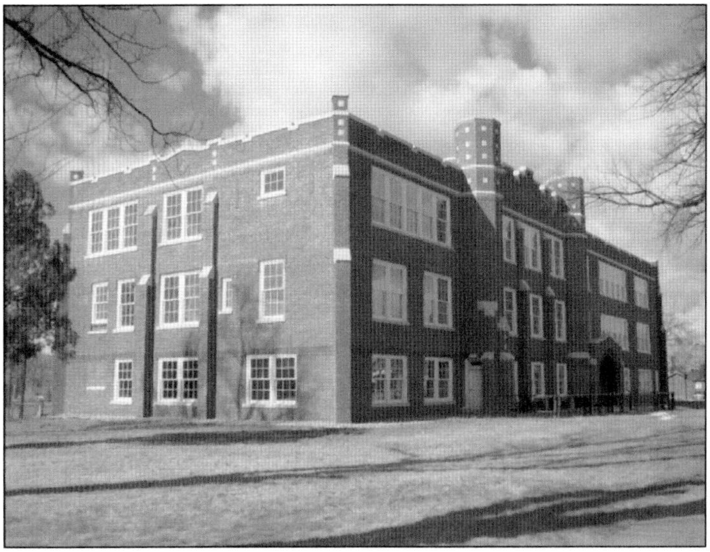

Walsenburg High School. Designed by Isaac H. Rapp, who was known for his work in Trinidad, the high school was completed in 1933. It is a beautiful redbrick building with octagonal towers and an arched entry. It has been restored and currently houses the Spanish Peaks Library on the first floor.

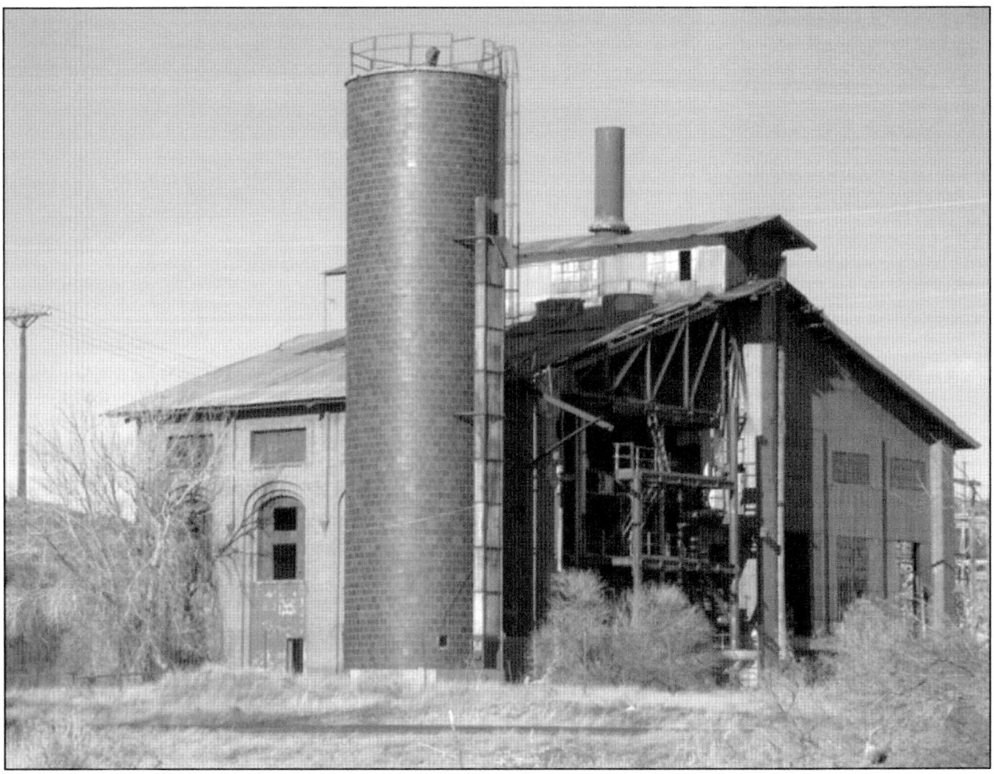

Power Plant At Walsen. The only remnant of the Walsen Mine still standing—the power plant—is easily visible just north of US Highway 160. When the mine closed in 1931, Walsenburg's economy took a dive from which it never fully recovered.

Six

Coal Camps North and South of Walsenburg

The Walsen Mine was the first established in Huerfano County, and it was the largest coal producer. However, coal camps were scattered all over the county, from west of La Veta to north and south of Walsenburg. One estimate counted a total of 100 mines in the county at various times. Existing mines often closed, and new ones opened nearby with the same name, confusing the total count. Also, some mines were known by both the name of the town they were near and by the actual name of the mine.

Stretching in an arc heading northwest from Walsenburg along present-day State Highway 69, mines at Toltec, Gordon, Delcarbon, Tioga, and Alamo are shown in the photographs on the following pages. Toltec was operated by the Aztec Coal Company, while Gordon was operated by the Gordon Coal Company. Delcarbon was the town that served the Calumet No. 1 and No. 2 mines. Tioga was the town that served the CF&I operations at the Kebler No. 1 and No. 2 mines. South of Tioga was the Alamo Mine, operated by the Oakdale Coal Company. A few miles north, the Alamo No. 2 Mine was opened in 1926 and was also known as the Barbour Mine and, later, as the Butte Valley Mine.

Directly south of Walsenburg, the CF&I Cameron Mine was located at the town of Farr. Farther south, the Pryor Mine opened in 1897, operated by the Union Coal and Coke Company. Southernmost of the CF&I mines in Huerfano County were the mines at Old Rouse and New Rouse. Old Rouse was flooded and closed in 1899. The homes, buildings, and machinery were moved five miles south to New Rouse, which expanded on the site of the old Santa Clara Mine. With all of this opening and closing, moving and shifting, it is easy to understand the difficulty of getting an accurate count of the actual number of mines. Currently, there is no large-scale coal mining in Huerfano County.

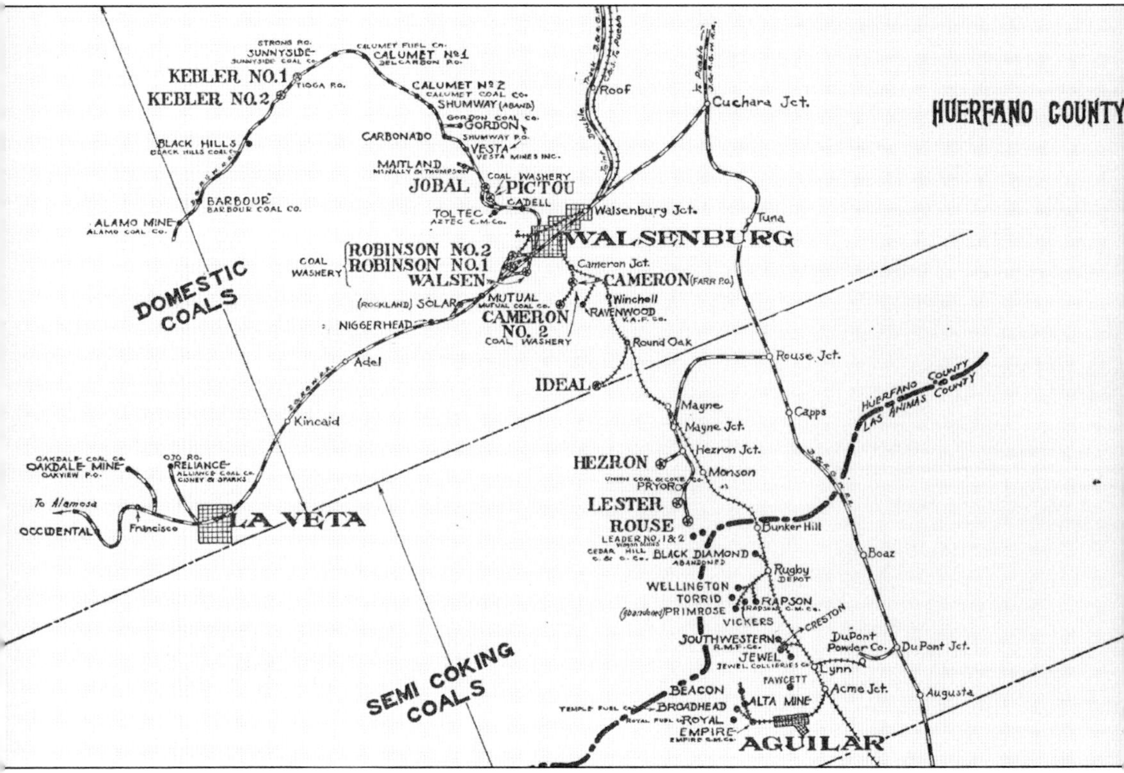

Coal Camps North and South of Walsenburg. CF&I mines north of Walsenburg included Pictou, Jobal, and Kebler No. 1 and No. 2. South of Walsenburg, CF&I camps included Cameron, Ideal, Hezron, Lester, and Rouse. Several independent coal companies also operated north and south of Walsenburg. (BHS/CFI.)

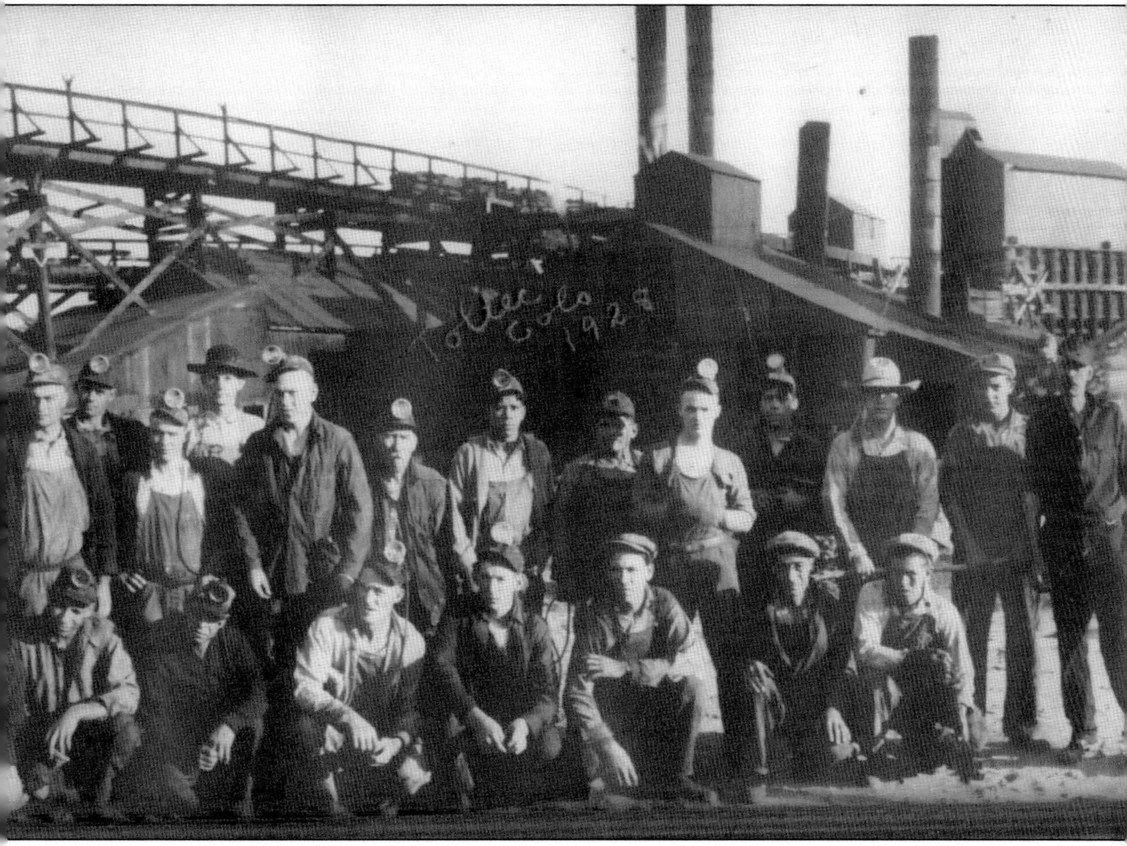

COAL MINERS AT TOLTEC, 1928. The Toltec Mine opened in 1894, and was owned by the Aztec Coal Company from 1916 on. Miners' children attended school at nearby Pictou, and most supplies were obtained from Walsenburg. By 1920, the camp had a population of about 200 and employed over 100 men. By the time the mine closed in 1944, it had produced 1,856,837 tons of coal. (HCHS.)

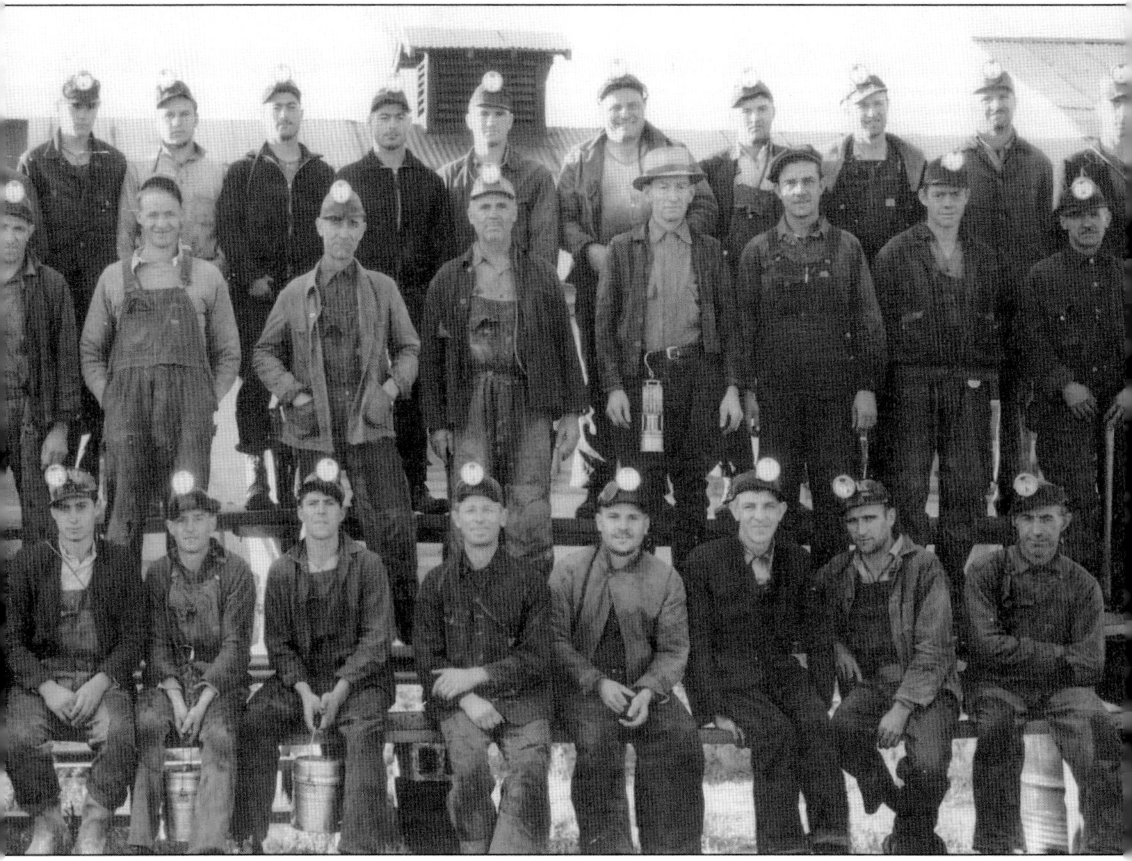

GORDON MINERS, OCTOBER 11, 1935. The Gordon Coal Company operated a mine from 1907 until it closed in 1965. Due to the lengthy production period, the mine was able to produce 2,239,763 tons of coal. The Gordon mining crew was brave and worked hard, as did all the miners in Huerfano County. A gas explosion in June 1925 killed three men at the Gordon Mine. (HCHS.)

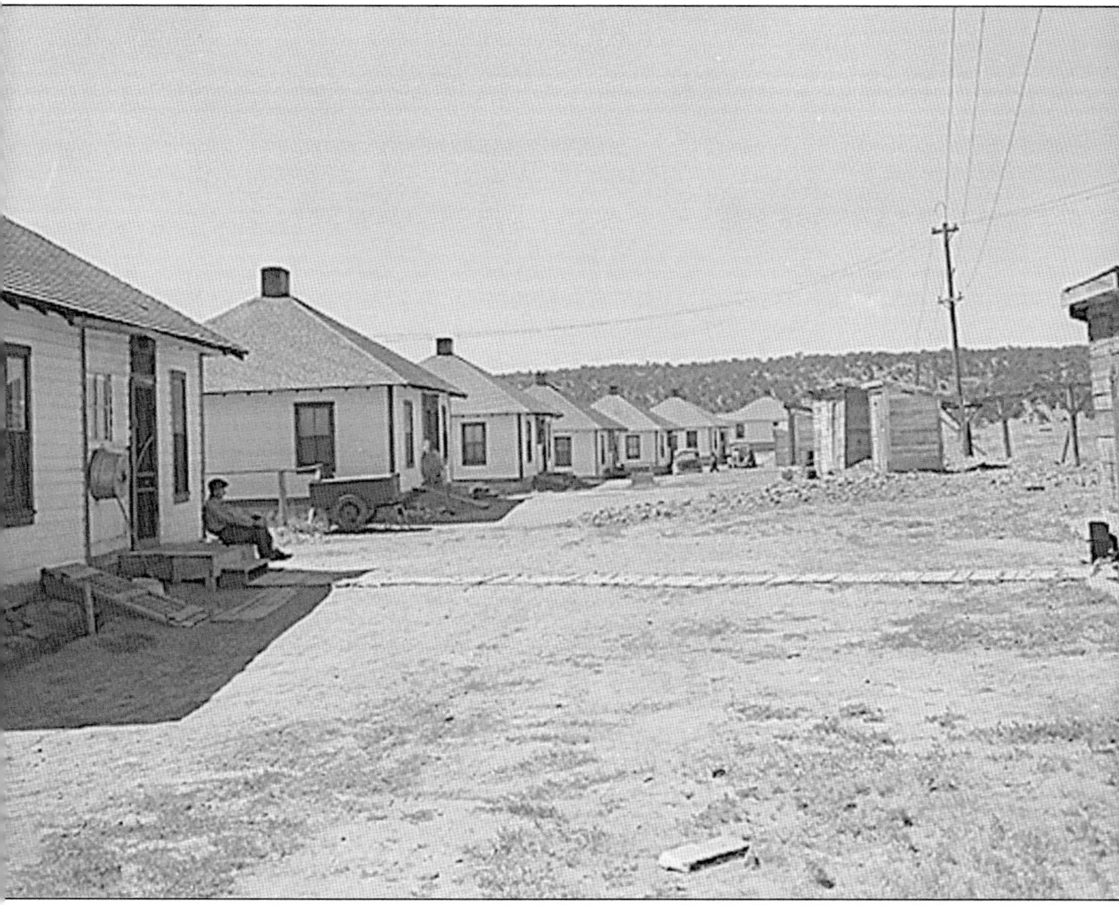

Delcarbon Housing, 1946. Delcarbon was the camp that served the Calumet No. 1 Mine to the north and Calumet No. 2 Mine to the south. Prefabricated company homes were common in the coal mining camps (see page 100). The Calumet Coal Company purchased the mines in 1931. Calumet No. 1 opened in 1911 and closed in 1933. Calumet No. 2 opened in 1918 and closed in 1971, having produced 2,916,273 tons of coal. Russell Lee took this photograph and those shown through page 90. (NAR.)

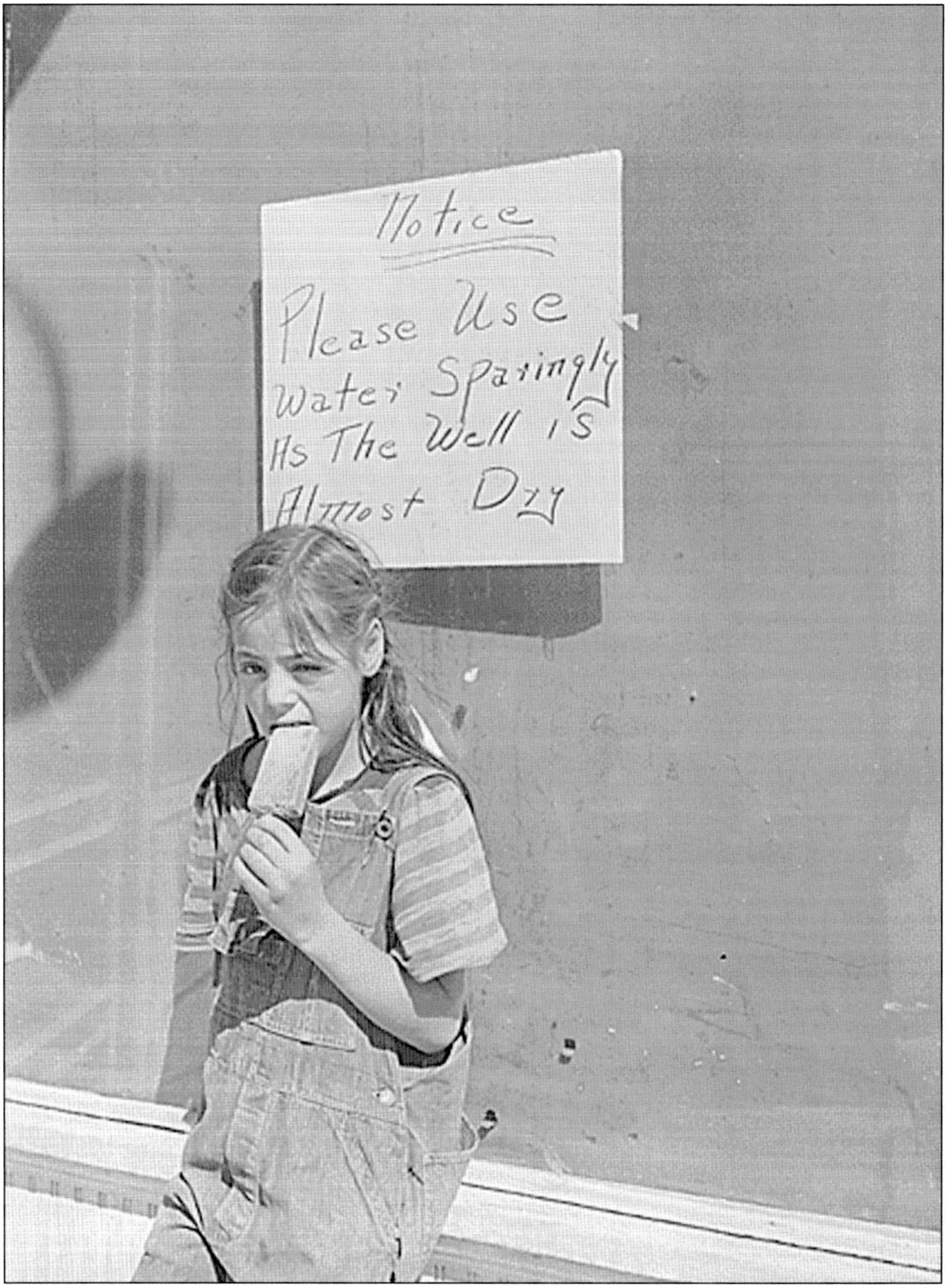

CALUMET COAL COMPANY STORE, 1946. Company stores provided necessary goods for the residents of the coal camps. Here, a miner's daughter enjoys an ice cream treat on a warm June day. Families were encouraged to conserve water at the Delcarbon camp. (NAR.)

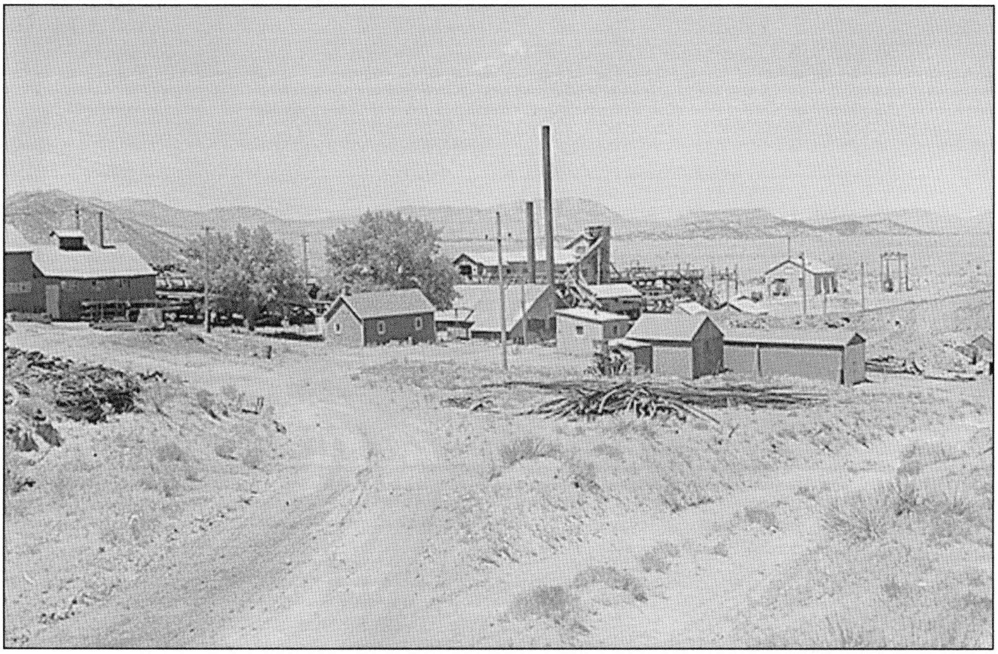

CF&I Kebler No. 2 Mine, 1946. Tioga was the company camp that served the Kebler No. 1 and Kebler No. 2 mines. Each mine was opened in 1907; Kebler No. 1 closed in 1923, while Kebler No. 2 operated until 1953. (NAR.)

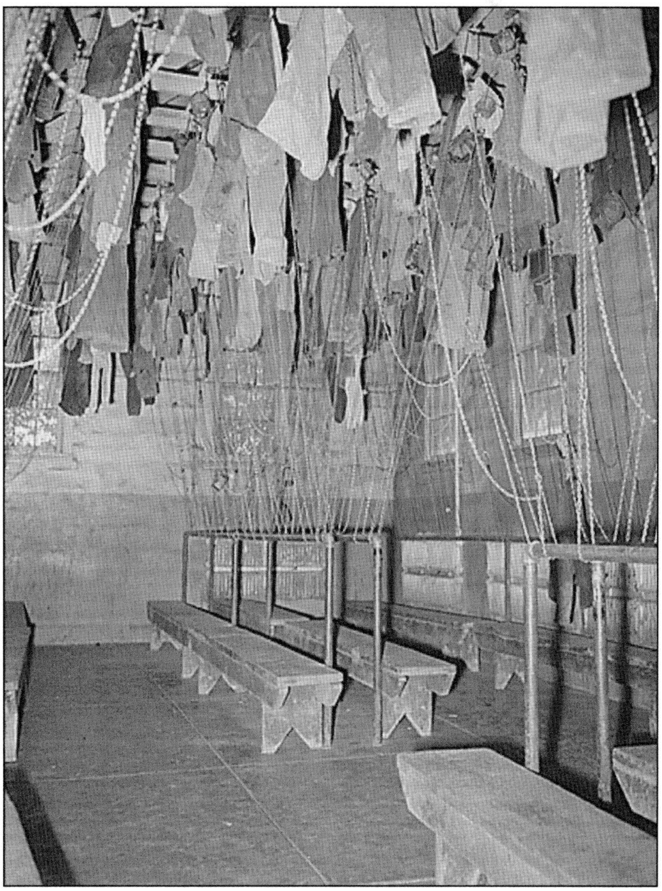

Kebler No. 2 Wash and Change House, 1946. At the end of a shift, miners left dirty coveralls here to be washed. Once cleaned, the garments were then hoisted by pulleys to the ceiling to dry. (NAR.)

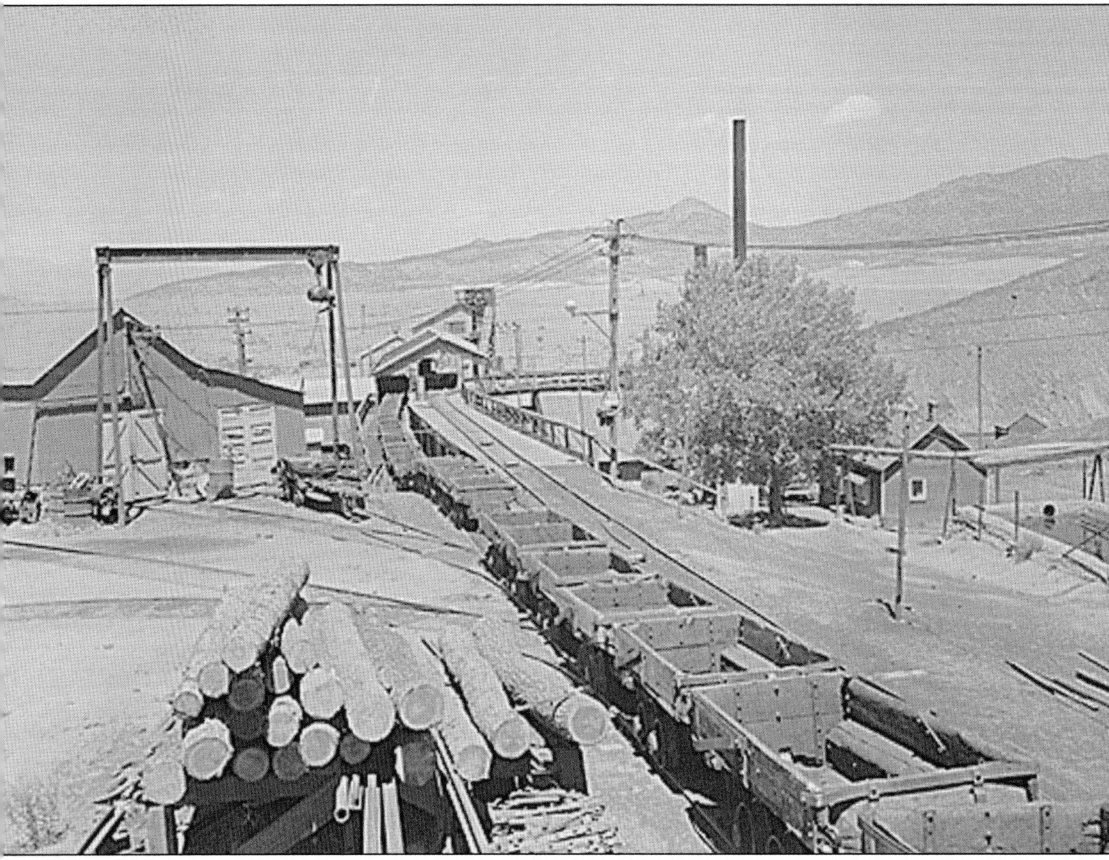

Kebler No. 2 Tipple, 1946. Empty ore cars head back to the mine after being dumped at the tipple. The D&RGW Railroad built a spur line from Walsenburg to Tioga to pick up the coal, and the railroad extended the line farther south to the Alamo Mine. The high peak in the right background is Greenhorn Mountain, with the Badito Cone just to the left. (NAR.)

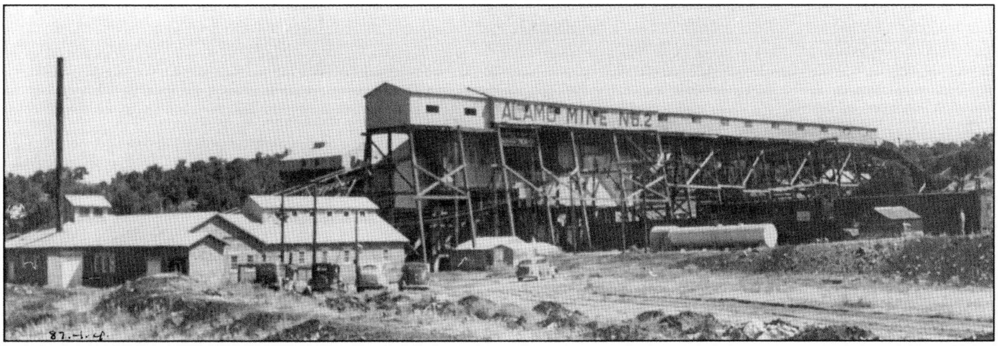

Alamo Mine No. 2, 1930s. The two Alamo mines were a few miles south of Tioga. Alamo No. 2 was also known as the Barbour Mine and then as the Butte Valley Mine. It operated from 1926 to 1952 and produced 1,211,331 tons of coal. (HCHS.)

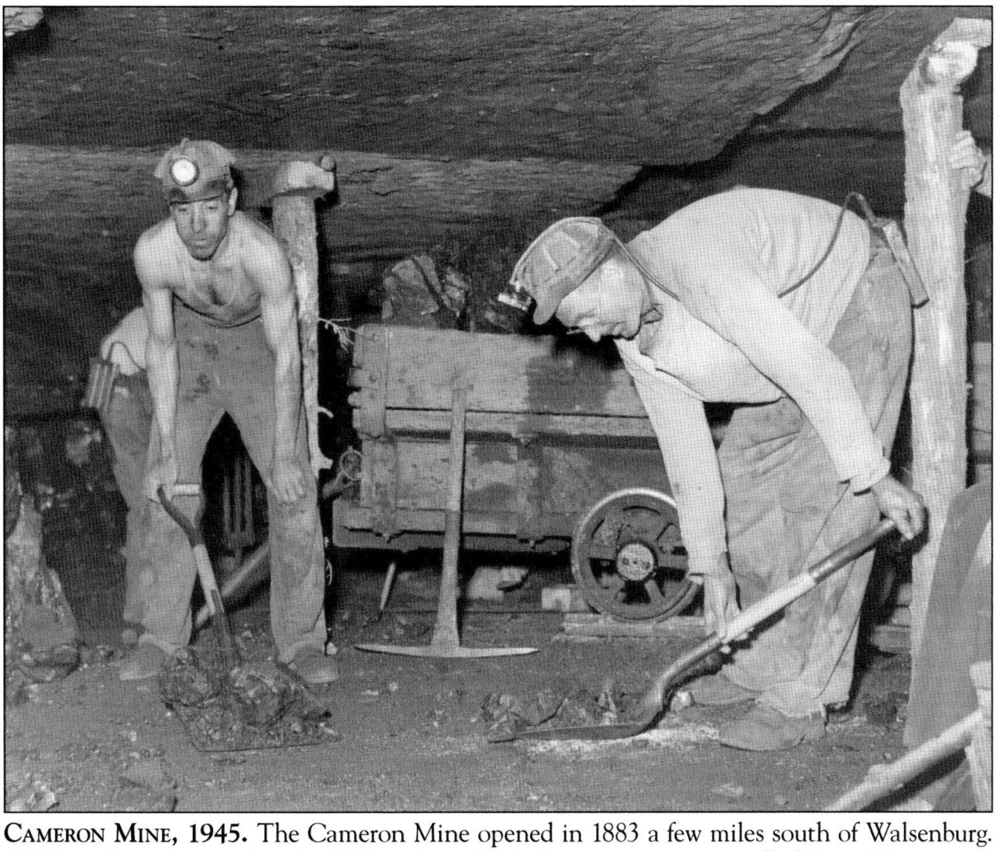

Cameron Mine, 1945. The Cameron Mine opened in 1883 a few miles south of Walsenburg. CF&I took over operations in 1907 and established a company town called Farr. Miners were still loading ore cars by hand at Cameron in 1945. (BHS/CFI.)

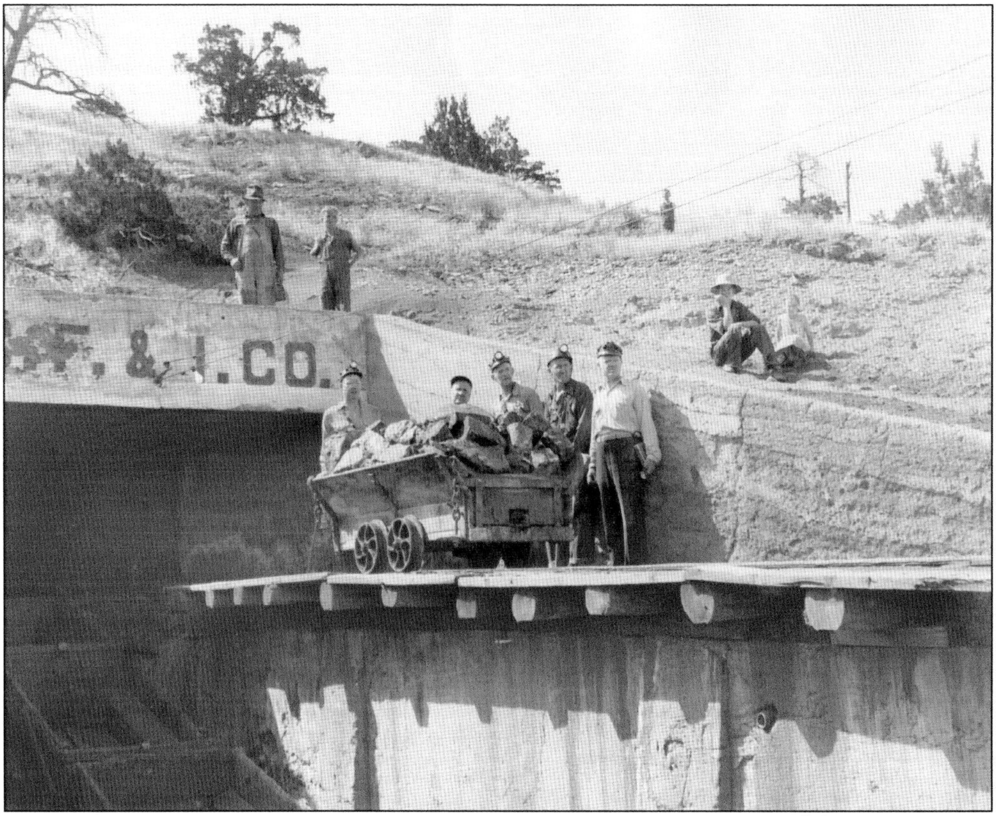

Cameron, January 1944. Miners pose with a loaded coal car at the entrance to the CF&I mine. The ore cars were hauled out of the mine by mules (see page 93). (BHS/CFI.)

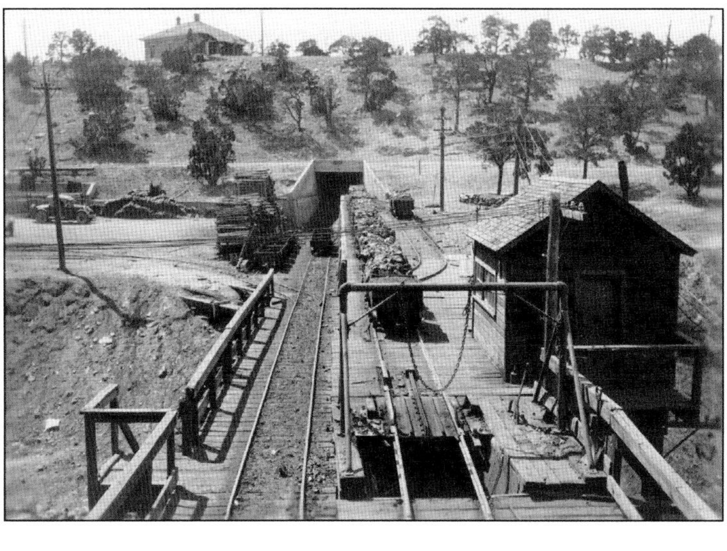

Cameron Mine Tipple. A more distant view of the area in the previous photograph shows ore cars lined up at the mine entrance, ready to be brought forward for dumping through the tipple hole into waiting rail cars. (BHS/CFI.)

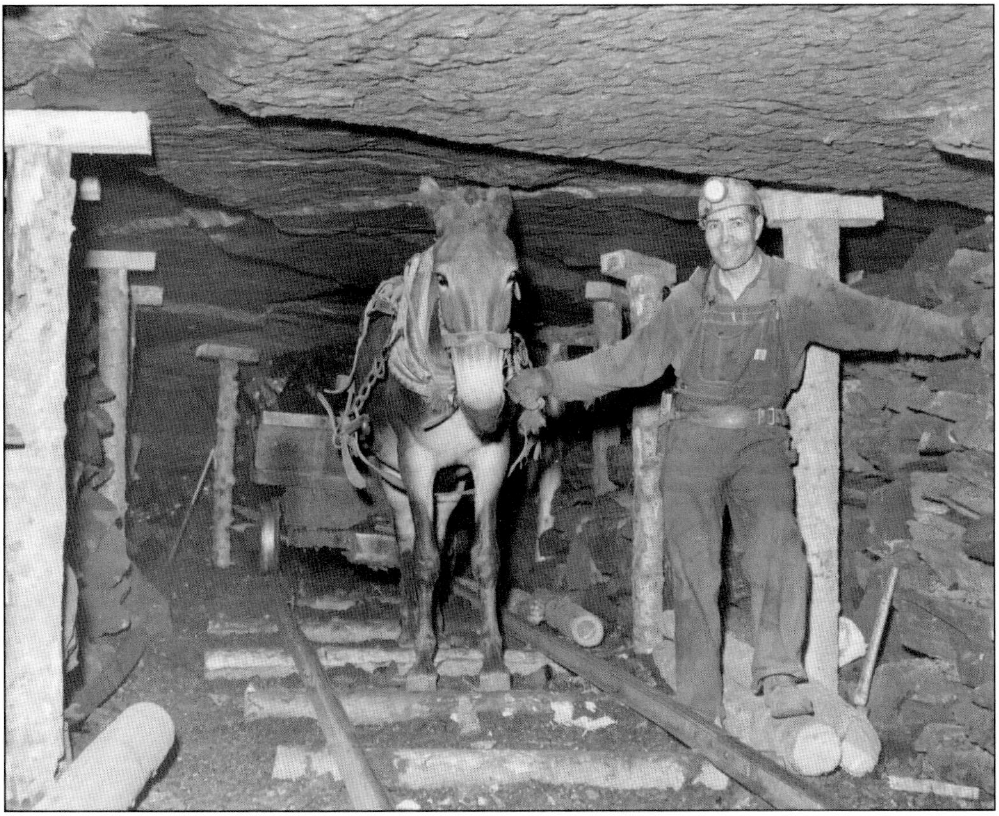

Cameron Mine, January 1945. A miner leads a mule and a loaded coal car out of the mine. Note the mule's ears and the miner's hard hat touching the top of the shaft. Timber props helped prevent collapse of the ceiling. (BHS/CFI.)

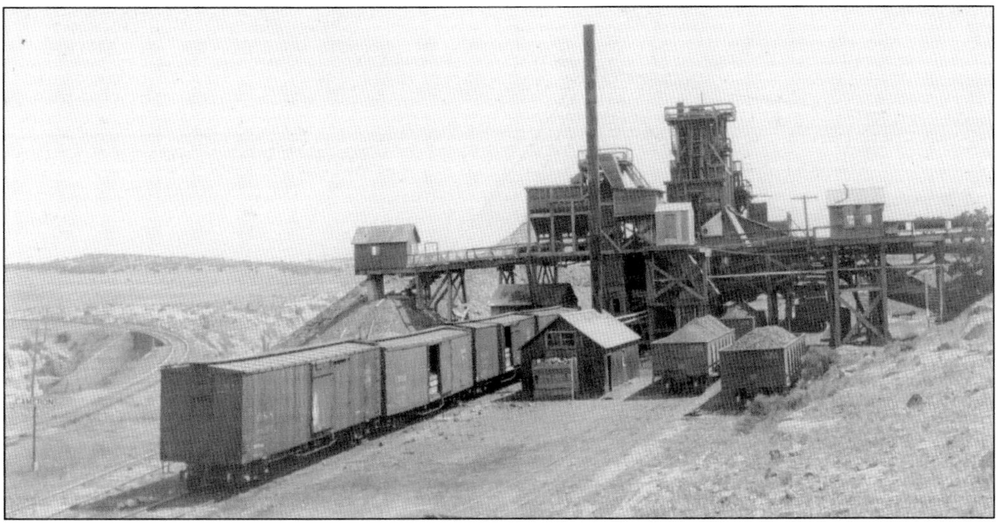

Cameron Loading Track. This photograph shows the underside of the coal tipple. Loaded ore cars enter from the top level at right and are dumped just past the shed with two windows (a different view of the same shed is on page 92). The dumped coal lands in coal cars waiting below. (HCHS.)

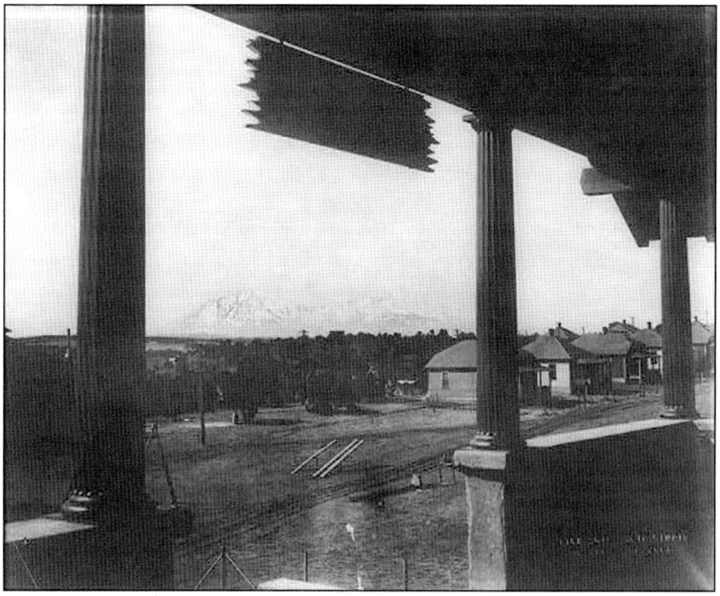

Cameron YMCA, 1918. This view looks southwest toward the Spanish Peaks from the top of the steps at the newly constructed YMCA. The YMCA had billiard tables, checker and chessboards, a library, and other facilities for miners' recreation. Cameron also had a swimming pool with a diving board (see page 114.) (LOC.)

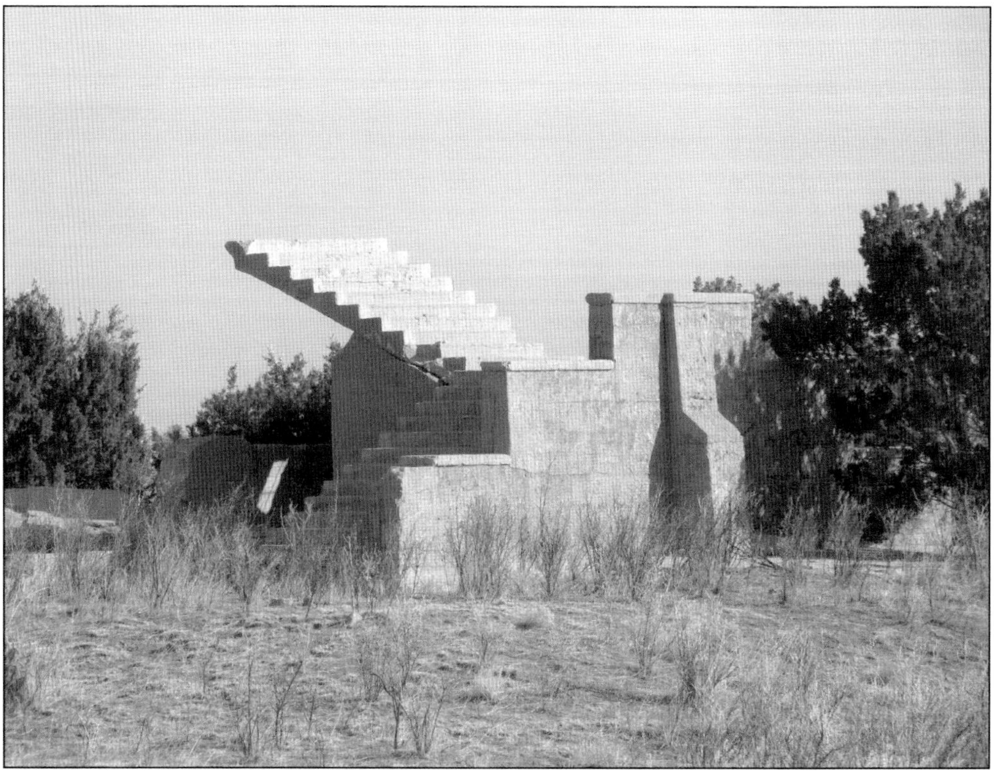

Cameron YMCA, 2011. All that is left of the Cameron YMCA are these stairs leading to nowhere. The previous photograph was taken from the top of these stairs, looking out to the Spanish Peaks.

Cameron School, c. 1924. This view from the steps of the Cameron YMCA shows the school, at left, which was completed in 1923 after the previous schoolhouse burned down. Enrollment in 1924 was 134 students. The Spanish Peaks are dimly visible in the background. (BHS/CFI.)

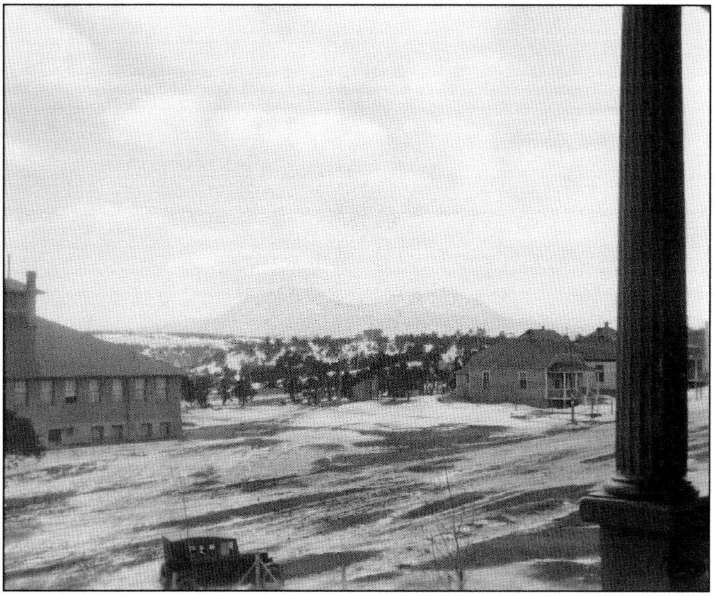

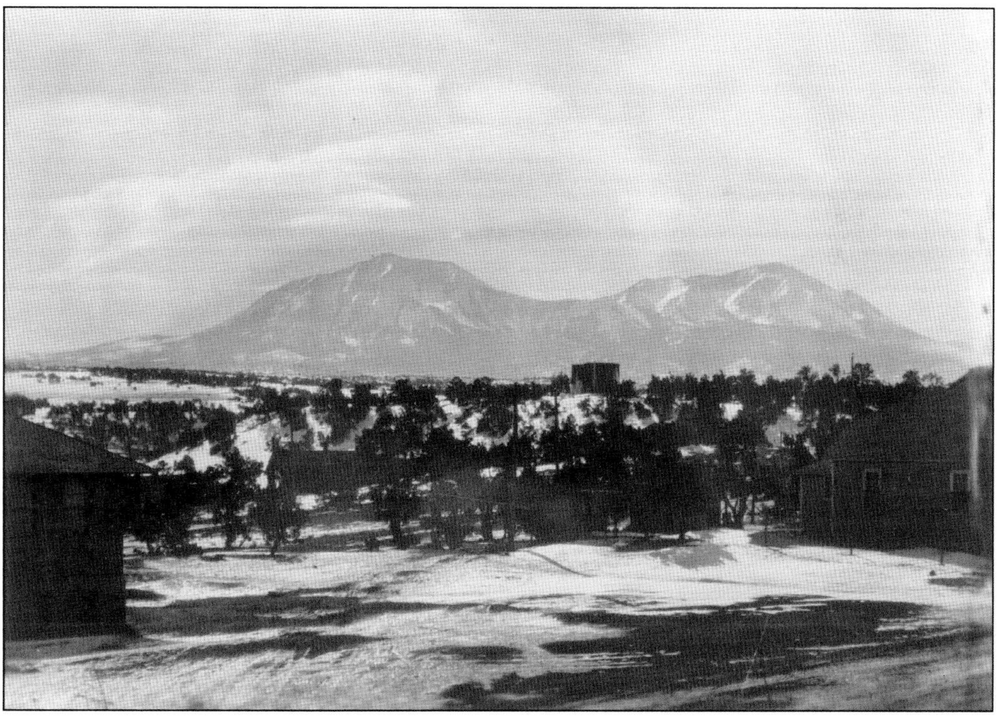

Spanish Peaks from Cameron YMCA. The peaks show up much more clearly in this photograph taken from the front of the YMCA. The edge of the school is visible at lower left. (BHS/CFI.)

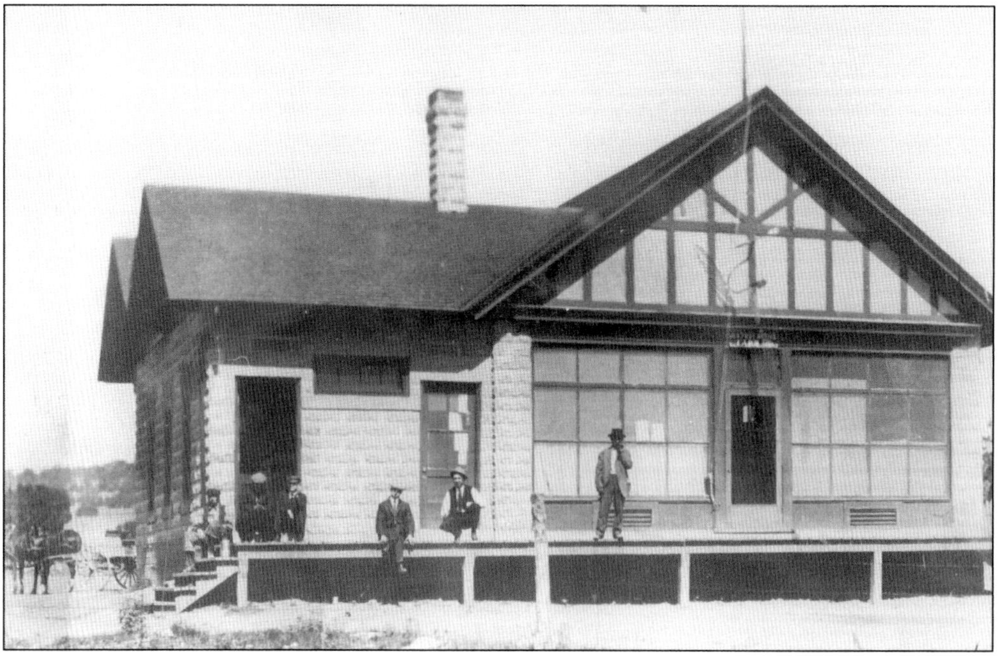

Colorado Supply Company Store at Farr. CF&I established a company store in Farr in 1907 and operated it until the Cameron Mine closed in 1946. Not all company camps had company stores, and it was a bit unusual for Cameron to have its own store, since it was so close to Walsenburg. (HCHS.)

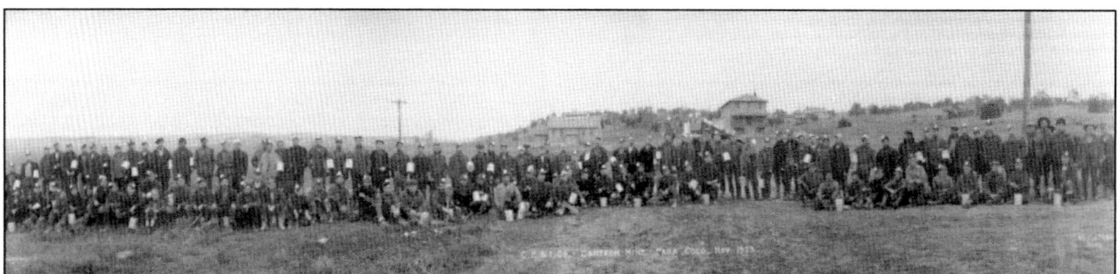

Miners at Cameron, 1923. Cameron (Farr) was a large camp with 117 houses and a boardinghouse, serving some 220 men and their families. When Cameron closed in 1946, most of the houses were sold and moved to other locations, and the machinery was moved to Pictou. (HCHS.)

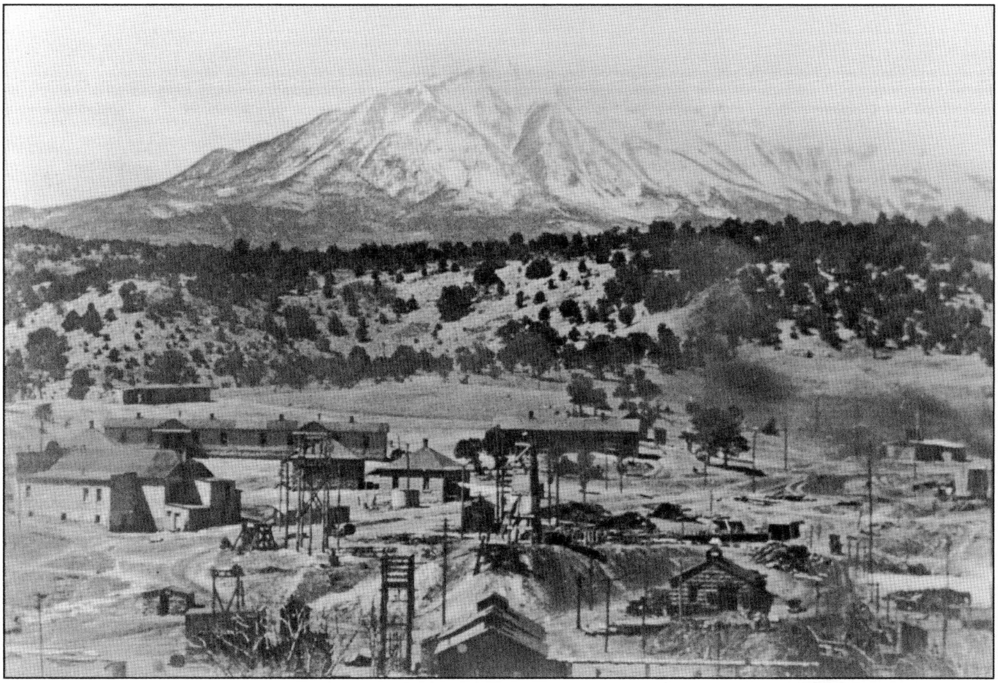

Pryor Mine, 1908. The East Spanish Peak dominates this view looking west from Pryor. Pryor was about eight miles south of Walsenburg. The mine was opened in 1897 by the Union Coal and Coke Co. and was named for Mack and Ike Pryor, early ranchers in the area. (DPL no. X-61917.)

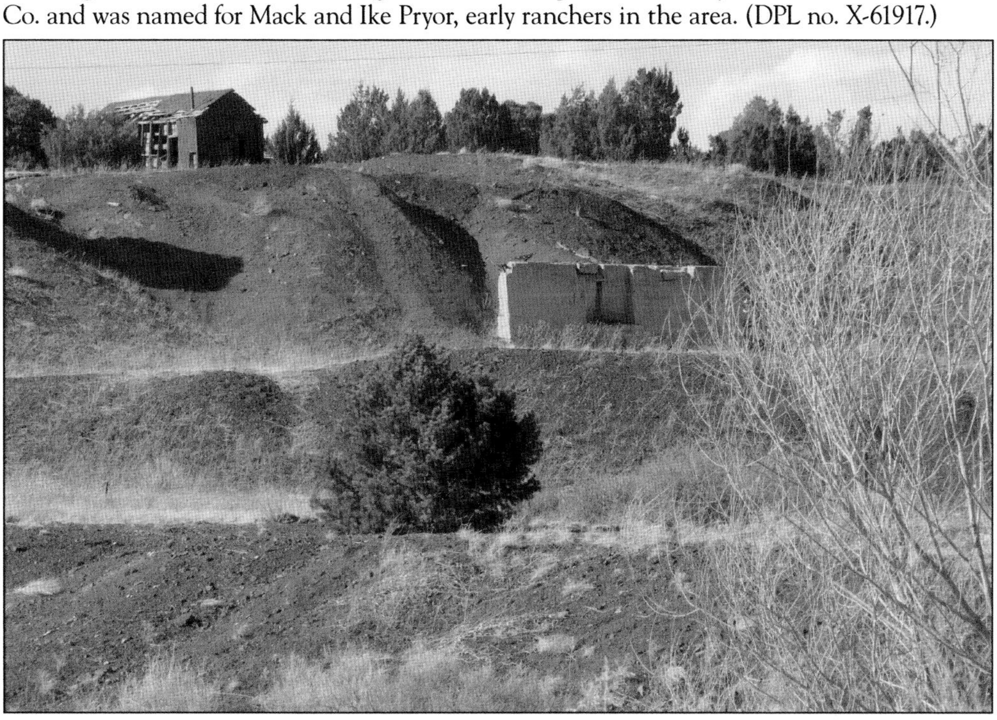

Remains of Pryor, 2011. Not much is left from the once bustling mining camp that had a population of 225 in 1920; Pryor had a post office, school, and two grocery stores. The mine closed in the early 1950s.

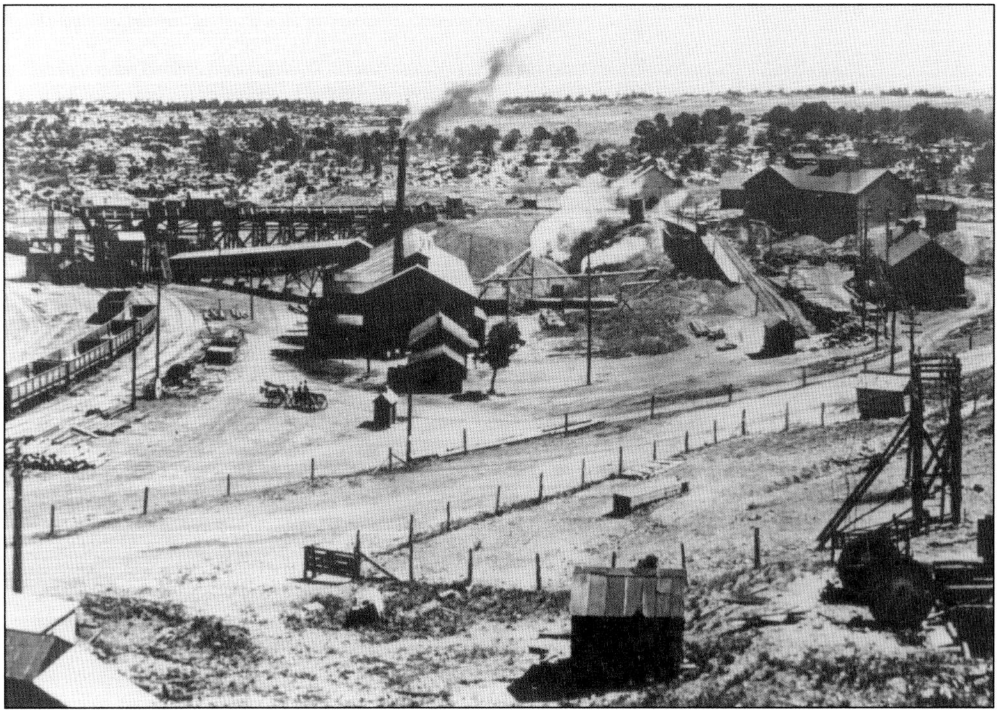

Rouse Mine, Early 1900s. The Old Rouse Mine opened in 1888 about 10 miles south of Walsenburg. The mine was flooded in 1899 and permanently closed. CF&I moved all the homes and equipment a few miles south to the old Santa Clara Mine site, which became New Rouse. The coal tipple and powerhouse are visible in this picture. (HCHS.)

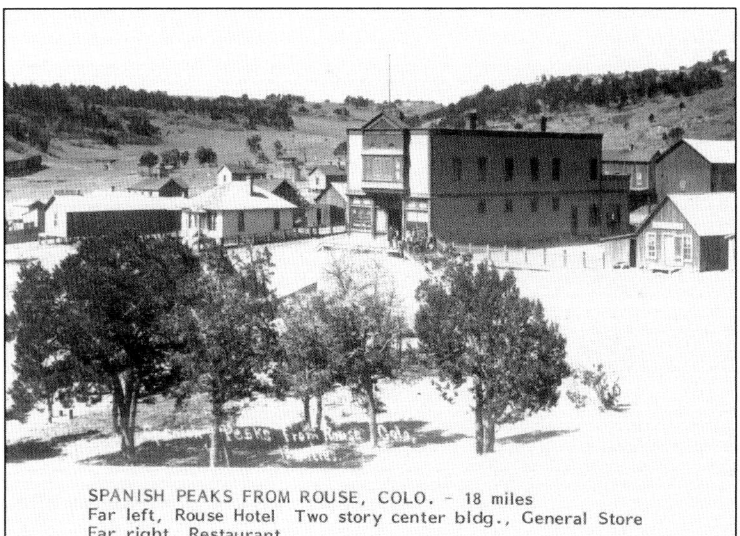

Rouse Hotel, General Store, and Restaurant. Rouse was a bustling CF&I camp with a population of over 1,000. Rouse had churches, hotels, grocery stores, blacksmiths, saloons, a newspaper, and the first CF&I high school established in a company camp, which graduated its first class in 1920. (HCHS.)

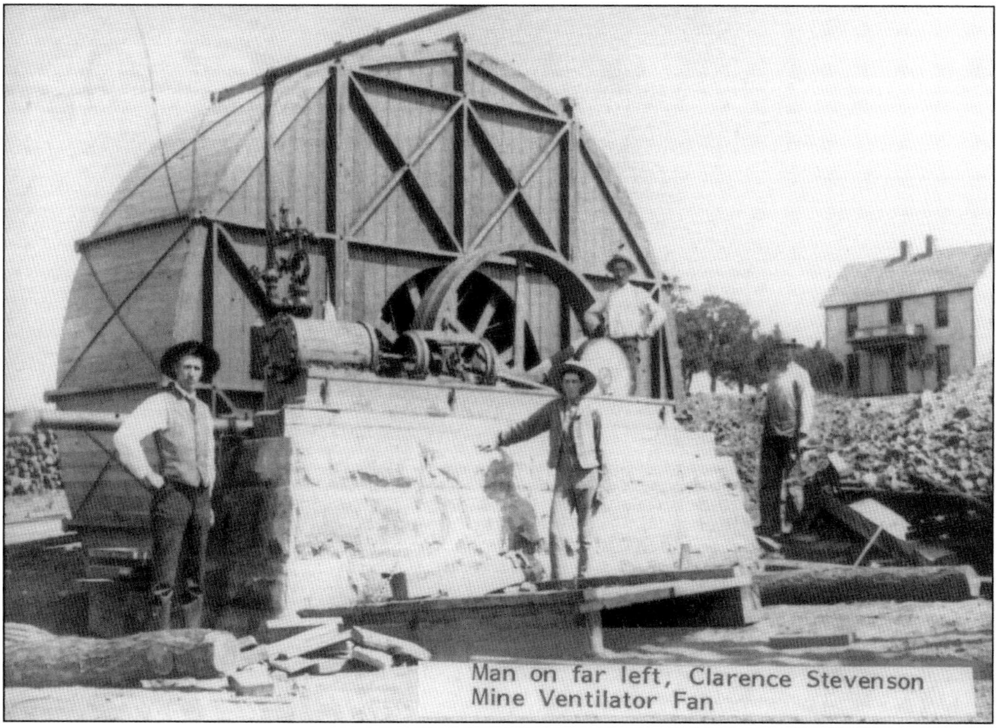

Rouse Ventilator Fan. Huge fans were brought to the coal mines to provide fresh air in the shafts and to disperse the explosive gases that built up in the mines. New Rouse was the third-largest-producing mine in Huerfano County, after Walsen and Cameron. (HCHS.)

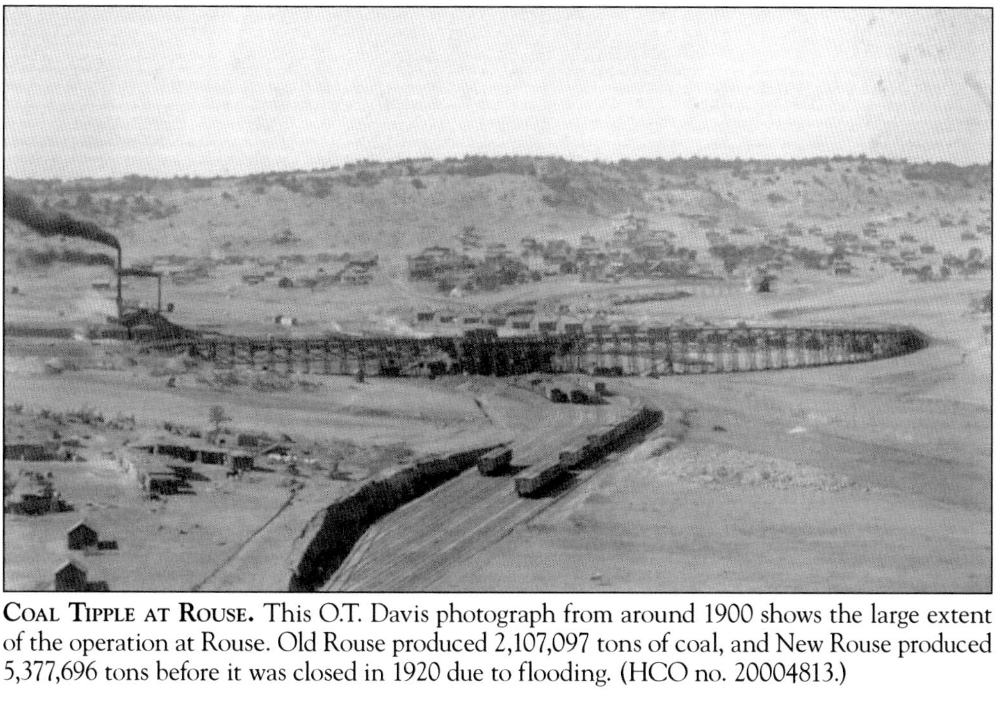

Coal Tipple at Rouse. This O.T. Davis photograph from around 1900 shows the large extent of the operation at Rouse. Old Rouse produced 2,107,097 tons of coal, and New Rouse produced 5,377,696 tons before it was closed in 1920 due to flooding. (HCO no. 20004813.)

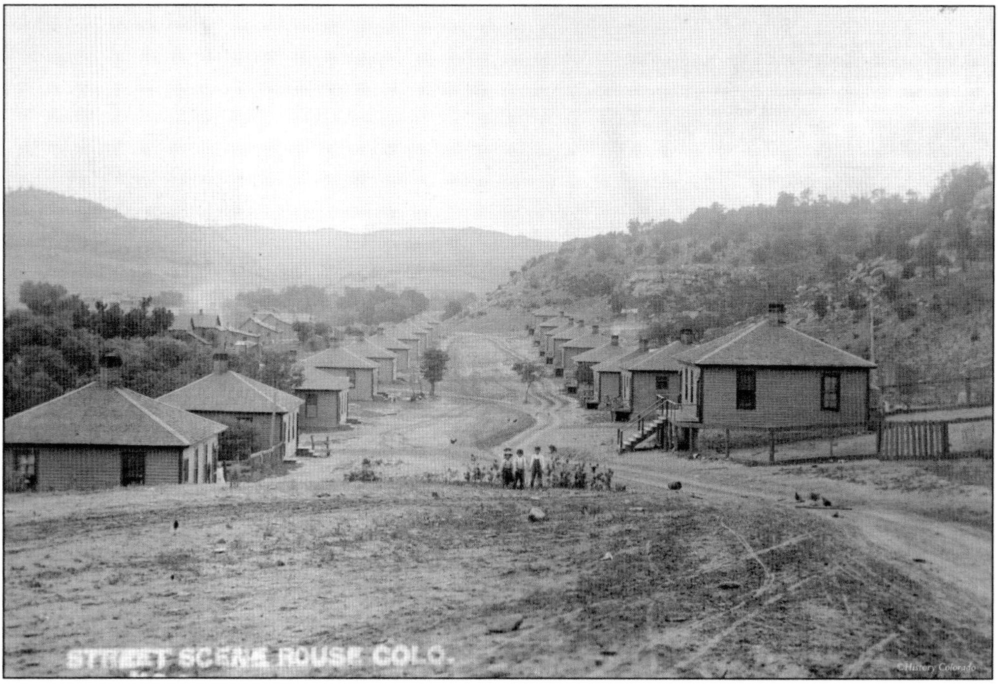

Rouse. Rouse was a typical CF&I company town, with identical prefabricated houses lining the street. Each clapboard home was four rooms square. Each structure is a duplex with two entryways. This photograph was taken between 1900 and 1920. (HCO no. 20004310.)

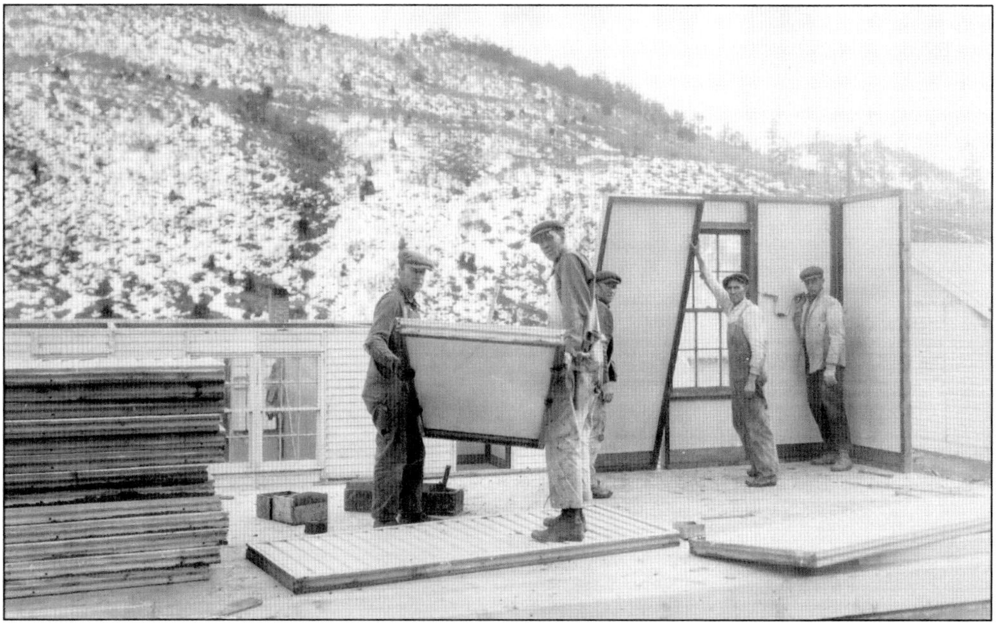

Prefabricated Company Housing at Toller. This is a great illustration of how houses were moved from one mining camp to another, as between Old Rouse and New Rouse. Toller was a mining camp in Las Animas County, between Aguilar and Trinidad. (BHS/CFI.)

Seven

Cuchara from Camps to Ski Resort

Eleven miles south of La Veta on Highway 12 sits the charming mountain community of Cuchara. *Cuchara* is the Spanish word for spoon. The neck of the spoon is the narrow Cuchara Pass at the top of the range, while the bowl of the spoon is the valley below, where the town is located.

In the early 1900s, campers and tourists discovered the beautiful Cuchara valley. With its crystal-clear air, cool summer nights, high peaks, and clean water, Cuchara soon began to attract folks from the hot, dusty plains of Kansas, Oklahoma, and Texas. One Texan, George Mayes, settled in Cuchara in 1908 and decided that the area would make a great summer resort. He set about adding rooms to the home that he bought so that it could serve as a hotel. He also built a few cabins, but since most of his guests would be staying in tents, he named the resort Cuchara Camps. This remained the name of the town until 1958, when the Post Office Department changed it to Cuchara.

When the downhill skiing boom came to Colorado in the 1970s, Cuchara did not want to be left behind, especially with its abundant 250 inches of annual snowfall. Cuchara resident Tom Watson secured financial backing and began building a base lodge and ski lifts two miles south of the town of Cuchara. The ski area was located next to Baker Creek, and since *panadero* is the Spanish word for "baker," the new resort was christened Panadero when it opened for business during the winter of 1981–1982.

Following expansion of the ski area in 1983 and 1984, the name was changed to Cuchara Valley Resort. The resort fell on hard times, opening and closing many times over the next decade. In 2000, it finally closed and never reopened. In 2010, local rancher Bruce Cantrell purchased the base area and eventually hopes to open his new Cuchara Mountain Resort with a mountain coaster and zip line, as well as sledding and skiing.

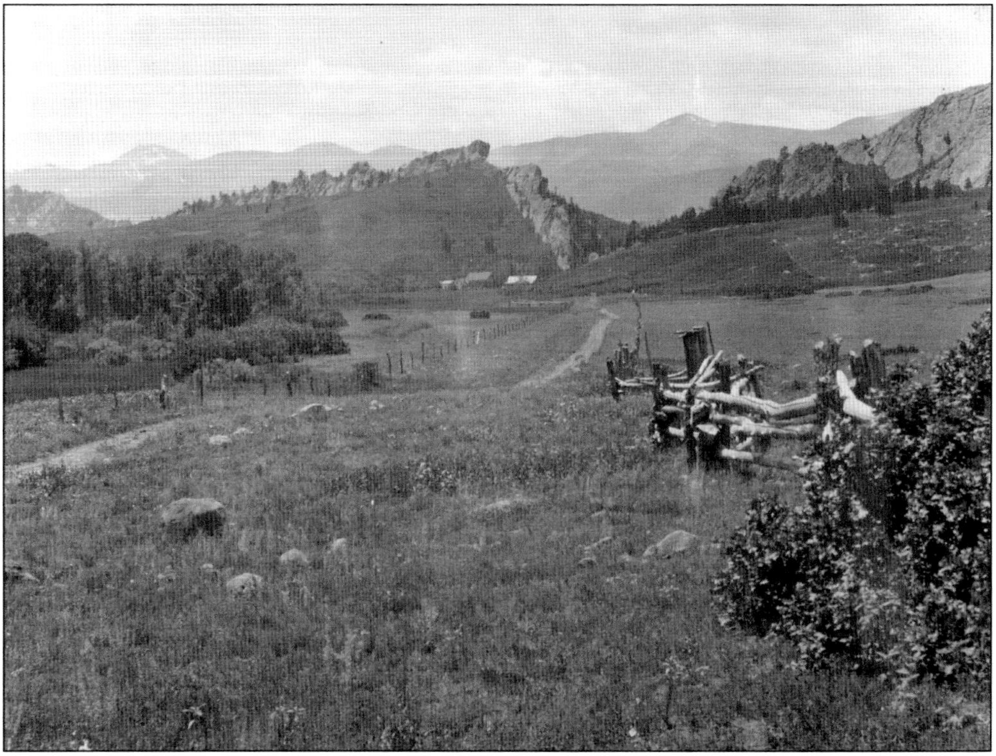

ROAD TO CUCHARA, 1910S. This view from the Eugene S. Vories ranch shows the route heading south from La Veta to Cuchara—a one-lane dirt road that was not paved until 1960. The road passed through the gap in the Dakota hogback just beyond the ranch buildings. (Eugene C. Vories.)

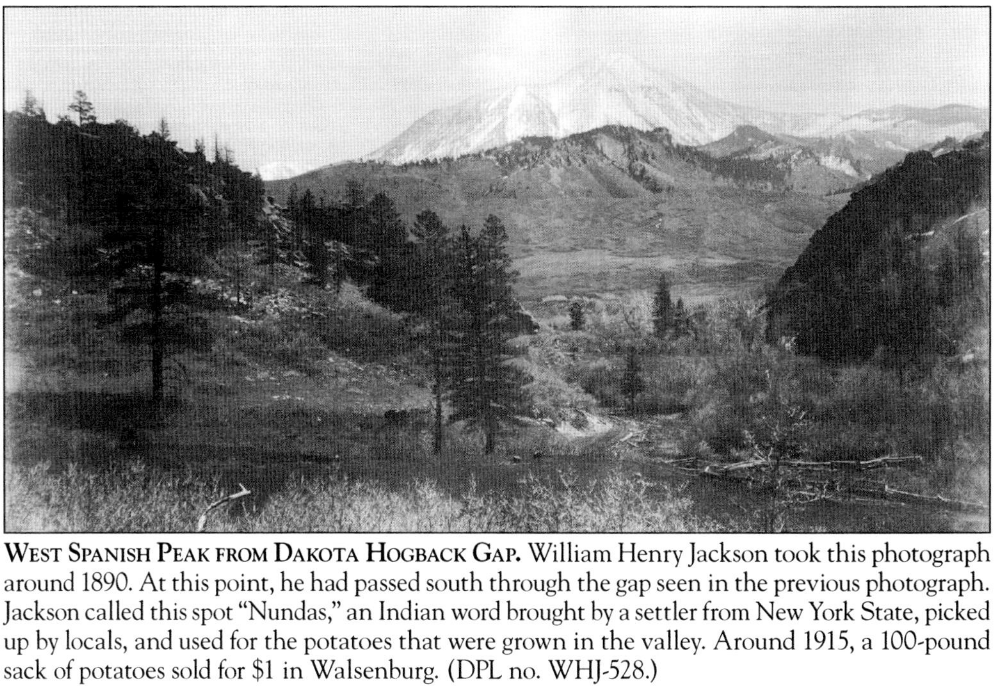

WEST SPANISH PEAK FROM DAKOTA HOGBACK GAP. William Henry Jackson took this photograph around 1890. At this point, he had passed south through the gap seen in the previous photograph. Jackson called this spot "Nundas," an Indian word brought by a settler from New York State, picked up by locals, and used for the potatoes that were grown in the valley. Around 1915, a 100-pound sack of potatoes sold for $1 in Walsenburg. (DPL no. WHJ-528.)

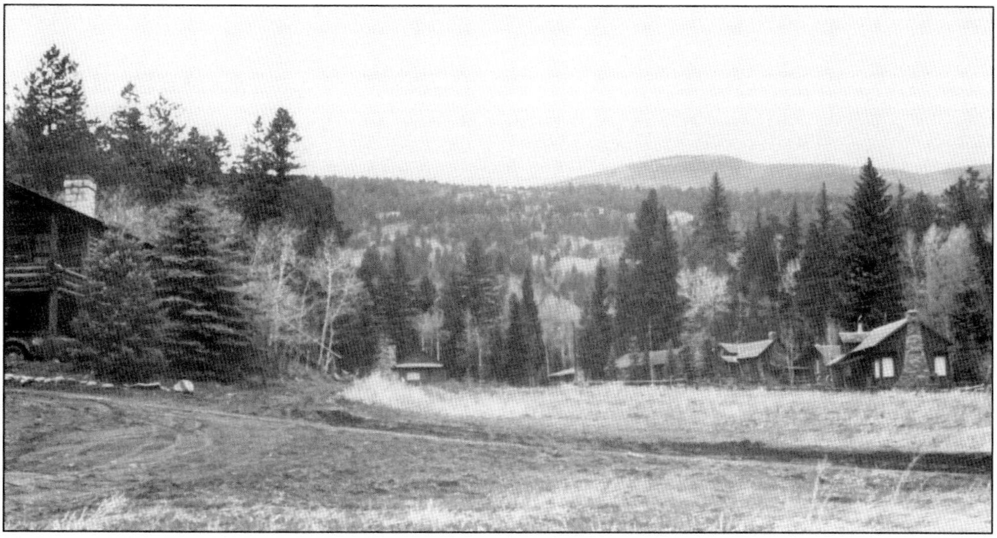

Cuchara Camps, c. 1930s. In the early 1900s, the camps were mainly tents for summer visitors, but by the 1920s/1930s, summer residents were building permanent cabins across the valley. (HCHS.)

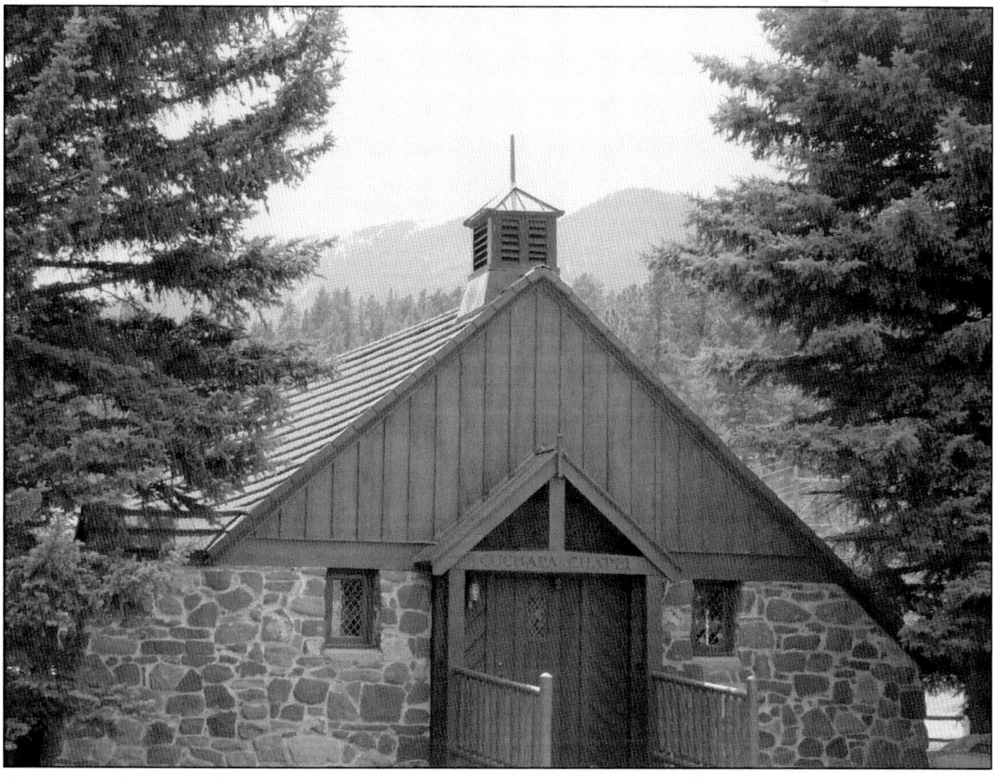

Cuchara Chapel. Summer residents were not inclined to make the trip to La Veta for church on Sunday, but they did want a place to worship. Resident Rae Albright wrote hundreds of letters to Cuchara camp residents soliciting donations for the chapel, and the building was completed in 1949.

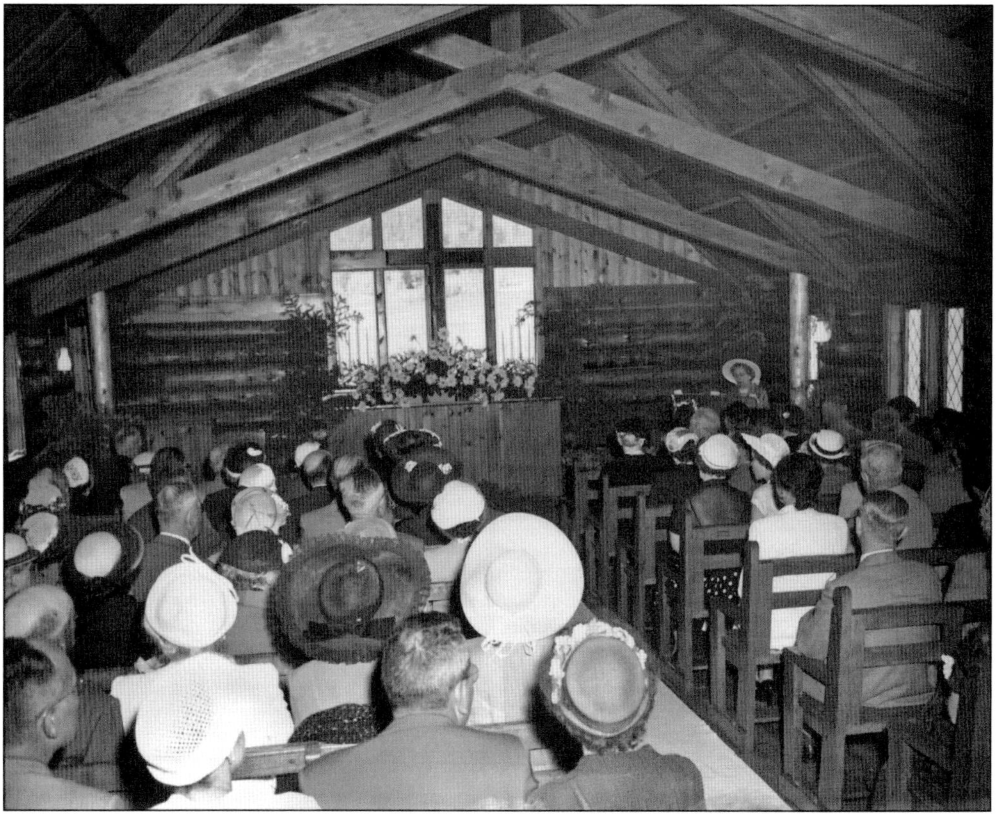

CUCHARA CHAPEL WORSHIPPERS. The chapel was formally dedicated in August 1950, and this 1950 photograph probably shows the dedication ceremony. Services are still held in the chapel from Memorial Day through Labor Day. (DPL no. X-14002.)

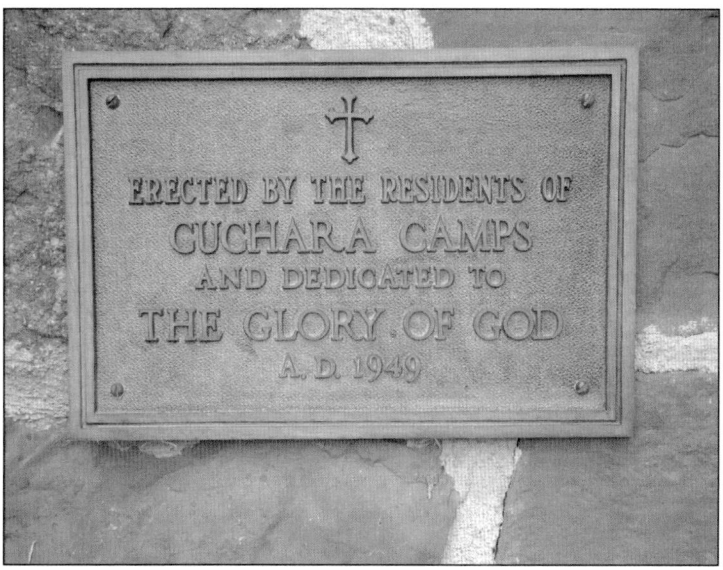

PLAQUE AT CUCHARA CHAPEL ENTRANCE. This is one of the few signs left that identifies the community as Cuchara Camps. The Post Office Department dropped the word *camps* in 1958, and the community became simply Cuchara.

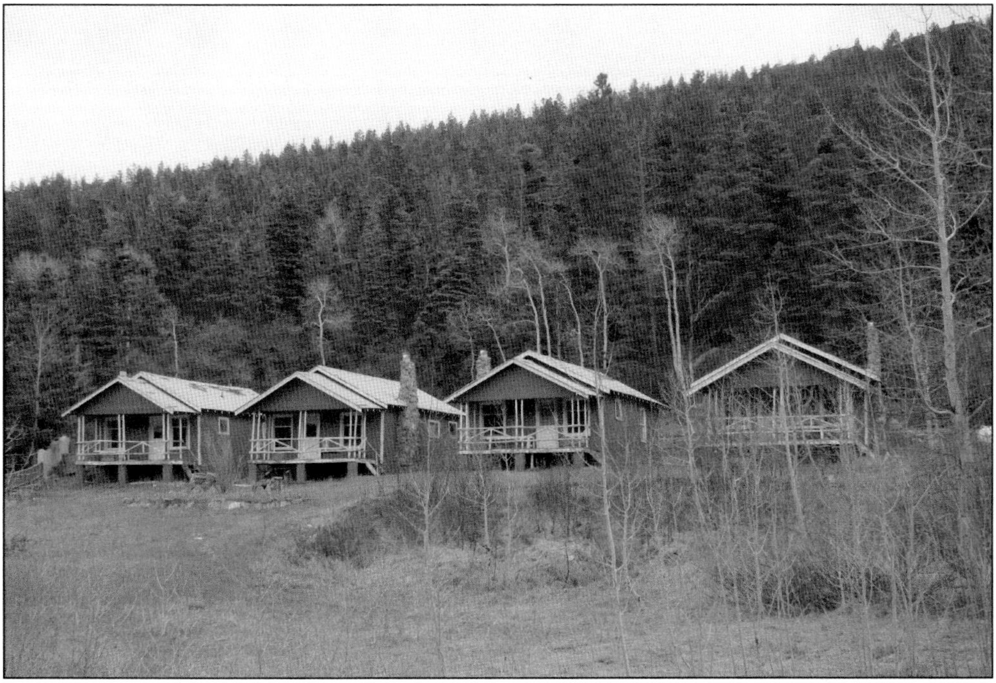

Cuchara Cabin Camps. After the road to Cuchara was finally paved in 1960, camps for motorists, at which cabins could be rented on a nightly or weekly basis, became popular. Enchanted by the area, many renters later came back and built permanent cabins.

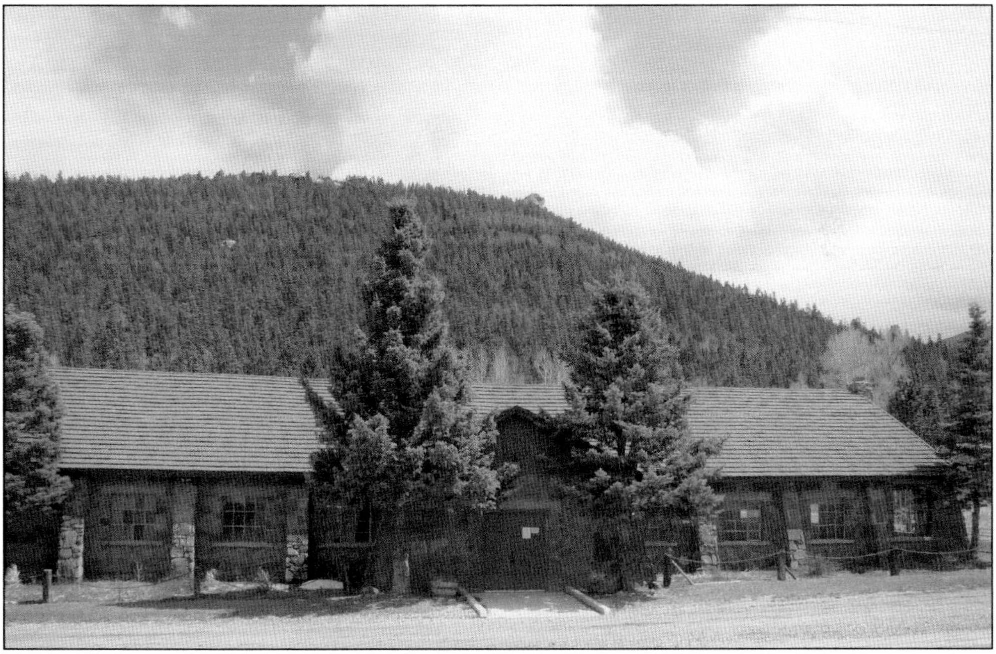

Cuchara Community Center. Construction began in 1955 on this beautiful stone-arched community center. All kinds of community events are held here, including an annual art show sponsored by Cuchara Hermosa, a women's group founded in 1964 to raise funds for beautifying Cuchara and La Veta.

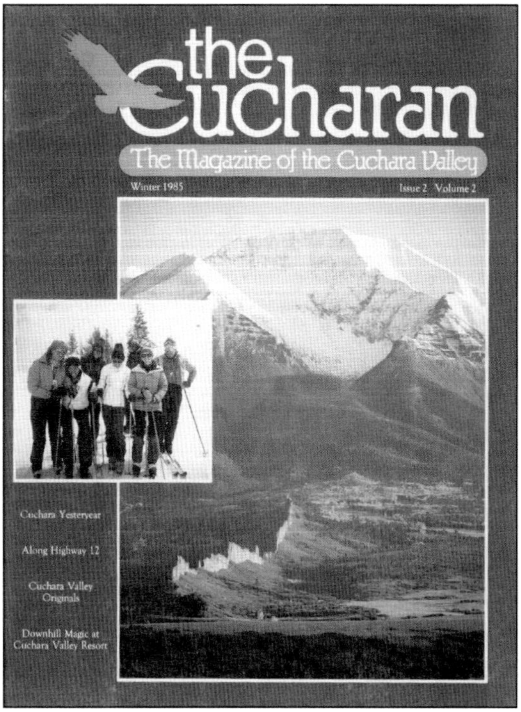

THE CUCHARAN. Publisher Dwight A. Harrison founded this magazine in 1984 to "spark your interest and enthusiasm for the Cuchara Valley." The winter 1985 cover shows a snowcapped West Spanish Peak and a dike wall, as well as skiers at Cuchara. (Dwight A. Harrison.)

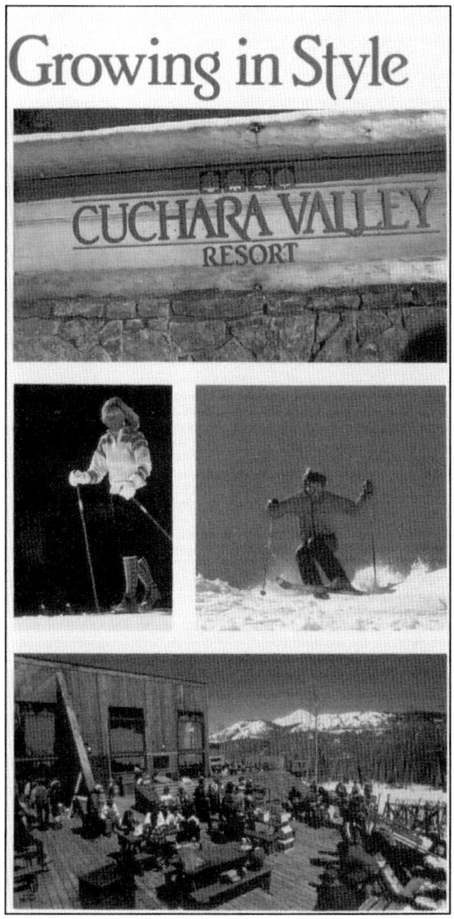

WINTER 1984 *CUCHARAN* MAGAZINE. This issue features the new Cuchara Valley Resort and its winter activities. Skiers enjoyed a fantastic view of the West Spanish Peak from the sun-splashed deck of the base lodge. (Dwight A. Harrison.)

CUCHARA VALLEY RESORT, 1985. The resort, opened in 1981 and expanded in 1983, was advertised extensively in the *The Cucharan*. Promotions featured the lodging facilities and real estate opportunities as well as great skiing. (Dwight A. Harrison.)

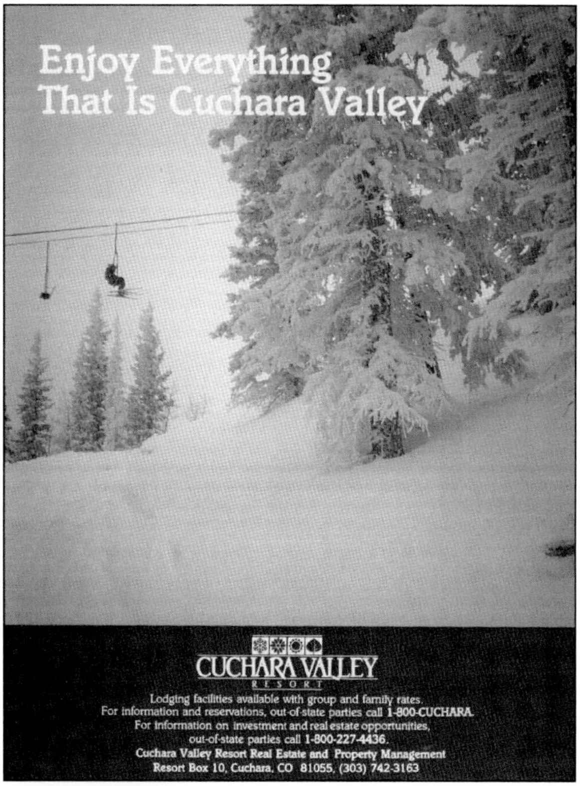

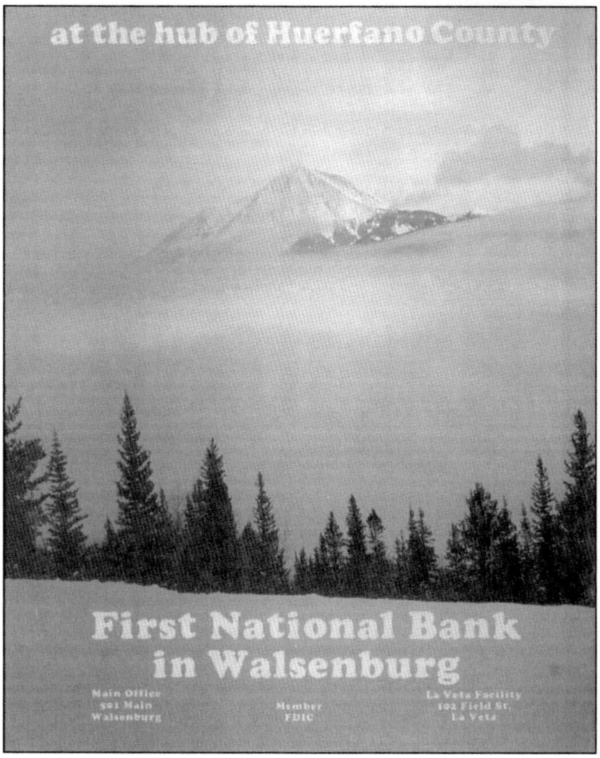

BACK COVER, CUCHARAN, WINTER 1984. The first run of printing totaled 25,000 copies for the first issue of the magazine, and was quickly expanded to 50,000 copies for the second issue. The West Spanish Peak, as seen from the ski area, was used in a promotional ad for a local bank. (Dwight A. Harrison.)

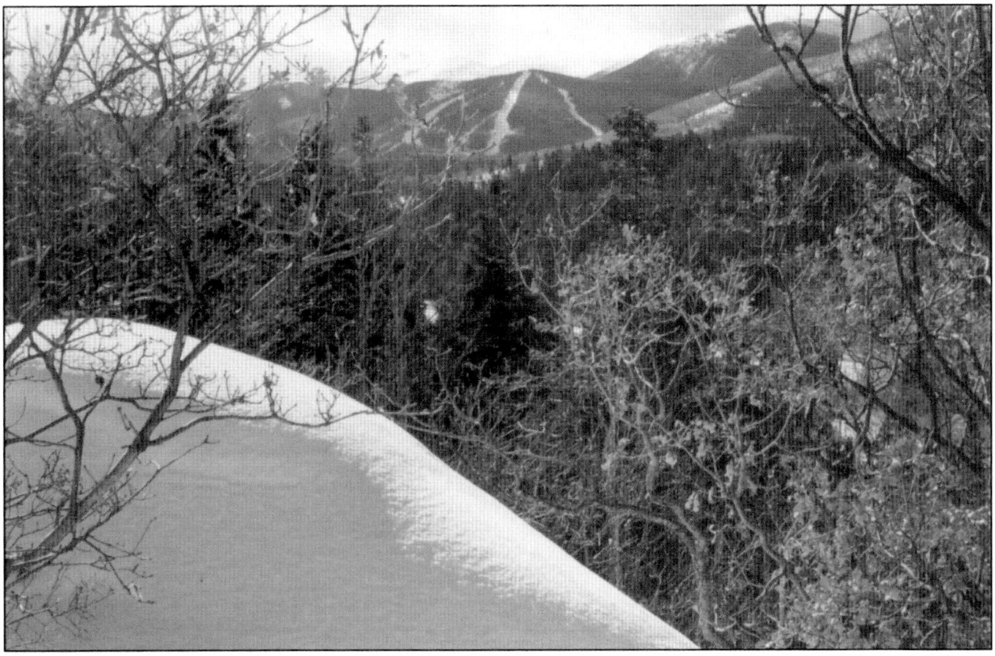

Cuchara Ski Slopes Viewed from Dike Trail. With an average of 250 inches of snowfall per year and plenty of beginner and intermediate ski runs, Cuchara successfully attracted families from Texas, Oklahoma, and Kansas in the 1980s.

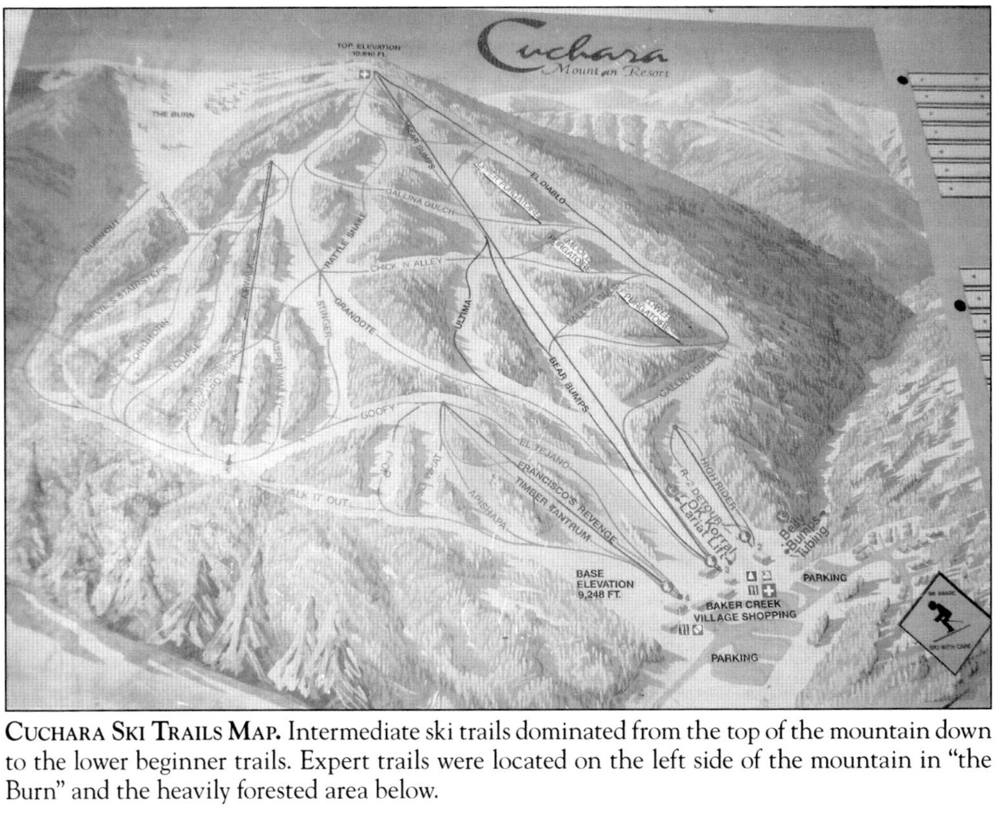

Cuchara Ski Trails Map. Intermediate ski trails dominated from the top of the mountain down to the lower beginner trails. Expert trails were located on the left side of the mountain in "the Burn" and the heavily forested area below.

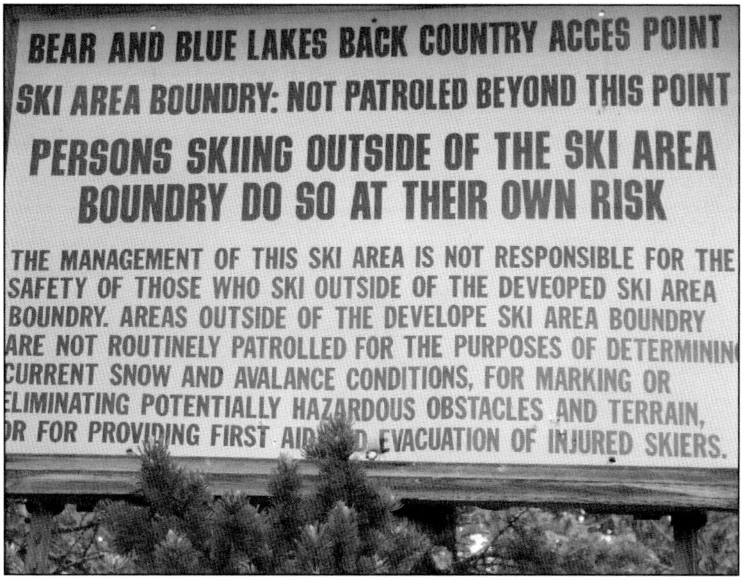

Warning Sign. This highly misspelled sign still stands near the Burn. From the top of the ski area, one can hike or ski over the ridge atop the Burn down to the Bear Lake campground. However, skiers do that "at their own risk."

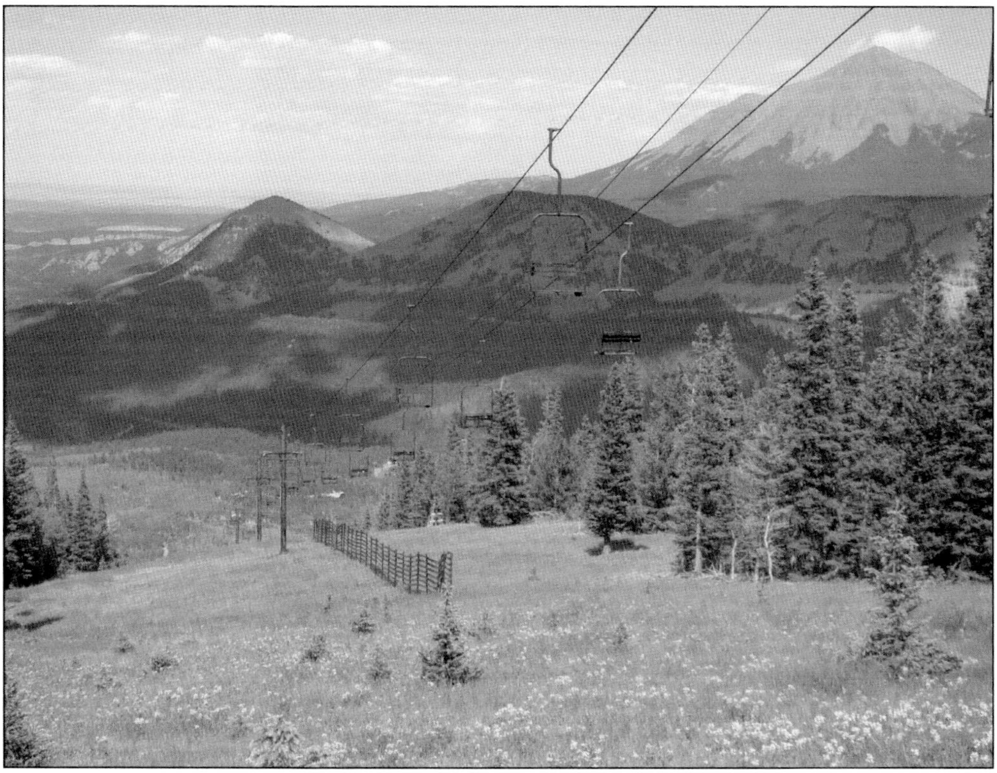

Abandoned Cuchara Ski Lift. The West Spanish Peak rises to the right, overlooking the forlorn ski area that closed in 2000. The savings and loan scandals of the mid-1980s ruined investors and made financing difficult for the resort.

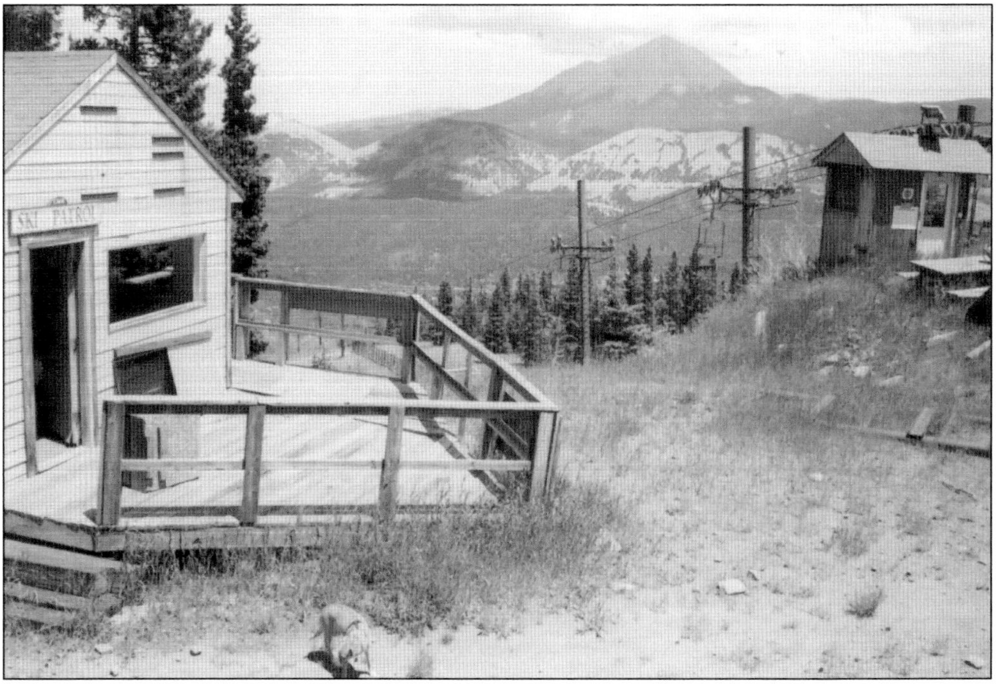

ABANDONED CUCHARA SKI PATROL BUILDING. The resort looks like a ghost town in this image made on a 2008 hike from Bear Lake Campground to the top of the ski mountain. Years of neglect by various owners and lack of financing contributed to the closing of the resort in 2000.

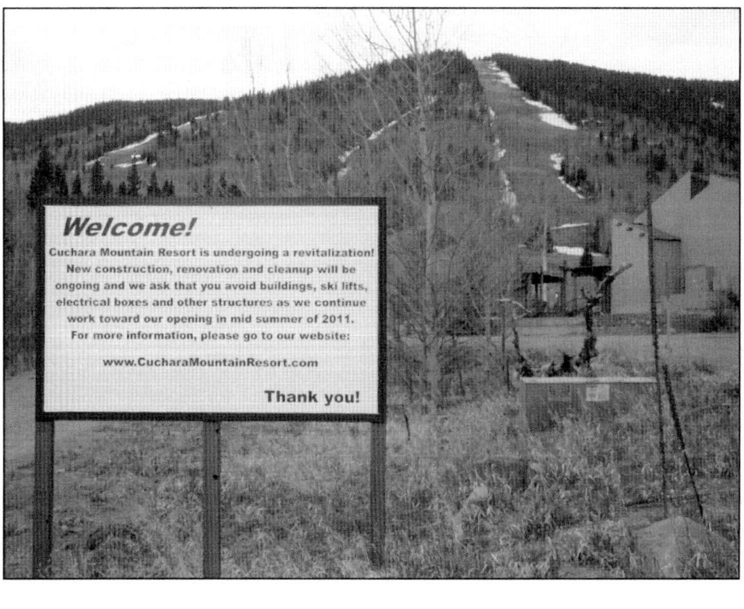

NEW HOPE FOR CUCHARA MOUNTAIN RESORT. This sign at the base of the mountain indicates new owner Bruce Cantrell's plan to open the resort for summer activities in 2011. A zip line and a mountain coaster are planned, and skiing may follow in 2012.

Eight

Recreation's Past, Present, and Future

With a state park, three wilderness areas, and a national forest within its boundaries, Huerfano County offers virtually unlimited recreational opportunities. It has not always been this way. The 20th century saw significant exploitation of the environment with coal mining, heavy forest cutting, and cattle grazing. Late in the century, efforts began to preserve the incredibly beautiful, pristine mountain scenery. In 1993, wilderness areas were established in the northern part of the county at Greenhorn Mountain, as well as in the northwest section of the county at the Sangre de Cristo Wilderness Area. In 2000, the Spanish Peaks Wilderness Area, in the southern portion of the county, was set aside for protection. The three wilderness areas offer wonderful opportunities for hiking, backpacking, and cross-country skiing.

The predecessor to the wilderness areas was Lathrop State Park, located three miles west of Walsenburg. Lathrop, founded in 1962, was Colorado's first state park. Named after Harold W. Lathrop, the first director of the state parks and recreation board, the park consists of 1,596 acres, including two lakes. Martin Lake offers powerboating, waterskiing, fishing, and swimming, and the more secluded Horseshoe Lake offers wakeless boating and fishing. The park also welcomes hikers and campers. More than 150,000 visitors come to Lathrop each year, many of them drawn by fantastic views of the Spanish Peaks from the lakeshores. Lathrop also has a nine-hole golf course—the only golf course located in a Colorado state park.

The San Isabel National Forest also extends through Huerfano County, and offers hiking, camping, jeeping, fishing, mountaineering, and skiing opportunities. The district ranger office in La Veta provides maps and information. The popular Blue Lake and Bear Lake campgrounds are just south of Cuchara. Fishing is permitted in both lakes, and hiking trails abound. While Huerfano County is fortunate to have an abundance of recreational opportunities, future threats to the environment and recreation include the proposed installation of high-tower electric transmission lines over La Veta Pass, natural gas extraction, and wind farms placed in scenic mountain valleys.

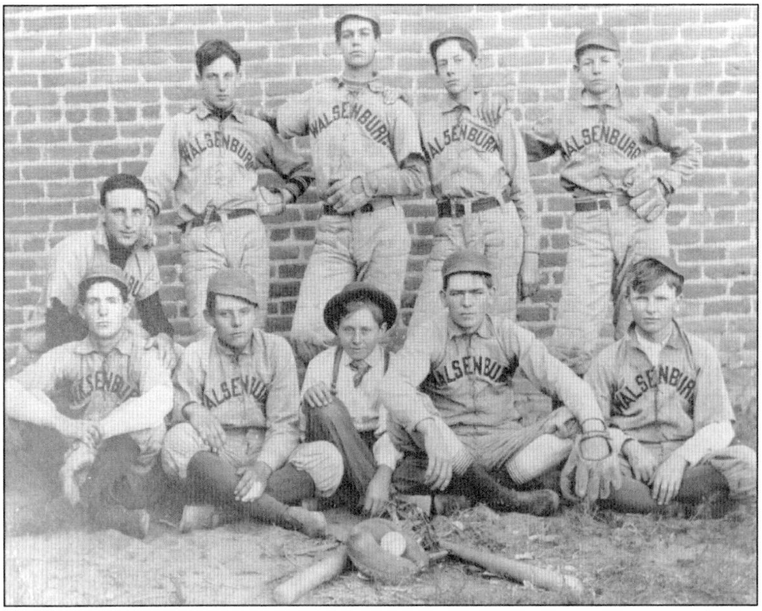

WALSENBURG HIGH SCHOOL BASEBALL TEAM, AROUND 1910. Organized team sports have always been an important part of the curriculum at local schools. Walsenburg and La Veta teams have had a great rivalry over the years.. (HCHS.)

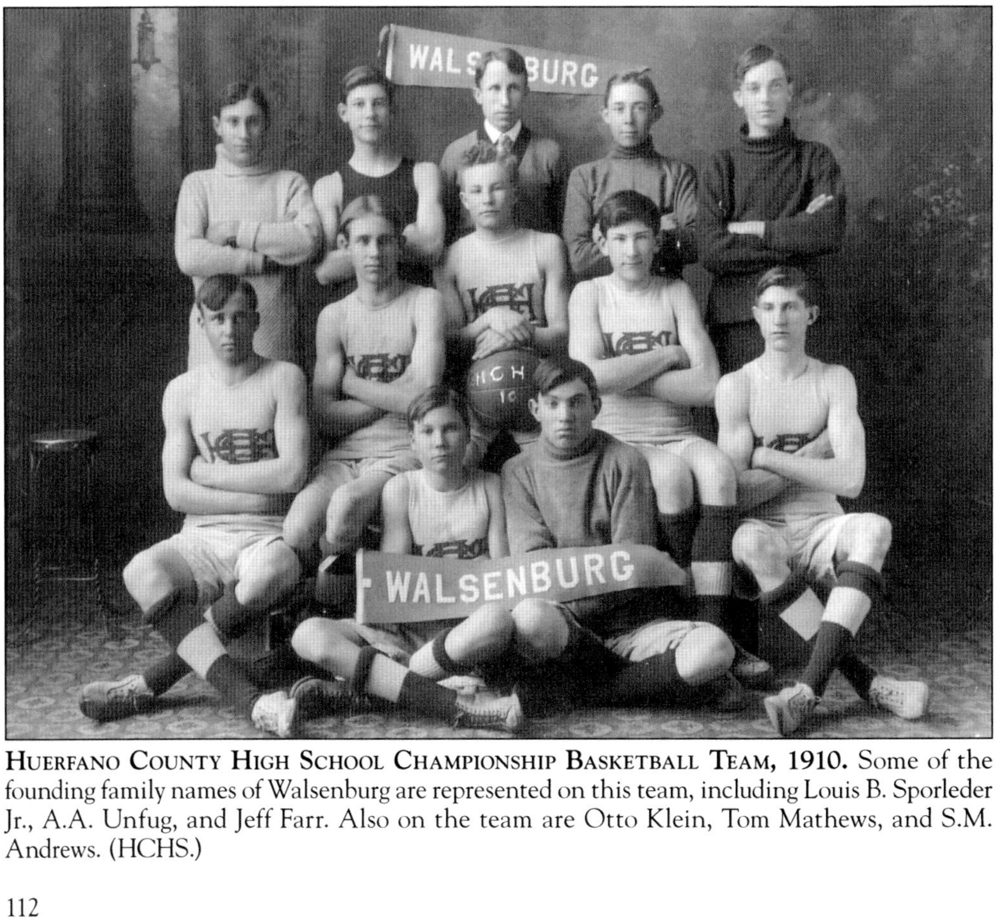

HUERFANO COUNTY HIGH SCHOOL CHAMPIONSHIP BASKETBALL TEAM, 1910. Some of the founding family names of Walsenburg are represented on this team, including Louis B. Sporleder Jr., A.A. Unfug, and Jeff Farr. Also on the team are Otto Klein, Tom Mathews, and S.M. Andrews. (HCHS.)

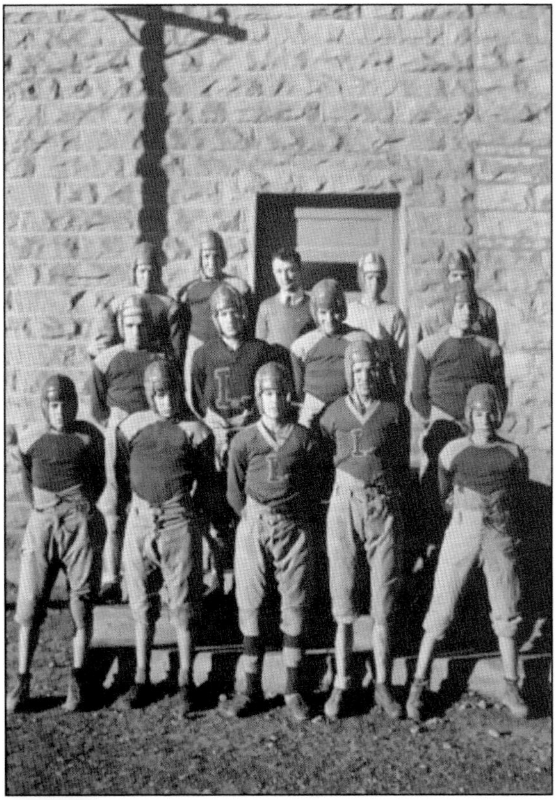

La Veta High School Football Team. Members of the team are lined up on the steps outside the sandstone walls of La Veta High School in the 1920s. Note the leather helmets (and lack of much other padding). (FFM.)

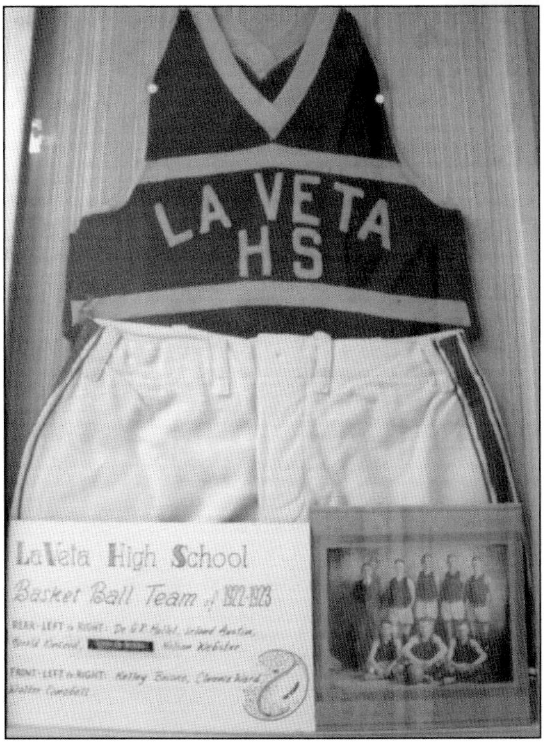

La Veta Basketball Team, 1922–1923. The uniform and team photograph shown here are on display in the Francisco Fort Museum in La Veta. (FFM.)

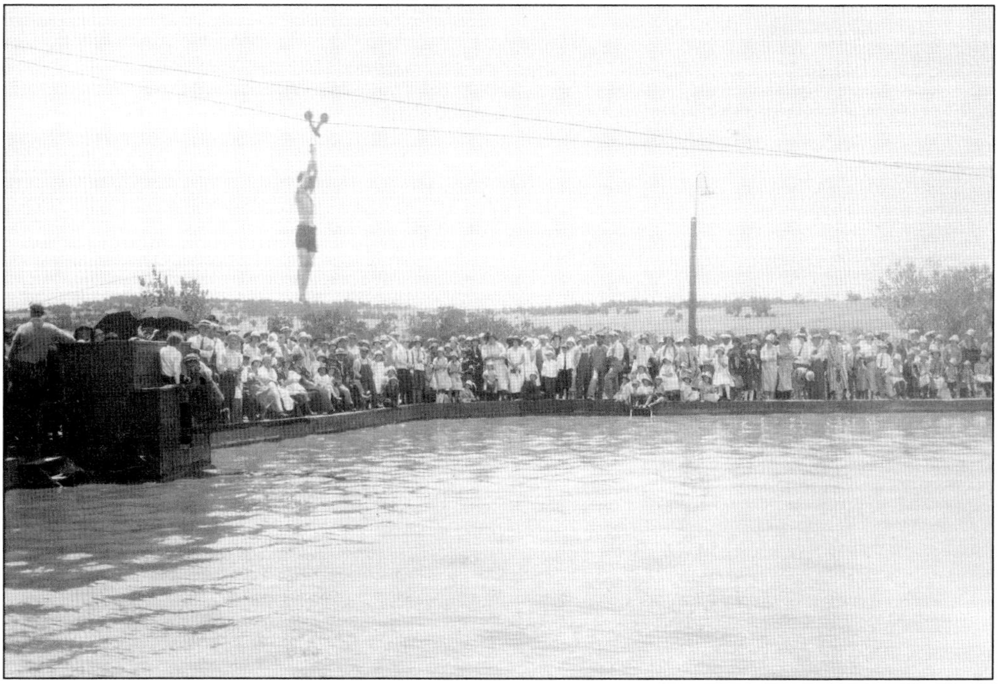

Cameron Zip Line Cruising. The mining camps had many recreational activities for families, particularly after the strikes of 1913 and 1914 led to better conditions. Cameron had a YMCA building and a swimming pool; daredevils could ride the zip line and drop off into the pool. (BHS/CFI.)

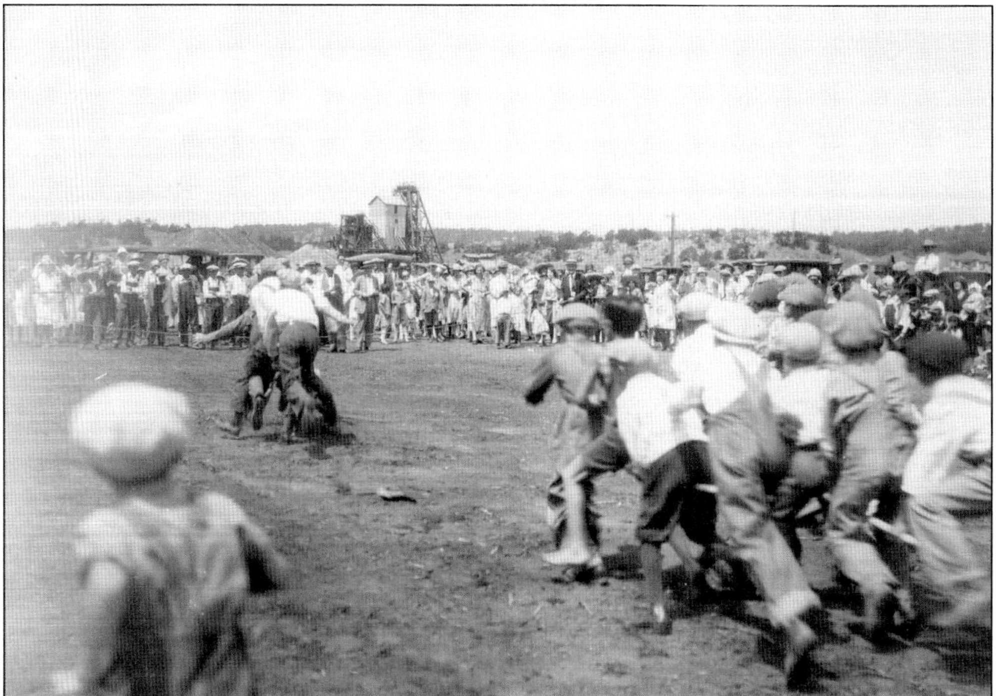

Huerfano County Picnic, 1926. Miners' families from around the county participated in events, like this boys' centipede race at the Walsen camp on August 7, 1926. (BHS/CFI.)

LATHROP STATE PARK, 1960s. State senator Sam Tesitor points to the new sign at Lathrop State Park, which opened in 1962. Located three miles west of Walsenburg, Lathrop attracts over 150,000 visitors annually. (HCHS.)

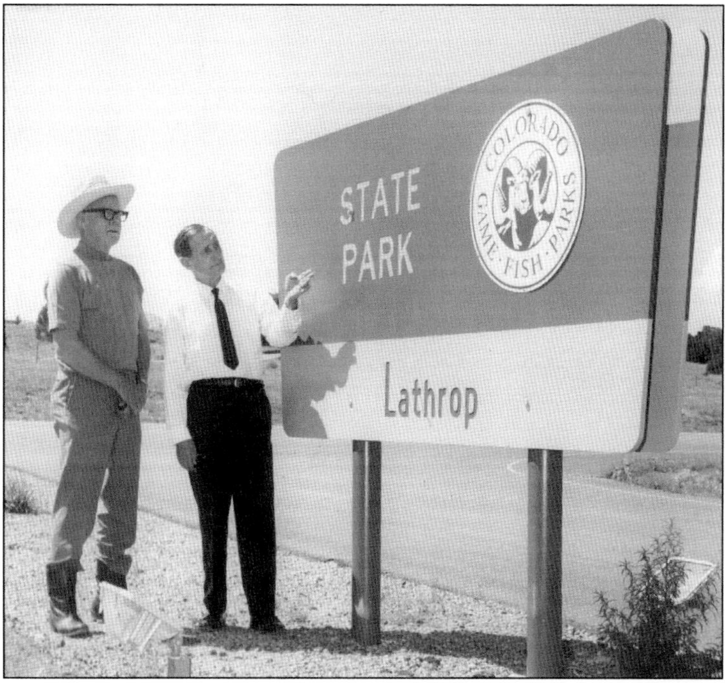

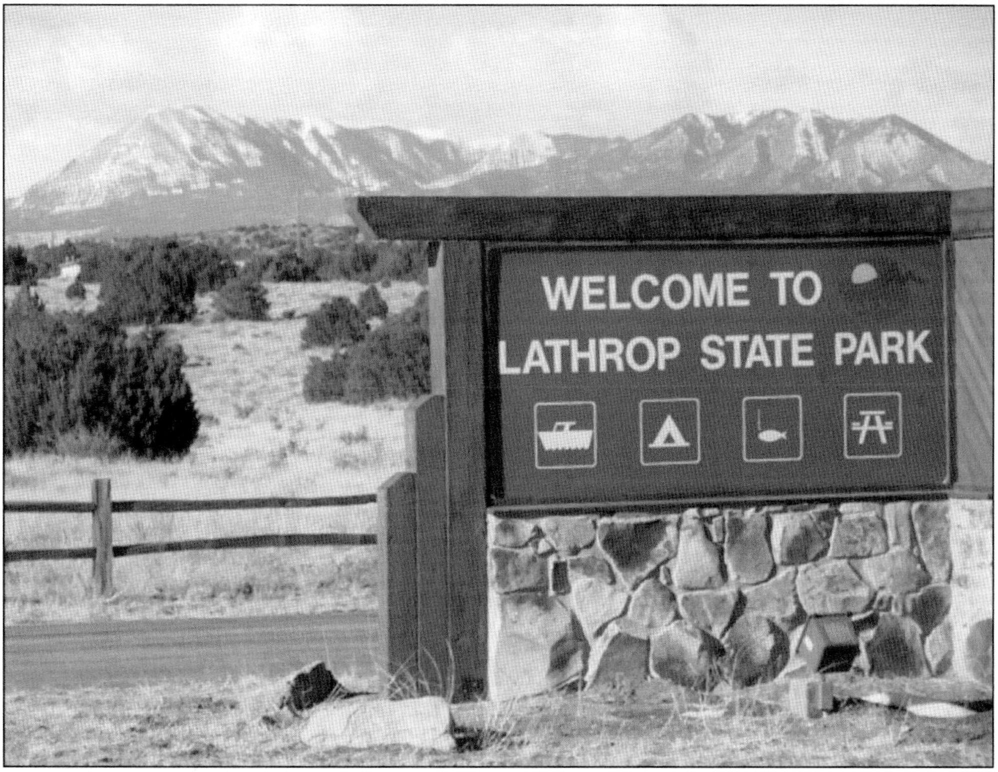

PRESENT-DAY LATHROP STATE PARK. The entrance sign has been updated, but the spectacular views remain the same. In this view looking west, Mount Mestas (left) and Silver Mountain rise up on the horizon.

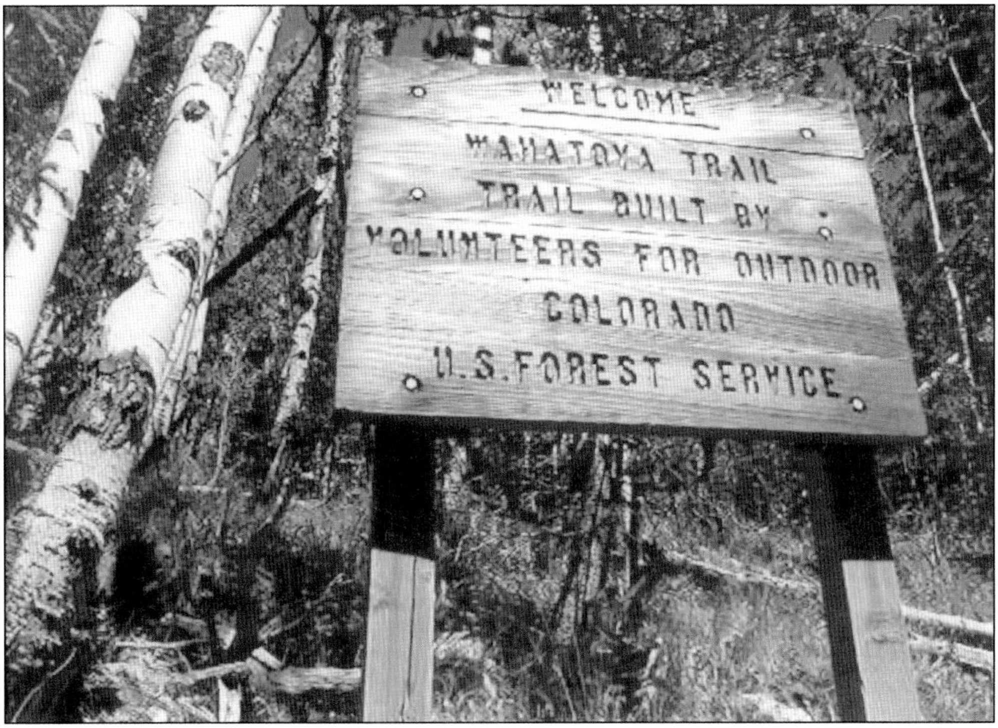

WAHATOYA TRAIL. This trail, on the south side of the West Spanish Peak, was constructed by a group called Volunteers for Outdoor Colorado that is very active in building trails around the state. The trail begins in San Isabel National Forest and climbs to several dike ridges in the Spanish Peaks Wilderness Area.

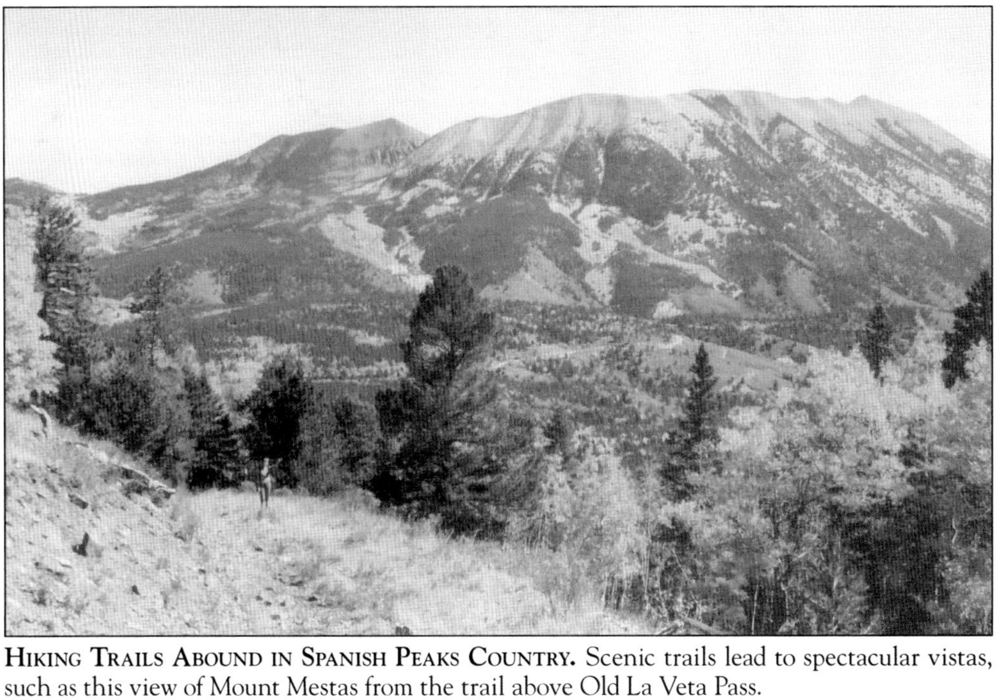

HIKING TRAILS ABOUND IN SPANISH PEAKS COUNTRY. Scenic trails lead to spectacular vistas, such as this view of Mount Mestas from the trail above Old La Veta Pass.

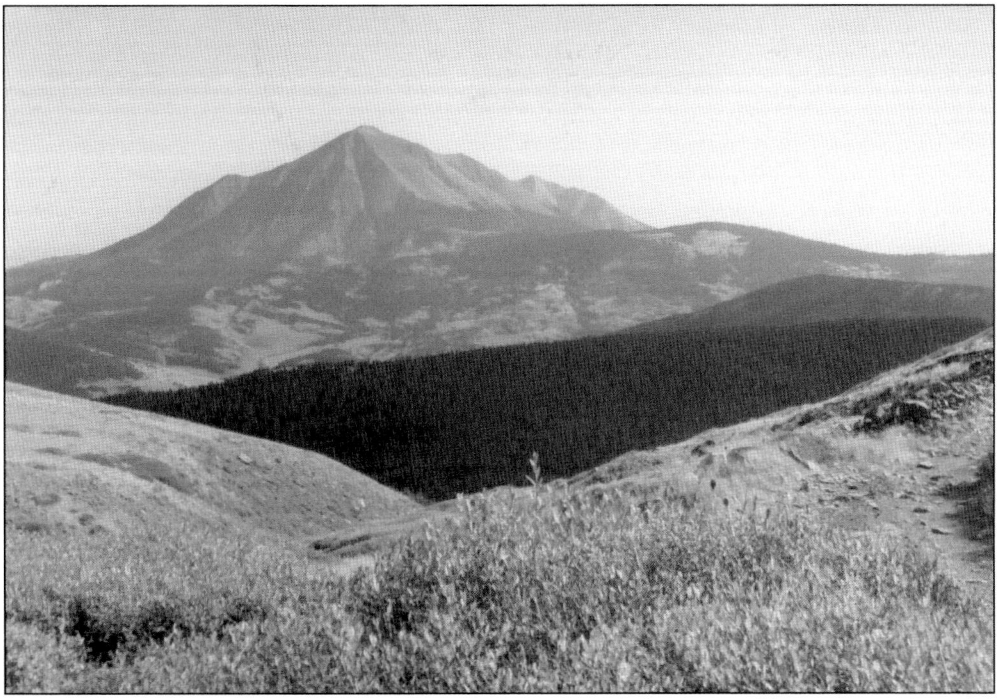

TRINCHERA JEEP ROAD. Starting from Blue Lake Campground, the jeep road (ruts seen on the right) climbs nearly to the top of Trinchera Peak, offering great views of the West Spanish Peak.

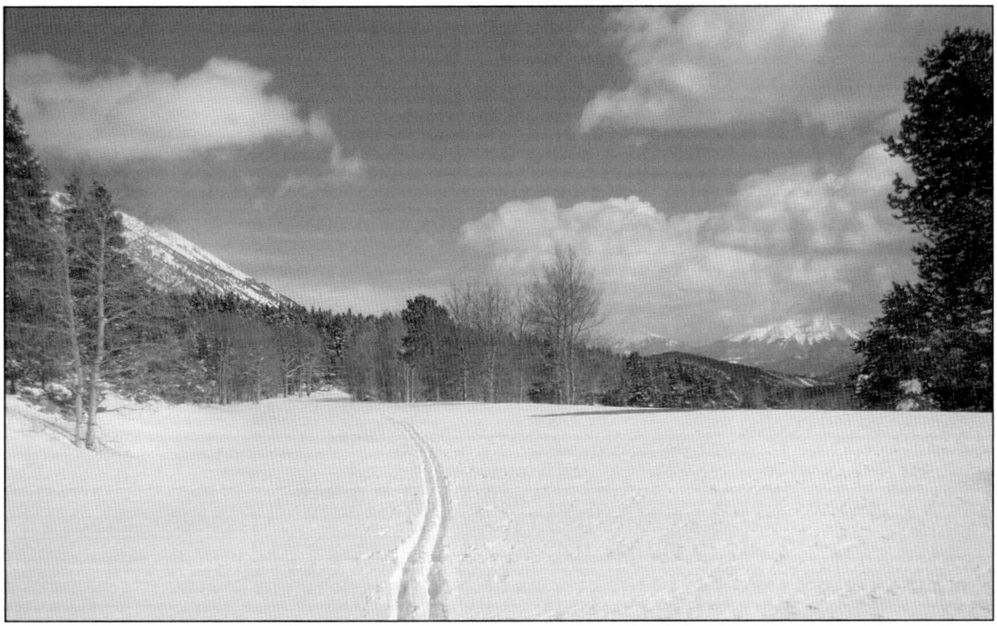

CROSS-COUNTRY SKIING ON OLD LA VETA PASS. Unplowed roads offer great opportunities for cross-country skiers. The Spanish Peaks are visible at right in this view from near the top of the pass, with Mount Mestas on the left.

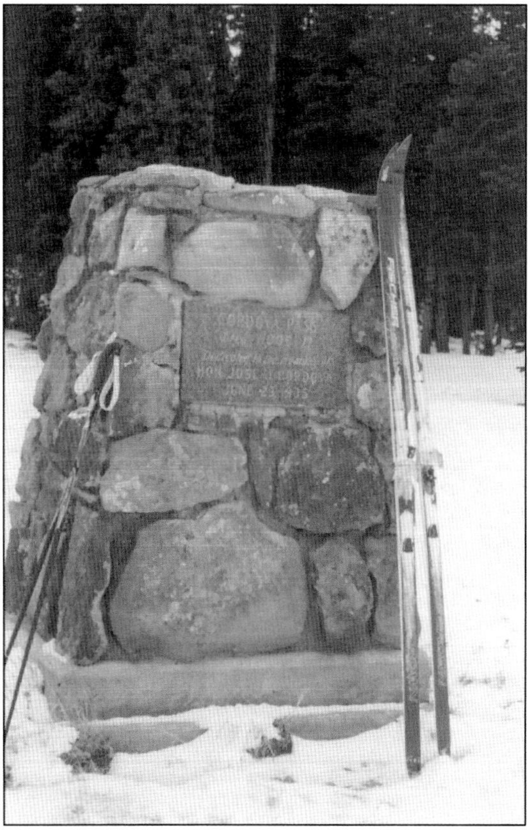

Cordova (or Apishapa) Pass. Cordova Pass is a strenuous five-mile climb for skiers from the Farley Overlook just east of Cuchara Pass. Windswept conditions and snowplowing often thwart skiing on this road, but when conditions are right, skiers are rewarded with terrific views from the top of Cordova Pass.

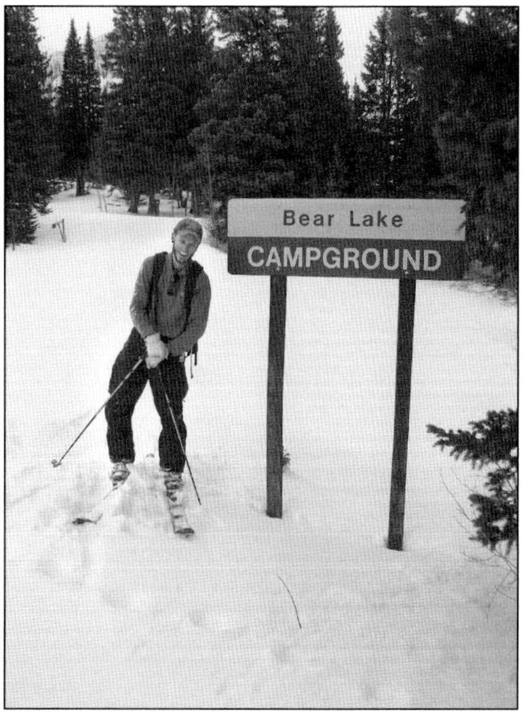

Skiing to Bear Lake Campground. Jason Butler enjoys cross-country skiing to Bear Lake, which can be a five-mile haul if skied all the way from Highway 12. Usually, there is insufficient snow on the road for the first couple of miles, so that portion may be traversed in a four-wheel drive vehicle.

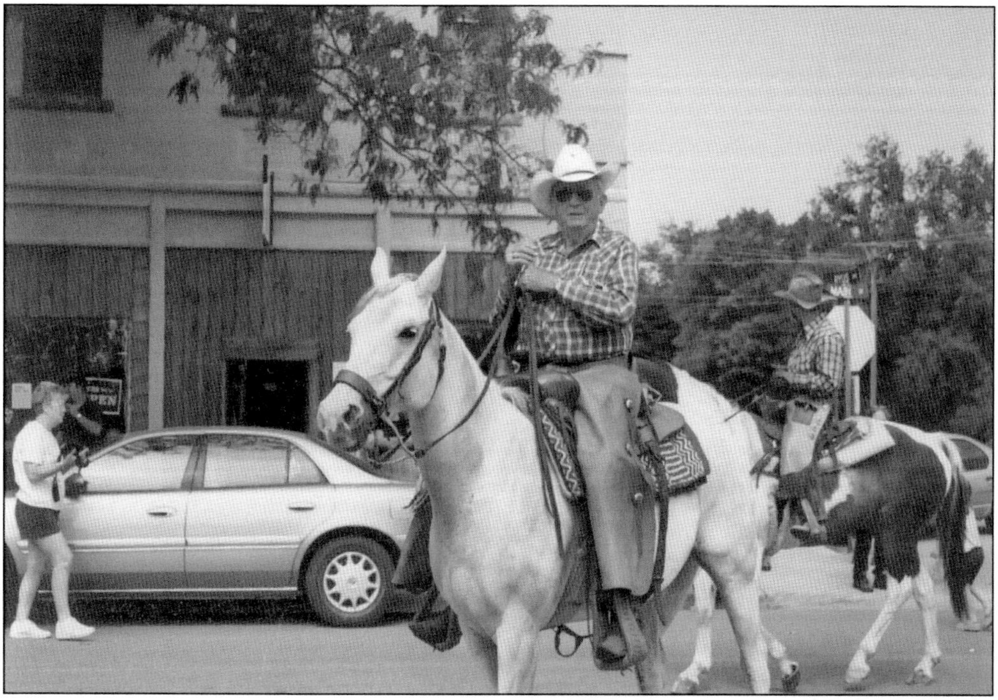

Western Author Eugene Capps Vories. Vories rode his horse in the Francisco Fort Day parade in La Veta on August 1, 2003. He is the grandson of Samuel J. and Amelia Capps, who ranched east of the East Spanish Peak in the 1890s (see page 122). (Eugene C. Vories.)

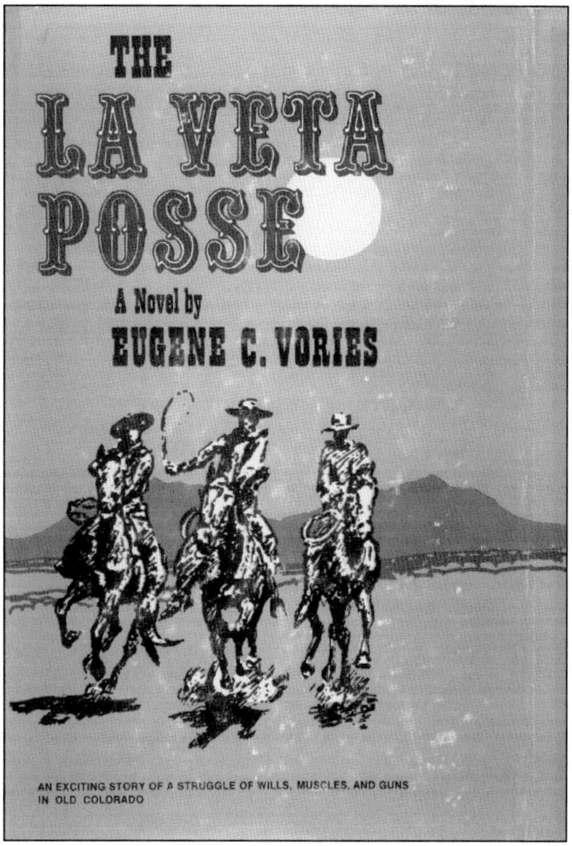

***The La Veta Posse*, by Eugene C. Vories.** The Spanish Peaks serve as the cover art of Vories' novel. Vories, born in Walsenburg in 1923, now lives in La Veta. He has written some 16 novels about the Old West, most of which are still in print. (Eugene C. Vories.)

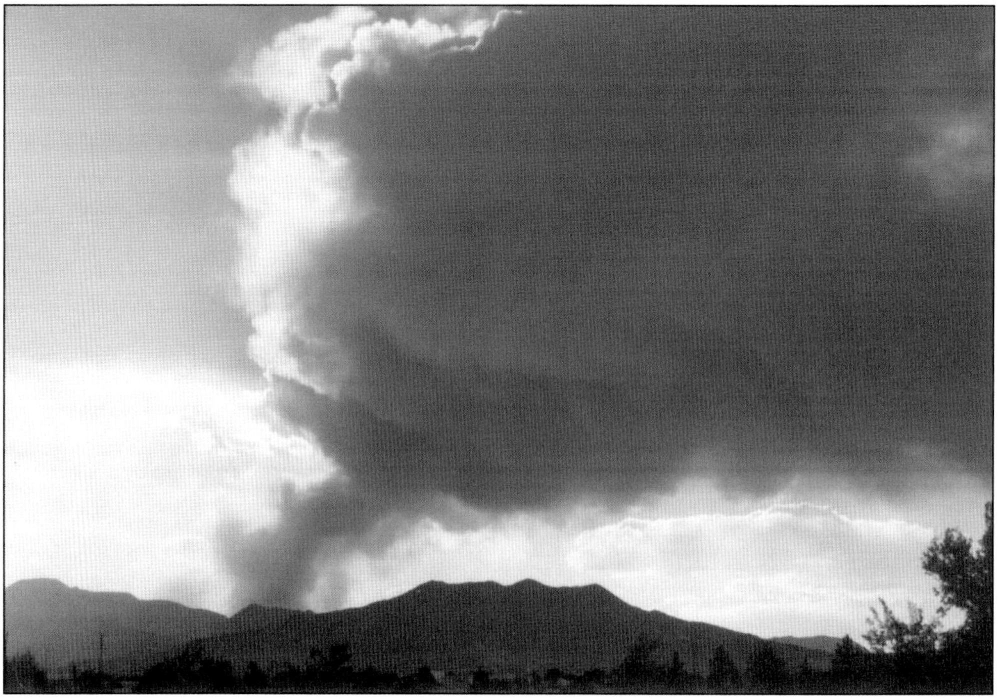

MATO VEGA FIRE, JUNE 19, 2006. Smoke from a huge forest fire west of La Veta Pass billows over Mount Mestas (left) and Silver Mountain (right). Forest fires represent an ever-present threat to recreational opportunities in the mountains.

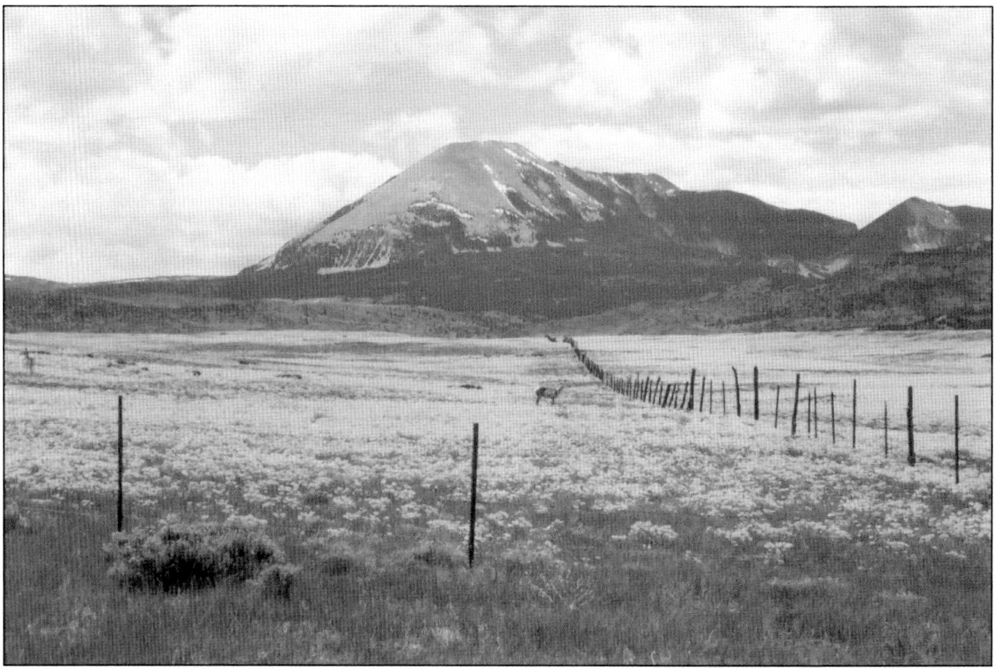

ANTELOPE AND MOUNT MESTAS. Antelope graze peacefully in the valley east of Mount Mestas. A wind farm has been proposed for this scenic location, threatening to drive off wildlife, as well as tourists who bring much support to the local economy.

Nine

Farther around the Spanish Peaks

Cattle ranching has always been an important part of the economy in Spanish Peaks country. The lush prairie grasses are sustained by fairly dependable water flow in creeks and rivers such as Santa Clara Creek, the Cuchara River, and the Huerfano River. Some very large ranches were established in the late 1800s, including as the Capps Ranch, with over 60,000 acres on the Santa Clara at the eastern foot of the East Spanish Peak. Samuel J. Capps founded the ranch, and his grandson, Eugene Capps Vories, of La Veta, has written 16 historical novels about the ranching era. Near La Veta, the Goemmer Ranch thrived along the Cuchara River, and the volcanic plug there is named Goemmer's Butte.

In the northwest part of Huerfano County, the Huerfano River originates in the Sangre de Cristo Mountains near the Lindsey and Blanca peaks, which both rise over 14,000 feet high. Flowing southeasterly, the Huerfano River fostered small communities such as Redwing, Malachite, Gardner, Farisita, and Badito to serve the nearby ranches. Badito, in fact, was the first county seat of Huerfano County, before the county seat was transferred to Walsenburg in 1872.

The Spanish Peaks are so high and large that they can be seen from great distances beyond Huerfano County. From the top of Raton Pass, on the New Mexico border, travelers on the Santa Fe Trail could clearly see the Spanish Peaks, as can travelers on Interstate 25 over Raton Pass today. South of Cuchara on Highway 10 (the Highway of Legends), the south face of the Spanish Peaks can easily be seen from Monument Lake. And on a clear day, the Spanish Peaks can be viewed from as far away as 10 miles north of the city of Pueblo.

Spanish Peaks country is filled with incredible mountain views and a legacy of cattle, coal, railroads, and historic communities scattered along river valleys. A warm welcome from local residents awaits visitors on any journey around the Spanish Peaks.

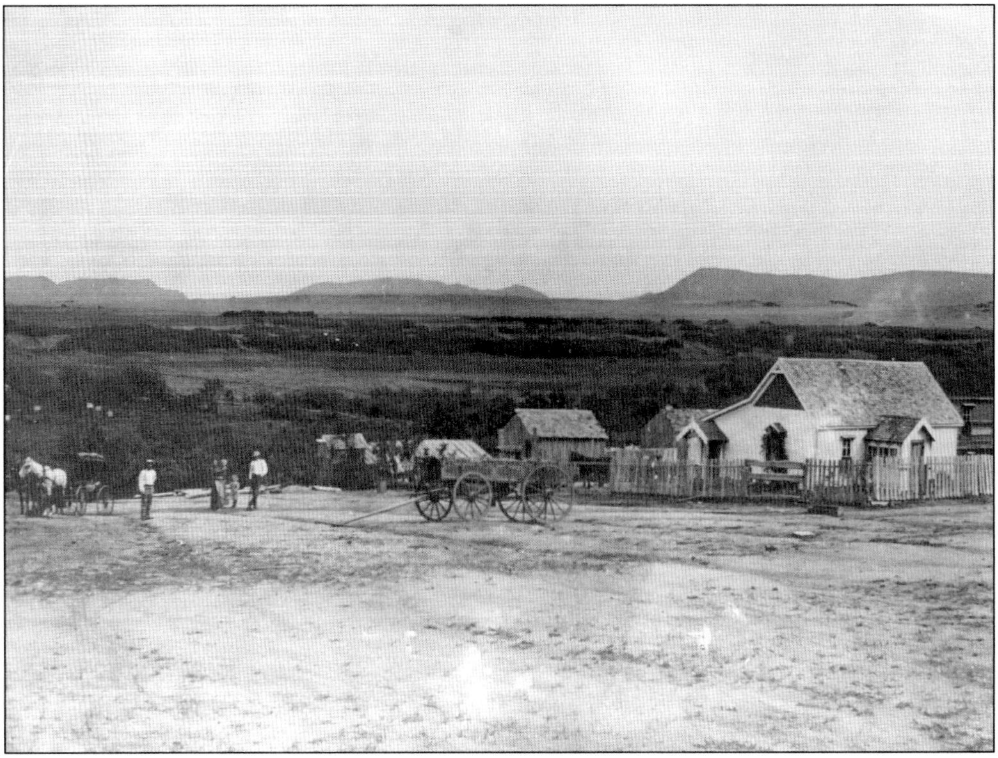

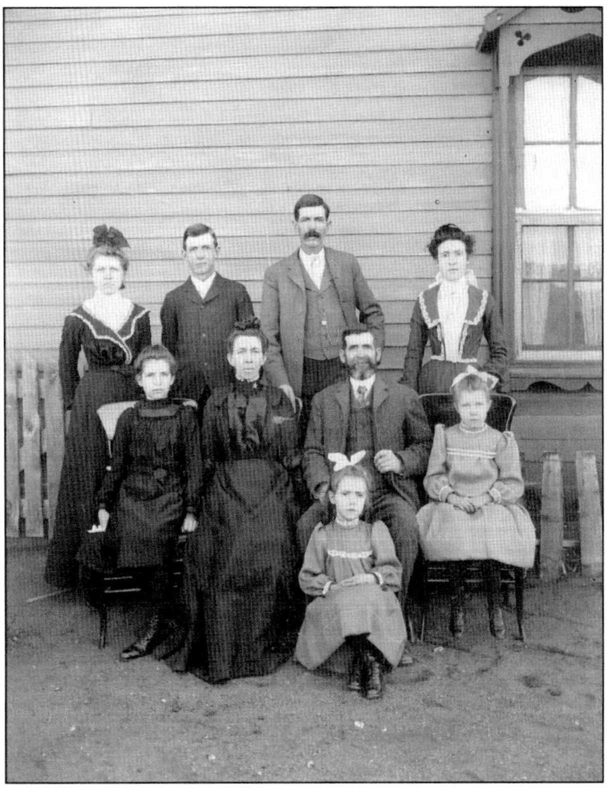

CAPPS RANCH, SANTA CLARA CREEK, 1890s. Samuel J. Capps and his wife, Amelia, settled east of the East Spanish Peak in the 1890s. They raised their seven children on the ranch, as well as several thousand head of cattle on 60,000 acres. (Eugene C. Vories.)

CAPPS FAMILY, C. 1900. The little girl seated in front is Evelyn. The other family members pictured are, from left to right, (first row) Ruby (Eugene C. Vories's mother), Amelia, Samuel J., and Emma; (second row) Rowena, W.C.H. "Claude," Harry J., and Susan. (Eugene C. Vories.)

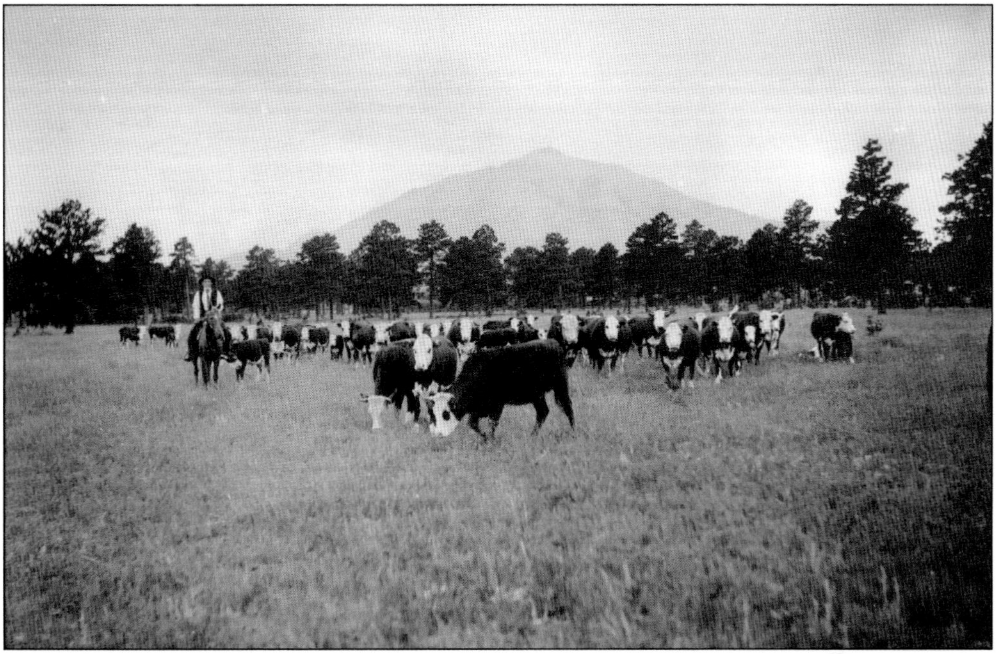

Capps Ranch. An unidentified cowboy watches over cattle as the East Spanish Peak looms in the background. (Eugene C. Vories.)

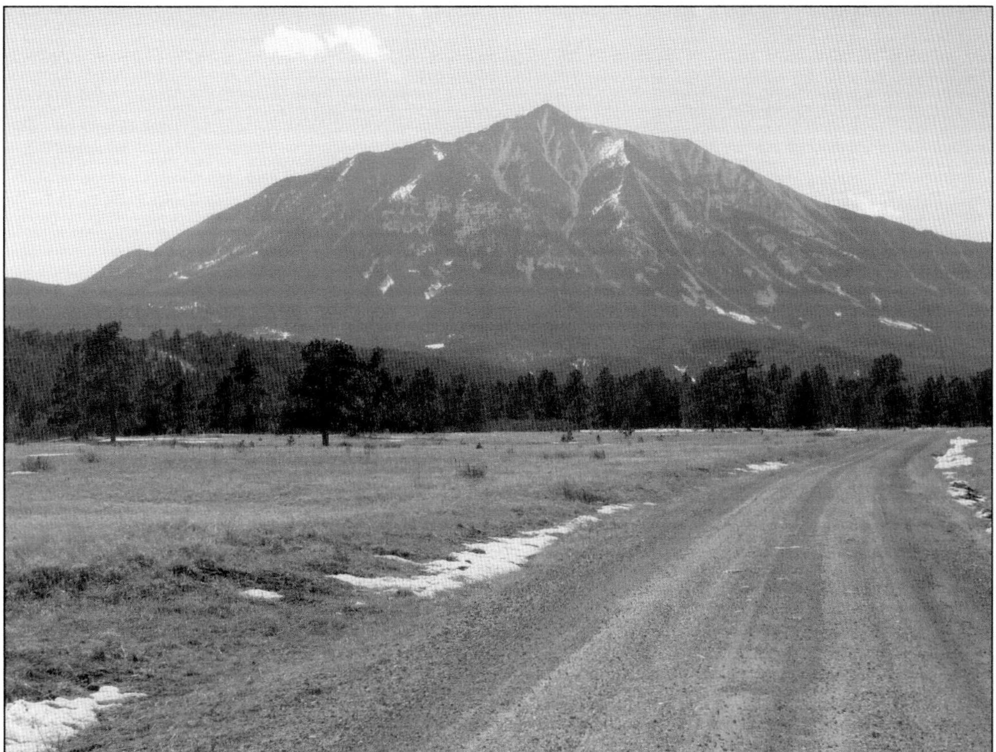

Present-day Capps Ranch. The Capps Ranch no longer exists, but cattle still graze along County Road 312 and the Santa Clara Creek at the base of the East Spanish Peak.

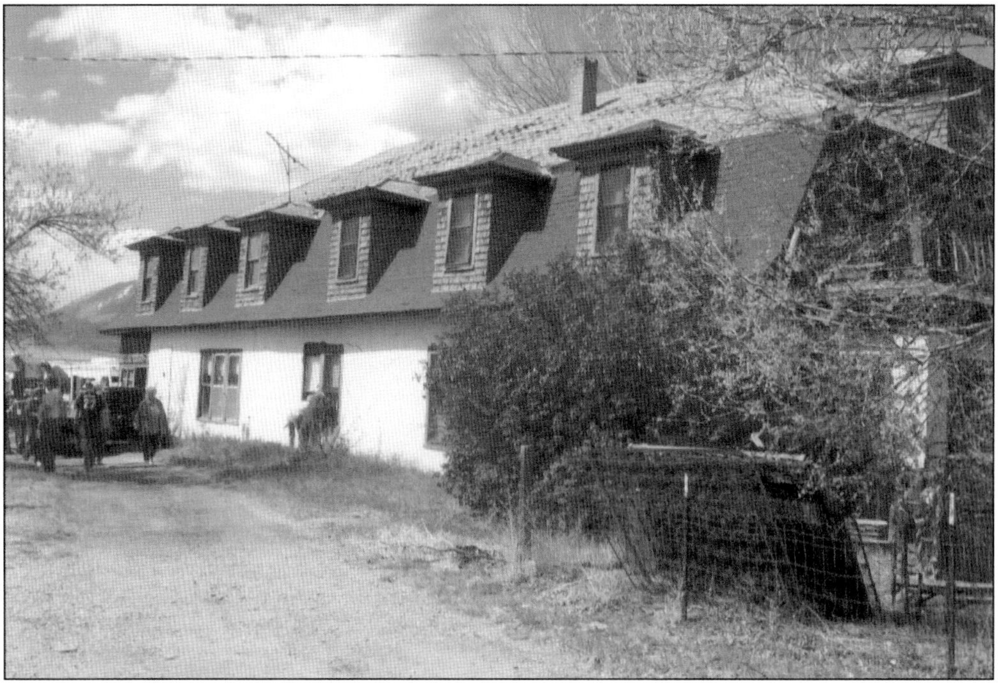

Gardner Hotel. In northern Huerfano County, the town of Gardner came to life in 1863 when Herbert Gardner opened a trading post and store. This adobe-and-frame hotel was built in 1915 by Dan Costello to replace an earlier hotel that burned down. (Carolyn Newman.)

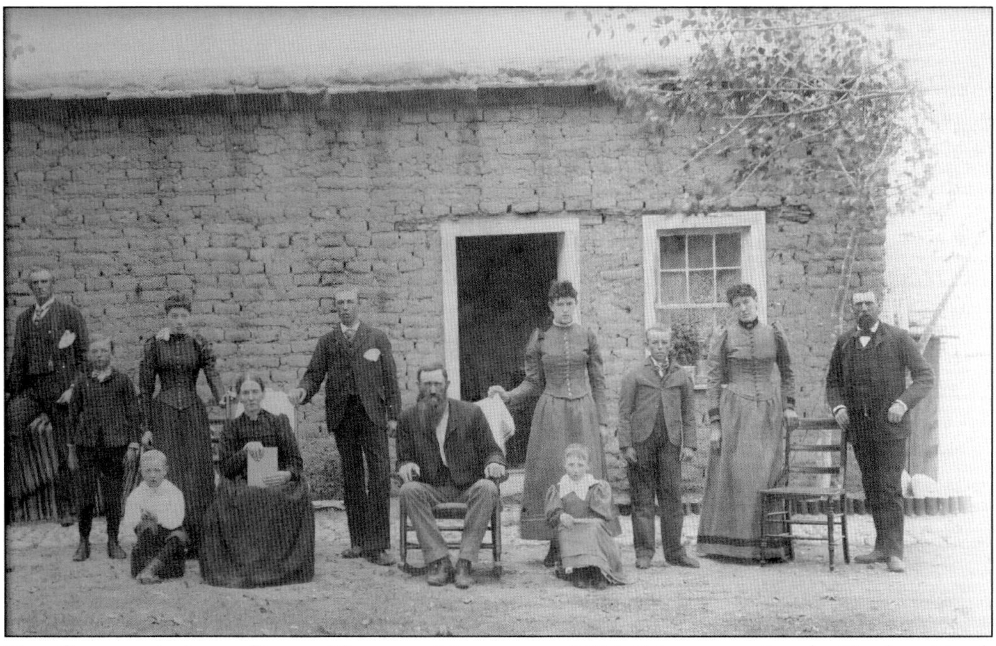

Dan Costello's Adobe Ranch House at Malachite, 1894. Prior to opening the Gardner Hotel, Dan Costello ranched at Malachite, west of Gardner. Dan is at the far right and his wife, Addie Addington, is to his right. Addie's mother, Sarah, and her father, March, are seated. (HCHS.)

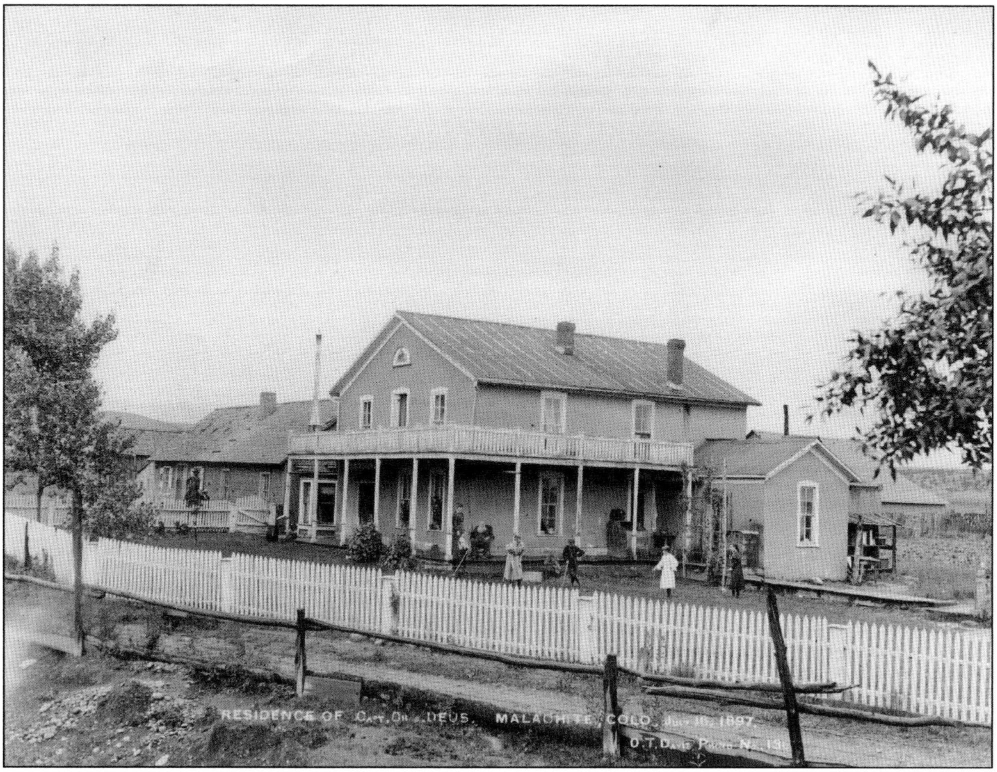

MALACHITE RESIDENCE OF CHARLES DEUS, JULY 16, 1897. O.T. Davis took this photograph of Capt. Charles Deus's lovely two-story home at Malachite. The captain is sitting on the porch while children play croquet on the lawn. (DPL no. X-12261.)

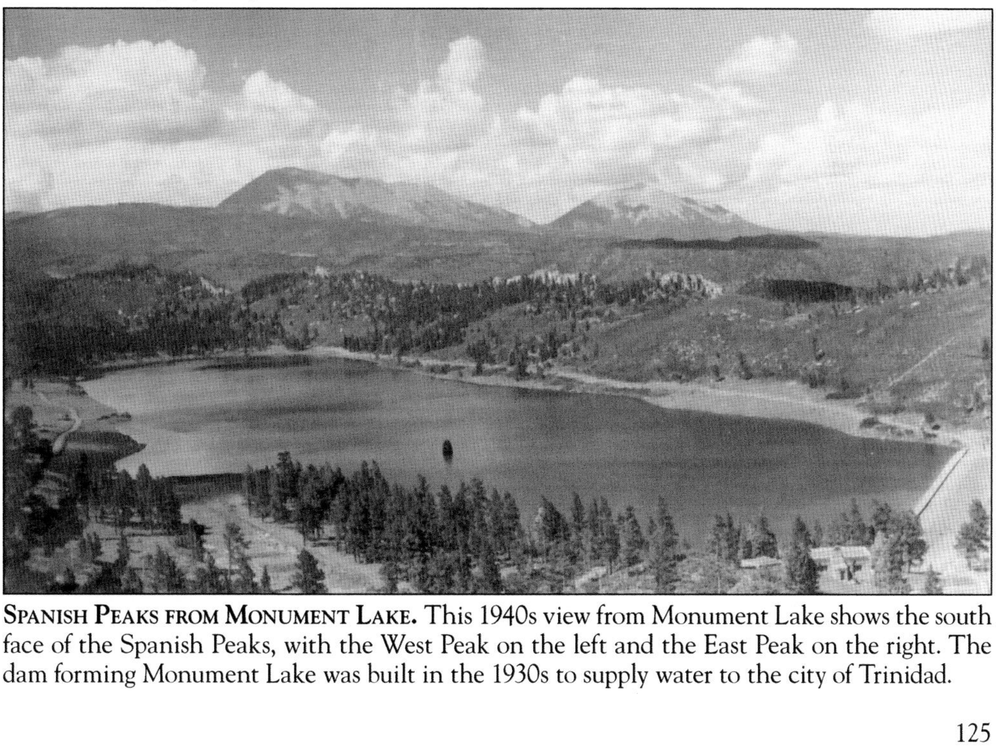

SPANISH PEAKS FROM MONUMENT LAKE. This 1940s view from Monument Lake shows the south face of the Spanish Peaks, with the West Peak on the left and the East Peak on the right. The dam forming Monument Lake was built in the 1930s to supply water to the city of Trinidad.

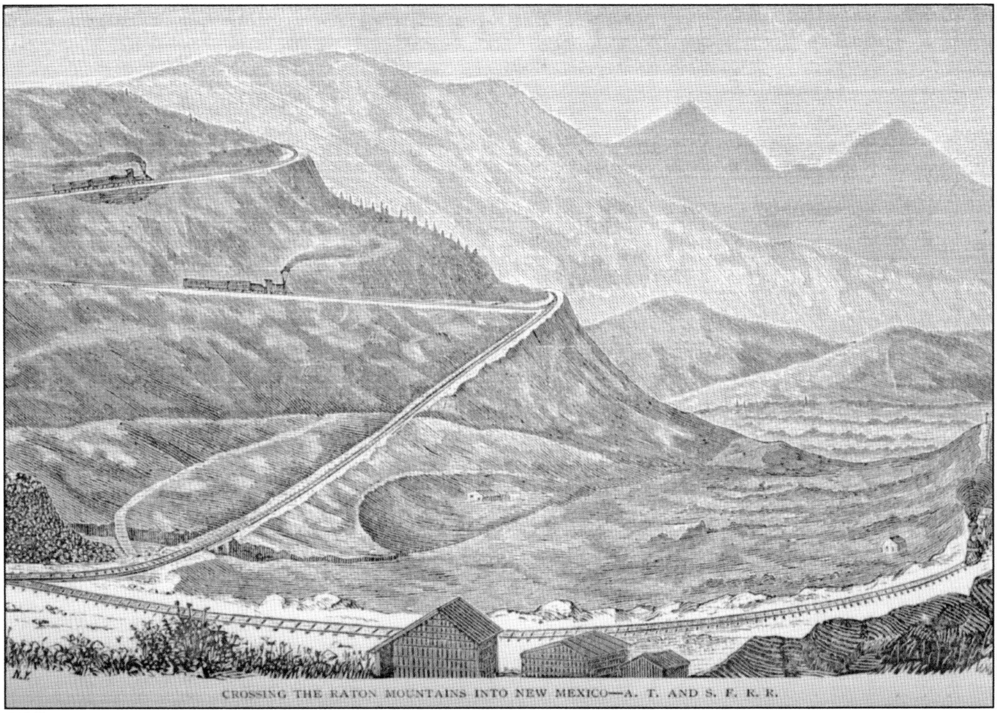

SPANISH PEAKS FROM RATON PASS. This 1880s magazine illustration shows the Spanish Peaks rising to the right, while the Santa Fe Railroad climbs precariously up the pass.

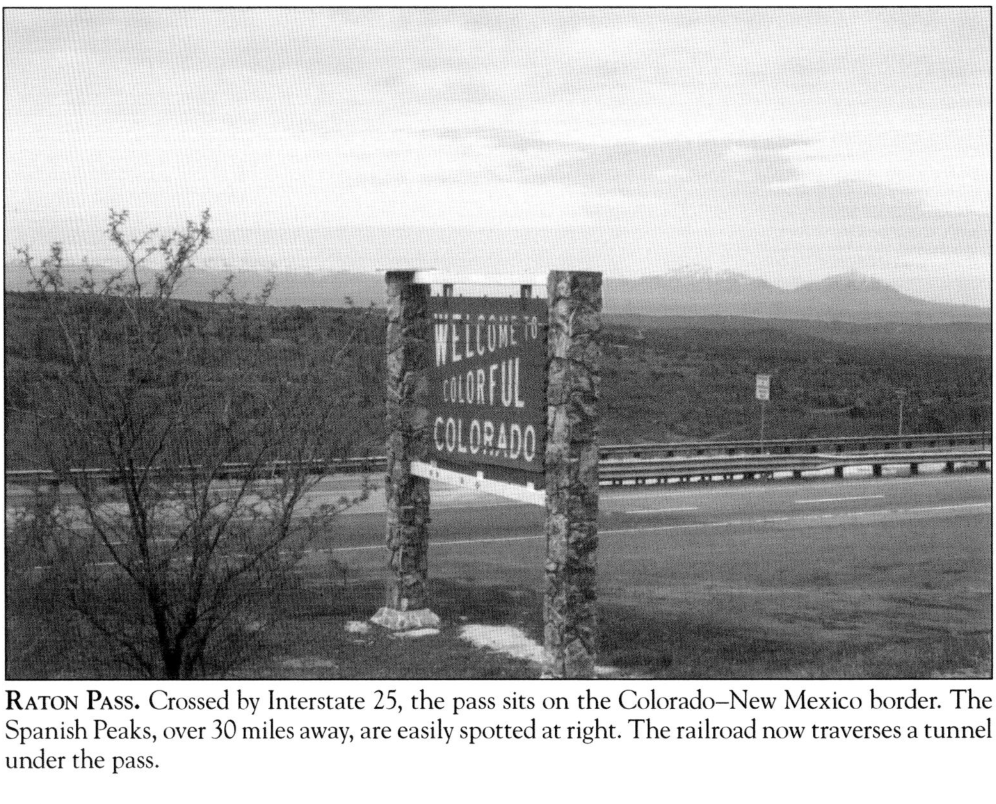

RATON PASS. Crossed by Interstate 25, the pass sits on the Colorado–New Mexico border. The Spanish Peaks, over 30 miles away, are easily spotted at right. The railroad now traverses a tunnel under the pass.

BIBLIOGRAPHY

Bronski, Peter. *Powder Ghost Towns: Epic Backcountry Runs In Colorado's Lost Ski Resorts.* Berkeley, CA: Wilderness Press, 2008.

Christofferson, Nancy. *Coal Was King. Huerfano County's Mining History.* La Veta, CO: Self-published, 2000.

———. *La Veta The First 40 Years: A History of La Veta, Colorado.* La Veta, CO: Self-published, 2001.

Copeland, James and R.W. MacCannon. *CF&I Coal Mines & Coke Ovens: A History.* Pueblo, CO: Bessemer Historical Society, 2008.

Cross, Hazel E. and Josephine C. Jochem. *River of Friendship: A Story of Early Cuchara Camps.* Chicago: Adams Press, 1970.

The Cucharan: The Magazine of the Cuchara Valley. 1, no. 2 (Winter 1984); 2, no. 2 (Winter 1985).

Fossett, Frank. *Colorado, Its Gold and Silver Mines: Farms and Stock Ranges, and Health and Pleasure Resorts: Tourist's Guide to the Rocky Mountains.* New York: C.G. Crawford Printer and Stationer, 1879.

Historic Preservation Committee. *La Veta's Stone Buildings.* La Veta, CO: Pamphlet and notes at La Veta Public Library, 2006.

Matthews, Vincent, Katie KellerLynn, and Betty Fox, eds. *Messages in Stone: Colorado's Colorful Geology.* Denver: Colorado Geological Survey, 2003.

Noel, Thomas J. *Buildings of Colorado.* New York: Oxford University Press, 1997.

———. Introduction to *The WPA Guide to 1930s Colorado* by Federal Writers Project. Lawrence: University Press of Kansas, 1987.

Osterwald, Doris B. and Becky Osterwald. *Sand & Smoke: A Mile By Mile Guide for the San Luis & Rio Grande Railroad.* Denver: Western Guideways Ltd., 2008.

Rasmussen, Stephen. *The Rio Grande's La Veta Pass Route: Gateway to the San Luis Valley.* Burlington, VT: Evergreen Press, 2000.

Sporleder, Louis B. Sr. *The Romance of the Spanish Peaks.* Pueblo, CO: Riverside Printing Company, 1989.

Discover Thousands of Local History Books Featuring Millions of Vintage Images

Arcadia Publishing, the leading local history publisher in the United States, is committed to making history accessible and meaningful through publishing books that celebrate and preserve the heritage of America's people and places.

Find more books like this at
www.arcadiapublishing.com

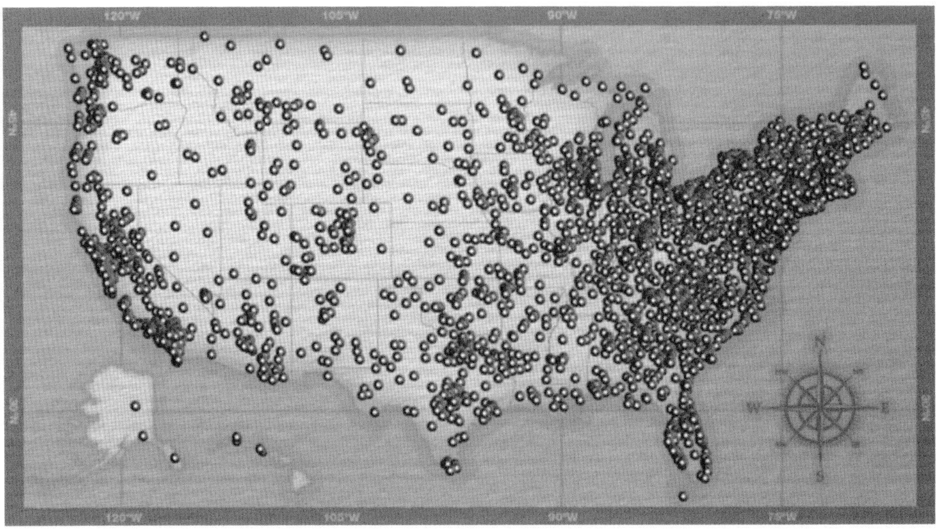

Search for your hometown history, your old stomping grounds, and even your favorite sports team.

Consistent with our mission to preserve history on a local level, this book was printed in South Carolina on American-made paper and manufactured entirely in the United States. Products carrying the accredited Forest Stewardship Council (FSC) label are printed on 100 percent FSC-certified paper.

MADE IN THE USA